MAKE A DIFFERENCE

D1018988

MAKE A DIFFERENCE

THE ULTIMATE
VOLUNTEER
HANDBOOK

arthur blaustein

Skyhorse Publishing

Skyhorse Publishing books may be purchased in bulk at special discounts for sales promotion, corporate gifts, fund-raising, or educational purposes. Special editions can also be created to specifications. For details, contact the Special Sales Department, Skyhorse Publishing, 307 West 36th Street, 11th Floor, New York, NY 10018 or info@skyhorsepublishing.com.

Skyhorse® and Skyhorse Publishing® are registered trademarks of Skyhorse Publishing, Inc.®, a Delaware corporation.

Visit our website at www.skyhorsepublishing.com.

10 9 8 7 6 5 4 3 2 1

Library of Congress Cataloging-in-Publication Data is available on file.

Cover design by Rain Saukas

Print ISBN: 978-1-5107-1429-8
Ebook ISBN: 978-1-5107-1431-1

Printed in China

CONTENTS

----------------------------------- ★ -----------------------------------

Preface

On April 21, 2009 our nation took an important step forward in re-affirming our historic commitment to citizen participation, compassion and generosity by expanding opportunities for civic engagement, community service and volunteerism. On that day President Barack Obama, who credited community service with giving him direction in life, signed a $5.7 billion national service bill that would triple the size of AmeriCorps, our national service program. The legislation extended AmeriCorps for eight years and expanded the ways that students could earn money for college and graduate school by volunteering to work in underserved communities across the country. ★

At the signing ceremony Obama said, "What this legislation does then, is to help harness this patriotism and connect deeds to needs." He pointed out that AmeriCorps creates opportunities not only for students but for seniors and everyone in between. In putting this landmark law into perspective Obama went on to say "It is just the beginning of a sustained, collaborative and focused effort to involve our greatest resource our citizens in the work of remaking this nation."

Obama was joined by Senator Edward Kennedy, (D-Mass) who was a co-sponsor of the bi-partisan legislation with Senator Orrin Hatch, (R-Utah). Kennedy reminded the audience that Obama's efforts echoed those of his brother, President John F. Kennedy. He said, "Today another young President has challenged another generation to give back to their nation," citing his brother's effort to establish the Peace Corps. Also present to lend their support to this endeavor were former First Lady Rosalynn Carter who, with her husband former President Jimmy Carter, are still volunteering to build housing for the poor by working with Habitat for Humanity, 35 years after leaving the White House. After signing the legislation Obama and First Lady Michelle Obama joined former President Bill Clinton who proposed and established AmeriCorps in 1994 in celebrating the event by planting trees in Washington's Kenilworth Park and Aquatic Gardens.

I know how valuable community Service can be because I experienced it first-hand as a volunteer in 1965 when President Lyndon Johnson initiated the War on Poverty. I participated in one of the anti-poverty programs, Volunteers in Service to America (VISTA often referred to as domestic Peace Corp, the fore-runner of AmeriCorps. I was assigned to teach and do community development work in East Harlem in New York City and my experience was eye-opening and transformative). The truth of the matter was that though I had received as good an education as I assumed one could get: an Ivy League prep school, an Ivy League undergraduate university and an Ivy League graduate school, I knew absolutely nothing about what life was like in inner-city ghettoes, Chinatowns and barrios; or the Appalachia's and the Native American reservations of America.

Thus, as a consequence of my own experience, many years later, in 1992, while a professor at the University of California at Berkeley, I decided that instead of giving a mid-semester exam I would give the students in all my classes the option of doing 16 hours of community service. The university has an outstanding Public Service Center that places students in volunteer opportunities with a diverse range of community organizations and institutions. I told the students, "If you want to go into the law, volunteer with a neighborhood Legal Services program; if you're pre-med volunteer to work at a local health center or hospital; if you want to go into the environmental sciences there are at least 10 environmental organizations in the San Francisco Bay Area; if you want to go into teaching, volunteer at an elementary or secondary school ...." And so it went. After their service the students were required to write a comprehensive essay on how they viewed their experience and what they had learned. (Over the 20 year period that I assigned community service I had joint appointments at the departments of Planning and Urban Studies, American Studies, and African-American Studies so the students came from different disciplines).) Yet, without exception the student's essays in all of the classes would warm the heart of even the most skeptical academic. And the students wrote, nearly uniformly, in the evaluations of each of the courses that their community service experience was "outstanding."

I can assure you, dear readers that 16 hours of community service beats the hell out of staying up three nights trying to guess and then memorize what might be on a mid-semester exam; regurgitating it in an in-class blue exam book; and then forgetting what you memorized two days later. Many students actually wrote that they would remember and value their volunteer experiences for their whole lives. In all of those years only one student chose to take the exam. (It was Spring semester and she was on the women's varsity softball team and they played games on weekends.)

In time, after reading the essays, talking with students, and seeing the course evaluations, I became convinced that community service was a far more meaningful and productive way for students to spend their time by engaging with, and gaining insights into, the real-world space that they hope to inhabit in the future. It gave them a practical perspective that would complement and enhance what they were learning intellectually. Both are valuable and necessary. Interestingly enough, some students wrote that they changed their majors after their service experience. For example, one student who was pre-med wrote, "I thought I wouldn't like working with children but I loved the children I taught and I now want to become an elementary school teacher."

In 2012, former Supreme Court Judge Sandra Day O'Connor the first woman appointed to the Court wrote about the fact that our educational system is failing to impart the basic knowledge that young people need in order to become effective citizens and leaders as they mature. More specifically she said that,

> "Statistics show that the problem is real and undeniable. On the last nationwide civics assessment test, two thirds of students scored below proficiency. Only about one-third of Americans can name the three branches of government, let alone describe their role in our democratic system.Less than one-fifth of high school seniors—citizens who might be eligible to exercise their franchise for the first time this November—can explain how citizen participation benefits democracy."

This is shocking and does not bode well for the future of democracy; as civic engagement and citizen participation are the life-blood of a democracy. This alienation from our nation's civic life and the workings of government at all levels, as well as the indifference to the role of citizenship are the main reasons

I decided to write this book. At the time of the beginning of our nation Thomas Paine wrote that "The highest vocation of an individual in a democracy is that of citizen." Or, as some of my students put it, "Use it or lose it." All over the world young people are struggling, and sometimes giving their lives, to help achieve democracy in their own countries, yet we seem to be frittering it away. Why is this happening?

Time and again I have been told by educators at all levels—as well as parents—that they cannot compete with the pervasive mass marketing of Entertainment Nation. The light that illumines is often no match for the glare that obscures. Our youngsters are constantly being bombarded with commercial messages that reinforce materialism, trivial amusement and gadgetry. They're fed a constant stream of popular music, film, junk food, video games, and iconic brands that are all meant to narcotize them. All of which distracts them from learning, reflecting, maturing, having genuine interpersonal relationships and being curious about the values of the society they live in. Just spend 10 minutes having coffee with a high school teacher and you'll hear about decay of classroom decorum and the drastic decline of student attention span.

Before you become despondent about this felonious assault on the sensibilities of our youth let me assure you that there are antidotes, cures, and solutions. I'll address some of these concerns in the next several paragraphs, and the book will focus on solutions. But keep in mind that it will require some effort on the part of adults. Young people learn by example so adults, as role models, also have to be engaged themselves. As the old saying goes, "If you're not part of the solution you're part of the problem."

Community service, my own and that of my students, also taught me an important lesson about our society: Ethical values and healthy communities are not inherited; they are either re-created through action by each generation, or they are not. Community service is unique and valuable because it helps us to regenerate our best values and principles as a society and as individuals. From

Plato to the present civic virtue has been at the core of civilized behavior. My experience as a teacher, as well as the faculty advisor to the Public Service Center at the university, has convinced me that ethical and moral values cannot survive from one generation to the next if the only preservatives are textbooks and research studies. Dr. Margaret Mead, one of my teachers at graduate school at Columbia, taught us that a truly healthy person is a thinking, feeling and acting person. She was right; real-life experience is the crucible for shaping values. Out of it develops an intuition and a living memory that are the seeds of a humane and just society.

I am thoroughly convinced that as we struggle to become a more humane and just society and to preserve our democratic values that a civics course and community service be required of every high school student in the 11th or 12th grade. And that a reasonable number of voluntary community service hours (16 hours a semester at a minimum) should become part of the required core curriculum at all colleges and universities.

It seems to me that another group that would benefit from community service is the U. S. Congress. Members of Congress spend far too much time with well-heeled contributors and pricey lobbyists leaving them with hardly any time for their less fortunate constituents. So, members should instead of, or in addition to, being feted at Super Bowls, golf tournaments or junkets to the Caribbean or to Hawaii be required to spend ten days a year in their home district pitching in at a Head Start program or at a soup kitchen for the homeless and hungry; or even at a neighborhood health center in a community that's adjacent to a chemical plant, a coal or copper mine or an oil refinery. This experience might be especially helpful to them when considering legislation related to early childhood education, food stamps or environmental health and justice issues. What could be an authentic and illuminating experience shouldn't be that much of a strain since the House, for example, is usually in session only about 135 days a year; while ordinary citizens clock in around 240 days a of work a year.

If this were to actually happen perhaps members of Congress could then become more exposed and sensitized to the problems and needs of a broader base of their constituency, in particular those citizens who do not have access, unlike the corporate and wealthy contributors to their campaigns, who are always seeking favors and tax breaks and whose audacity is boundless and who always have the access they need. How's that as a novel political concept—paying attention to the needs of ordinary citizens.

Congress might then seriously consider the very kind of initiatives that Pope Francis spoke about during his historic visit and speech to Congress in 2015; one that was enthusiastically received by the members. Yet one is hard put to find, in turn, the initiatives from Congress that would translate the Pope's eloquent and compelling words into deeds to actually come up with a legislative plan of action for economic and social justice. Unfortunately, too many legislators fail to understand the difference between moralistic posturing and authentic moral behavior. Once they put their minds to it they might even also consider passing campaign finance reform legislation that could restore democracy, fairness and honesty to our elections.

In another policy matter related to Congressional action, Senator Bernie Sanders, during the course of the Democratic presidential primary campaign, proposed that all young Americans be given the opportunity for a tuition-free higher education at colleges or universities in their home state. Though his goal is well-intended, I think the means he has outlined are ill-conceived. First of all the opportunity should not be universal, as I do not think that working class and middle class taxpayers should foot the bill for children of the wealthy. (There should be a means test for eligibility that the annual family income be below $150,000). As a practical matter I'm certain that this proposal, as Sanders outlined it, would be a non-starter in Congress; since both the House and the Senate are controlled by conservative Republicans who have been opposed to increasing the number of Pell grants for needy students, as well as reducing the crushing burden of debt for students and their families. Since I am in full agreement with Sanders' and Hillary Clinton's goal, that of providing a tuition-free higher education for all young Americans whose families find it unaffordable, let me suggest a legislative strategy to achieve the same goal with more practical and realistic means. It's a strategy that I'm convinced, has a much better chance of being supported by a large majority of the public as well as being considered more favorably by Congress.

What is most crucial to success is that the legislation should be modeled after the G.I. Bill of 1944 which offered educational (among other) benefits to veterans of the armed services since WWII. That landmark legislation had a positive and powerful impact on our society by improving the economic and social well-being of millions of Americans. It also helped spur the growth of our national economy. What is needed now is a National Community Service and Education Act. It would provide for the following: Any high school graduate who volunteers for AmeriCorps and completes two years of service shall be eligible to receive four years of tuition-free education at a home state college or university. If they have graduated from college and then volunteer for AmeriCorps and complete two years they can receive four years of tuition-free graduate school. It is critically important that a tuition-free education not be viewed as a freebie; but rather as just compensation for performing a vital national and community service. The legislation should also have an incentive for seniors who have much to offer as there are a substantial number of baby-boomers who are near retirement; many of whom want to remain active. For every one or two years of service a senior can accumulate two or four years of credit for a tuition-free higher education for a grandchild to be held in trust by the federal government.

For those who are not familiar with the program, AmeriCorps volunteers work with local non-profit or public institutions and organizations in the fields of: education; environmental protection; health and mental health; and public safety; in underserved communities across the country. If seems to me that if we, as a nation, can mobilize young men and women to fight in the jungles of Southeast Asia or have them volunteer to fight in the deserts of the Near East, we most certainly can afford to have them volunteer to improve the quality of life in America while making our communities and citizens healthier, smarter and safer. Community service is not just about lending a helpful hand; it is about learning: duty, ethics, leadership, patriotism, teamwork and valuable skills; all of which will make the volunteers better students when they get to college … and most important as a consequence of their service better citizens. I am of the firm belief that the time has come when America the land of opportunity does for class inequality and racial injustice, as well as for domestic tranquility and for peace what we have done for war.

On January 20, 2016 a huge step forward was taken in making the case that community service should become an integral part of the education of all young Americans—a case that I make in this book. On that day admissions deans and other leaders from over 50 of the nation's top colleges and universities (including all the Ivy's) announced a national and comprehensive effort to reshape the college admissions process and promote concern for the common good. At that time a report, "Turning the Tide: Inspiring Concern for Others and the Common Good through College Admissions" made concrete recommendations to reshape the college admissions process and promote greater ethical engagement among aspiring students. Richard Weissbourd of the Harvard Graduate School of Education and Co-director of the Making Caring Common Project said, "Too often today's culture sends young people messages that emphasize personal success rather than concern for others and the common good." He further stated that, "As a rite of passage, college admissions play a powerful role in shaping student attitudes and behaviors. Admissions deans are stepping up collectively to underscore the importance of meaningful engagement in communities and greater equity for economically diverse students." The message of the report and the project is to remind us that both ethical civic engagement and intellectual engagement are highly important and more fairly capture the strengths and potential of students across race, class and culture. This approach is right on the mark; it not only levels the playing field for students but it advances the struggle for civic virtue, as well as economic and social justice for our nation.

When Obama signed the AmeriCorps legislation into law he put the issue of community service into a perspective that every American should reflect upon. He said,

> "I'm asking you to help change history's course, put your shoulder up against the wheel, and if you do I promise you your life will be richer, our country will be stronger, and someday, years from now, you may remember it as the moment when your own story and the American story converged, when they came together, and we met the challenges of our new century."

I couldn't agree more. While thinking about Obama's remarks, I'm reminded that Eleanor Roosevelt arguably the most influential American woman of the 20th century said, "It's far better to light the candles than to curse the darkness." It's better because actually doing something is healthier, smarter, and infinitely more rewarding than complaining or feeling hopeless and depressed. The very act of affecting change is empowering and hopeful and it nourishes the heart, mind, and soul.

Introduction:
A Nation Challenged

Americans have been a very fortunate people. Indeed our nation and our people have been blessed with: abundant natural resources; a temperate climate; a Bill of Rights and Constitution bequeathed to us thanks to the genius of our founding fathers; the protective geography of two oceans and friendly neighbors to the north and south; waves of immigrants, who fleeing religious and political persecution, as well as economic deprivation, were thankful to arrive at Ellis Island or Angel Island; and a citizenry with boundless energy, openness and generosity. Americans have taken great pride in being the world's oldest democracy and the land of opportunity. ★

Yet, that is not the America we know today—one that is still reeling from the economic fallout from the Great Recession and the worst environmental disaster in our history; a housing mortgage meltdown with families losing their homes; skyrocketing student debt and health-care costs; unacceptable levels of unemployment and underemployment; and an ageing and broken infrastructure. If this were not bad enough, local governments, states and cities—some close to bankruptcy and others bankrupt—are faced with massive layoffs of teachers, police, fire fighters and human service professionals. These are hard times and a growing majority of Americans have been telling the pollsters, for the past twelve years, that "our nation is headed in the wrong direction" and "that their children will be the first generation to do worse that their parents." Among other issues, this book will focus on two critical questions. They are: How did we get into this mess? And what can be done to turn things around? There is a critical role for you in helping to reverse this downward trend.

Volunteers are needed in America today in record numbers. People are in trouble—and they are turning to voluntary organizations in their communities for help. Millions of Americans—middle class, working class, professional and business executives—have experienced a loss of job, a home, a business or small farm failure, a personal bankruptcy, a loss of pension or retirement income. Poverty and homelessness have increased. And millions more are only a layoff, an illness, a divorce, or an accident away from falling into poverty. And recent studies have found that the largest increase in homelessness was among families with children. Food banks—even in upscale suburban areas—are serving families who, a couple of years ago were the ones who did the serving and the donating of the food. The environment is in trouble too, and environmental organizations need volunteers to be effective in combating global warming.

Above all, public debate on where this country is headed is in trouble. The Republican presidential primary debates are but one example. The political deadlock and poisonous partisanship in Washington does not help matters either. Organizations that work on public policy need volunteers to keep public debate alive, to keep democracy viable, and to make a better future possible.

Voluntary efforts, however, should not be a substitute for the government's failure to act. And that's the great danger today because the federal government has been cutting back on social and human services for thirty-five years—since the Reagan administration—while slashing funds for basic social service assistance to state and local governments. This could not happen at a worse time.

Our nation is in an extremely precarious position. It looks like we could well have a double-dip recession and even stagflation over the next several years. Yet while President Barack Obama has put forth several important initiatives to: stimulate the economy; provide needed financial aid to local government; offer loans to help small business; and extend unemployment benefits; the Republicans in Congress have opposed him in every instance. This makes it extremely difficult to pass legislation that can alleviate the suffering that cash-strapped families are experiencing.

What is needed is a coherent and comprehensive understanding of how we got into this economic mess as well as an understanding of the public policy initiatives—economic, environmental and social—that it will take to assure a full and healthy recovery. Yet this is not happening. Why not? There are several reasons, but initially I'll touch on three: 1) Because of the way that economics is taught; 2)Because of the way that the mass media covers politics; and 3) Because the Republicans seem to think that it's in their political interest to oppose every necessary reform that President Obama proposes.

First, the way economics is taught. Education in economics is almost non-existent at the high school level (a few random pages of charts and curves) and on the college level it's far too abstract and theoretical. Thus the vast majority of Americans do not understand how economic policy is made and how it affects them. Nowhere have the mass media, politicians, the experts, and our education system failed us more than in the area of economic education. It is amazing how so many intelligent people get nervous at the sound of the word "economics." What's more, the so-called experts have confused us so much that we don't even trust our common sense. The truth of the matter is that we have an appallingly low level of economic literacy with most people buying into myths rather than truths. It is for precisely this reason that independent likely voters were telling pollsters that the Democrats are responsible for our economic woes, particularly the deficits and debt; when in fact it was eight years of George W. Bush and a compliant and enabling Republican Congress that gave us these failed "trickle-down" economic policies.

Next, it's important to examine the critical role of the mass media, the dominant means of conveying information to the American public. In the past thirty years we've experienced a steady and marked decline in the quality of journalism.

To a great extent, we have not had a serious national public policy debate because the mass media, with few exceptions—NPR, PBS, and some print journalism—have treated politics, as well as economic and social policy, as entertainment: a combination of hype and palliative. There's an unconscious cynicism in the way the mass media has reported the previous day's happening; OBAMA WINS or SENATE DEMS BEATEN. The political and economic life of the country has been reduced to little more than a struggle for political power, the results not unlike the score of a football game. There seems to be no higher good, no national purpose, no critical judgment. The problem is that 75 percent of the public get their news from television and talk radio, the worst offenders. And with the advent of 24/7 cable TV, the internet, and the blogosphere, traditional news sources have dumbed down content to compete for revenue and audiences with short attention spans.

Most of us should know that our dependence on mindless, endless, irrelevant evening news and cable-news sound bites and talk radio ranting creates the illusion that we are learning something. We are not. In the process of being bombarded by de-contextualized and useless information, we lose our freedom to make genuine choices based on the coherent, rational ideas about our economy and how it affects social policies and the well-being of our communities. Hype has impoverished our political debate. It undermines the very idea that public discourse can be educational and edifying—or that national public policy can grow out of reflective discussion and shared political values. This "MacNews" approach has undercut our moral values and civic traditions. We have sought simplistic answers to complex problems without even beginning to comprehend our loss. The Donald Trump campaign is but one glaring example. Anger is not a policy.

But now we're getting ahead of ourselves. A more detailed analysis, as well as a healthy antidote to media hype, is discussed in the chapter, "The Reading Cure".

The loss of coherent and comprehensive public discourse raises some difficult and complex questions about the relationship between policy and community service. Volunteers work in a context, and that context is shaped by America's social and economic policy. That policy, in turn, is shaped by politics in Washington D.C.

Next, let's look at Republican opposition to Obama's policies and the political deadlock in Washington. It would appear that the GOP. leadership, Mitch McConnell, the Majority Leader in the Senate and Paul Ryan, the Speaker of the House, are convinced that the way for their party to climb the greasy pole back to the White House is to attack anything Obama says and to oppose any and all legislation that Obama or Congressional Democratic leadership propose. And to do so without any concern as to what is best for the country. They have opposed: the economic recovery stimulus package; health care reform; climate change reform; banking and financial services reform; campaign finance reform; extension of unemployment benefits; consumer affairs reform; a partial ban on deep sea drilling and immigration reform, among other legislative initiatives. Moreover, they have not even bothered to offer any constructive or reasonable alternatives whatsoever. It's just like they dusted off and put on their old Nancy Reagan JUST SAY NO buttons.

Instead of offering creative alternatives, Ryan and McConnell slavishly recite—as does the Republican Congressional Chorus—the same repetitive 30 second sound bites for the evening television news, day in and day out. They could just as well put a parrot before the mike. Apparently their handlers and pollsters—with fresh research from a focus group of 15 folks in Hammond, Indiana—have told them that the mantra of "lower taxes, less government" is the winning slogan that will play in Peoria. What's really scary is that this mindless strategy might even win.

If it does work, and the Republican Party—shoved and shouted further to the right of George W. Bush by the Tea Party—stays in power by winning the House and Senate in 2016, as well as the White House, we'll be in far bigger trouble than we were during the Bush era. We'll have to contend with a more extreme version of Bush's ruinous policies. Republican leadership, who for eight years partnered with Bush in taking us to the economic abyss are now doubling down their political bets because of pressure from their right-wing base, Trump, and the Tea Party and their belief that the voters have short memories.

In July of 2010 thirty-eight Republican members of the House, including two in critical leadership positions, formed a Tea Party Caucus, now called the Freedom Caucus. They are playing with fire as the angry populism and simplistic rhetoric they are promoting is not a substitute for coherent and comprehensive public policies. For want of creative and serious ideas and policies, the GOP and Trump are practicing the art of superficial posturing and caving in to what is called "crackpot realism". The consequences of this kind of cynical pandering—if they win—will be government by provisional catastrophe; which could well lead to man-on-the-white-horse authoritarianism. Just thinking about this possibility reminds me of the words of Robert Frost, "I have seen the future; and I don't advocate it."

If this sounds gloomy, unless you hadn't noticed, we're going through bleak times. But it need not be that way. We have been through bad times before. First, we have to confront the reality that there is no easy or simple solution to the problems we face as a nation. For too long we put our faith in incompetent pitch-men posing as leaders (Ronald Reagan and Bush II) who, with bad ideas and worse policies, have frittered away our natural resources, human capital and financial security. The deficits and debt that have piled up over the past thirty-five years are not only economic—they are also moral and social.

Another reality we have to face is that Obama is a political leader, he is not a wizard. He cannot wave a magic wand to change reality and make our problems disappear. Problems and policies that were thirty-five years in the making do not go away in two terms. What Obama has done is put our problems into perspective and offer reasonable, doable—and sometimes painful—solutions that require patience. Fortunately for us, he is an intelligent, competent and decent, and he's displayed qualities of leadership under the most difficult of circumstances. The week of his inauguration the headline in The Onion got it right: America Gives Its Worst Job to a Black Man. All things considered, he's done a commendable job without any help from the opposition party and with vicious attacks from the reactionary media.

If Obama had a difficult time getting the Republicans in Congress to cooperate his first two years, the past six were all but impossible. Having won control of the House and gained several seats in the Senate in the 2010 midterm elections, the GOP was emboldened to block all legislation proposed by the White House. Their motto was "No We Can't."

Obama has to accept some blame for this stinging political defeat. The two issues uppermost in the minds of voters were the economy/unemployment and health care. The administration dawdled far too long on health care, talking about a bipartisan approach that was going nowhere. Meanwhile, the Republicans and the Tea Party were spreading false myths about "death panels" and frightening senior about big cuts in their Medicare. White House strategists also failed to clearly and coherently explain to the American people the long-term benefits of either their healthcare reform initiative or their economic stimulus package.

The inability of the White House to communicate effectively on these two issues gave the opposition the opportunity to frame the debate on their own terms; and the mass media had a field day fueling extraneous controversy, especially Tea Party rallies. Facts and truth are no match for angry guys with powdered wigs and tricorn hats. This media diversion and the failure of the White House to provide a coherent message undermined Obama's credibility on other issues and detracted from his solid accomplishments. In politics, perception is often more important than substance. Negative public perceptions–as well as a steady dose of attack ads—made it extremely difficult for Democratic House and Senate candidates to compete in tight races.

Now that the Republicans have a majority in the House and Senate, they have absolute power of chairing all legislative committees. They've used these powers in the past to freeze out the Democrats, as they did from 2001 until 2007. The Republican chairs hire staff, decide which issues to consider, set legislative priorities, issue subpoenas, and determine when to hold investigations,

press conferences, and hearings. During the recent Bush administration, legislative oversight and accountability of the financial sector were no more than a wink and a nod, and a whitewash. That's
how we got into this economic crisis in the first place and GOP
leadership, having learned nothing from the past, will continue to
try to repeal crucial parts of the financial reform legislation passed
in 2010. Now, more than ever, the Republicans are beholden to
corporate vested interest, who shoveled huge amounts of money
into GOP campaign coffers.

Many pundits are drawing parallels between the 2010 and
2014 midterm elections and the 1994 midterm elections, when
Republicans captured both the Senate and House after two years
of Bill Clinton's first term. But there is a huge difference. The economy was in fairly good shape then. Now, the economy is extremely
fragile and uncertain. If Republicans are hell-bent on destroying
the Obama presidency—as their leadership has repeatedly said is
a priority—they could very well continue to oppose legislation crucial to putting the nation's economy back on track. This legislation
includes extension of emergency unemployment benefits; more
federal aid to state and local governments to stave off the loss of
essential jobs in public safety and education; and a stimulus package targeted toward creating more jobs in infrastructure—roads,
sewer systems, airports, bridges, mass transit, and the energy
grid—is extremely important if we are to effectively compete in the
global economic market. Republican opposition to these job-cre-
ating initiatives could well deepen the consequences of the Great
Recession, causing untold pain to millions of American families
now living on the margins.

Not only did the Democratic Party take a big hit in the midterm
elections, so did democracy. Secret money was pumped into the
campaign in huge amounts, like toxic waste being dumped into
reservoirs across the country. This shadow money was provided,
in the main, to Republicans by corporations and wealthy individuals—through the Chamber of Commerce and vested interest

groups legitimized by the recent Citizens United decision—who expect dividends in return for their investments. The cash was primarily used for attack ads—targeting Democrats—that flooded our airwaves and mailboxes. At the end of each ad, there should have been a disclaimer: "This message is a dangerous blow to democracy and was made possible by the John Roberts gang-of-five reactionaries on the Supreme Court." Since when is the sanctioning of legalized bribery "judicial restraint" (as the conservatives preach to us) and a "strict construction" of the Constitution? It took a particularly contorted form of intellectual and moral jujitsu for the Roberts 5–4 majority to pin that decision on our nation's founders.

If the Tea Partiers and Trumpites have the genuine concern they claim to have for the demise of republicanism in our country, and a decent eleventh grade understanding of American civic history, they'd plant their "Don't Tread on Me" flags around the Supreme Court, the U.S. Chamber of Commerce, the Republican National Committee headquarters, and Fox News. Patrick Henry could then stop turning over in his grave. The stakes are very high, as the flood of plutocratic undisclosed and unregulated dark money poured into our electoral system not only contaminates our politics and undermines our republican values but it threatens to destroy the integrity of American democracy.

What allowed an American president in the past to lead us out of adversity was their ability to focus the American people on the challenges our country faced, in an open and honest way. But it was up to the American people to bear the burden—to pull together to persevere and succeed. What made a big difference in the past was our ability, as a people, to confront reality. Though the problems may be different today, the means of solving them are the same. It is up to us, individually and collectively, to become part of the solution rather than being part of the problem.

We have to put aside irrelevant distractions, mindless entertainment and false assumptions that somehow everything will work out for the best if we just sit on our rear ends. For example, when we went to war in Iraq, Bush went on television and told the American people to go out to the malls and shop; spend until they maxed out their credit cards. Guess what? That didn't work, because it was the thumb-sucking materialistic equivalent of binge drinking and denial. No sacrifice, no belt-tightening, no introspection, no questioning, no problem. That's what people do in television commercials or in sit-coms; not in real life. Can you imagine Washington during the Revolutionary War, or Lincoln during the Civil War or Roosevelt during World War II asking Americans to go out and shop?

Next, Bush told folks—particularly working-class and minorities—to become stakeholders in his "home ownership society". That was going to be the key to solving our social and domestic problems. Just go down to your friendly neighborhood bank and take out an adjustable interest, sub-prime loan and join the middle class. We know how that turned out.

The Iraq war, shopping at malls and sub-prime loans; if you meld all these together—a failed foreign policy with a failed domestic policy—what you get is a national economy in the tank and international banking chaos—the Wall Street Sharpies call it synergism; but it's spelled catastrophe. Only through civic engagement and citizen participation can we turn things around. We only have to look at our recent past to see how our nation was changed, for the better, by home-grown grass roots movements. When our leaders could or did not act the people did. The civil rights, anti-war, environmental justice, consumer, anti-apartheid, disabilities, gay and lesbian rights, anti-nuke and anti-sweatshop movements—among others—are a few examples of how citizen action has had a profound effect on American law, society and culture.

Let me share a more recent story about what I'm getting at. About three weeks after 9/11, I was listening to NPR. They were doing interviews with New Yorkers about how that tragedy had affected their lives. One of those interviewed was a seventeen-year-old high school student. He told the interviewer, "Before 9/11, when my friends and I went into a music store to get CDs, or a fast food place, if we weren't served in 2 minutes I'd get antsy and irritated. Last week I went down to the Red Cross Center to volunteer to give blood. I had to wait three hours and I never felt better in my life." This story is both real and metaphoric.

The lifeblood of a democracy, in the real world, is volunteering, community service, civic engagement and citizen participation. And that's what this book is about. It's a win-win-win situation: it's good for you, vital to those being served and healthy for your communities and our nation.

There is a postscript to this story that is worth thinking about. My twenty years of working with volunteers has confirmed what my intuition told me: that volunteering for community service could well be the quickest, most rewarding and least expensive way of gaining healthy self-esteem and a life-affirming sense of purpose.

PART ONE

UNDER-STANDING COMMUNITY SERVICE

When you volunteer, it helps a lot to understand the economic and social problems that impact the communities where you donate your time. It is also important to become aware of the political decisions and/or the policies that are causing the problems you're trying to deal with through your volunteer work. Often, by necessity, volunteers must become advocates for changing those political decisions or policies.

Volunteers can become advocates as individuals or through public interest groups that lobby for systemic change. If a volunteer does not become an advocate, the problems will keep recurring over and over again. The volunteer will either burn out or succumb to "compassion fatigue." ★

Volunteering, Public Policy, and Politics

L et's review the economic and social problems facing our people, our communities, and our nation. We have recently experienced the Great Recession that had been 30 years in the making. It is absolutely essential that we comprehend the policies and politics of how we got into this colossal mess. Otherwise, as George Santayana observed, "Those who cannot remember the past are condemned to repeat it."

The Census Bureau report of September 2010 on increased poverty in the United States should have been a wakeup call. Four million additional Americans found themselves struggling with poverty in 2009, with children comprising the biggest percentage of this population. This increase brought the total number of people in poverty to 44 million—one in seven Americans—the highest level recorded since 1994.

In addition, the states, individually and collectively, were experiencing their biggest budget deficits since World War II because of the loss of federal aid. The reason for the decline of federal aid is that after four consecutive years of federal surpluses under the Clinton administration, the George W. Bush administration managed to give us eight years of the largest federal budget deficits in our history. It is important to understand this and put it in perspective because all the GOP presidential candidates in 2016 were blaming President Obama.

The biggest culprits behind the deficit and the soaring national debt were the two Bush tax cuts. The sad truth is that what Washington giveth in tax cuts, the states taketh back in regressive tax increases and service cuts. But there's one critical difference: the state tax increases caused by federal tax cuts were mainly shouldered by the middle class and the poor. The state cuts in education, health care, nutrition, and job training especially hurt 44 million poor Americans and another 55 million who are near-poor. Local cuts in education, environmental protection, public safety, libraries, the arts, and mass transit hurt everyone. These are not abstract statistics, but the fate of millions of human beings living in real communities. And this happened at a time when over 46 million Americans did not have health insurance. It's not a pretty picture, and the painful consequences will be felt for decades, even though the Bush administration is gone. The futures of our children and grandchildren were mortgaged without a serious national debate.

The Bush tax cuts may have been popular, but like snake oil, they sold but they didn't cure. Lost in all the superficial coverage of the tax cuts was the reality that someone making $1 million annually got a break of $92,000, while an average working family got $256.

MAKE A DIFFERENCE

Just like in the "The Wizard of Oz," when we finally get to see who was operating the smoke-puffing machine, we find a consummate pitchman. In Bush's case, the man behind the screen was a flag-waving, anti-terrorist fear monger who labeled his opponents anti-patriotic. Early in his administration, following the tragedy of 9/11, Bush and his party cooked up the ultimate recipe for keeping political power. A nation in a constant state of anxiety—over the threat of terrorism, or a potential war—is a nation off balance. The Bush administration exploited that insecurity and used it as a cover to divert public attention from the country's serious domestic economic and social problems and the administration's political agenda.

The "Bush doctrine" opened the door to a series of pre-emptive wars against "evil" regimes, ostensibly to protect the United States and bring security, stability, safety and democracy to the citizens of Baghdad and Kabul. These two wars cost over two trillion dollars and thousands of lives. Meanwhile, the administration showed little or no concern for the security, stability and safety of the citizens of New York, Los Angeles, Detroit, Cleveland, or thousands of other cities and small towns across America, who were facing enormous economic and social difficulties.

Bush did a clever job of manipulating the mass media, but in reality his smooth imagery and charming personality were steadily and subtly undermining America's values. While he composed hymns to individualism, Sunday piety, trickle-down economics, and family values, he tried to gut most programs providing for social, economic and environmental justice. America's families needed less pious rhetoric, and more policies geared toward a healthy economy, secure jobs, decent health care, affordable housing, quality public education, renewable energy and a sustainable environment. Bush seemed unable—or unwilling—to grasp that the government has an important leadership role in this. In fact, the only policy that Bush seemed energized by was one of tax giveaways for the rich and for corporate America.

Bush did not seem to understand that, while it is not a sin to be born to privilege, it is a sin to spend your life defending it. John F. Kennedy and Franklin D. Roosevelt understood that. They knew the narrowness that privilege can breed. Bush's policies amounted to a war against the poor and the middle class. The tax and budget cuts were not made, as he claimed, to jump-start the economy or balance the budget. They were simply massive cash transfers. Social programs were slashed to pay for tax giveaways for the wealthy and new defense contracts for arms makers, pharmas, insurance companies and war contractors (think Haliburton and Blackwater) who just happened to be big campaign contributors.

Bush's economic policies hammered the middle and working class. An economic research study done for the Rockefeller Foundation measured the percentage of Americans who experienced a decrease in their income of 25 percent or more in a given year, without having the resources to make up for the loss. During the Bush years, the percentage of insecure Americans, relative to the given level of unemployment, rose steadily. In 2008 alone, more than 20 per cent of Americans experienced a 25 percent or greater loss of household income over the prior year—the biggest income decline for the most Americans in 25 years.

In the eight Bush years overall, our nation experienced the weakest post-recession job creation cycle since the Great Depression, record deficits, record household debt, a record bankruptcy rate and a substantial increase in poverty. If that's not enough, we shifted from being a nation with substantial federal surpluses to

ith major deficits. The United States became orld's biggest borrower; we exported far less ve imported; we produced far less than we sumed; and foreign investors own more of merican assets than Americans own of foreign assets. That's the Bush economic record, d the horrendous mess that Obama inher-

As bad as the Bush years were, many of the economic and social problems we have been experiencing began before Bush; and can be directly traced back to the 1980s and the Reagan era. It was Reagan's administration that foisted "supply-side economics"—also known as "trickle-down" or Reaganomics—on the nation. To justify their plan to kill the safety net of federal support programs established under President Lyndon Johnson, Reagan's economists claimed that Reaganomics would eradicate poverty. Yet the best research indicates the opposite. Growth in the private economy has had a declining role in reducing poverty, and virtually all of the reduction in poverty since the mid-1960s has been brought about by the expansion of federal social insurance and income transfer programs of the kind attacked by the Reagan and Bush administrations. In point of fact, eighteen months after Reagan took office and "trickle down" economics became a reality; five million Americans were driven into poverty (a 17 percent increase)—85 percent of whom were women and children.

In addition to the massive cuts, the Regan administration's strategy was to privatize or turn over to the states specific social, education, housing, and health programs, historically the responsibility of the federal government.

In the 60s, thanks to Prescient Lyndon Johnson's Great Society programs, there was hope: Upward Bound (provided basic academic prep support for low-income high school students who want to go to college), the Neighborhood Youth Corps (provided summer jobs for "at risk" low-income teenagers) and the Job Corps (provides basic technical skills training and education for disadvantaged 16-24 year olds) held out a helping hand. Youngsters who had never before had a chance believed that the dream of achieving selfhood could become a reality. By the early 80s, though, with budgets slashed, that hope had been dashed, and it was replaced with despair, as youngsters turned to drugs, crime and violence.

In deliberate efforts to destroy the credibility of these programs, conservative politicians began manipulating symbols in order to stigmatize them. During the Nixon era, they cleverly and cynically began to refer to them as "minority" and "welfare" programs, rather than as "opportunity" programs, which they were. That switched the message from positive to negative. This kind of deceit and distortion was not an accident; it was designed to exploit fear and racial divisiveness.

These appeals to bigotry worked. They allowed Republicans to defeat moderate Democrats across the South and pick up a substantial number of seats in Congress. This "Southern strategy" of Nixon— a veiled racist strategy that was part of a deal he cut with arch- segregationist Senator Strom Thurmond of South Carolina in order to secure Nixon the Republican presidential nomination— ultimately provided the political cover, and congressional votes, for Reagan and Bush II to enact their reactionary economic and social agenda.

The Nixon administration also tried, illegally (like so much else they were doing), to kill the War on Poverty. Fortunately, a federal judge prevented them from abolishing the anti-poverty efforts. And Nixon resigned in disgrace, faced with an impeachment trial over Watergate, shortly thereafter.

Once the United States reached the Reagan era of the 80s, we had entered a period that officially—at the highest levels of government—condoned and even encouraged negative attitudes, code words, and symbols directed against the poor in particular and toward basic human and social service programs in general. Conservative politicians were adept at moralizing endlessly over the problems: the unemployed and underemployed, the homeless and hungry, alcoholism, drug abuse, mental illness, infant mortality, child and spouse abuse, and disrupted families. But they had neither the heart nor the will for the rigorous thought and work of finding cures or even just relieving some of the suffering and symptoms.

Let me give an example. During the course of the 1980 presidential campaign, then-candidate Reagan would entertain crowds with the line, "Do you know how much it costs to keep a kid in the Job Corps? (pause) and how much it costs to send a kid to Harvard? Well, I'll tell you: $13,000 for the Job Corps and only $12,500 for Harvard." This usually elicited gales of smug laughter. But it was a false comparison. The alternative to the Job Corps was not Harvard, it was despair. There were substantial costs to eliminating the Job Corps. At the time Reagan compared the Job Corps to Harvard, it cost $20,000 a year to keep a youngster in prison, and $26,000 to keep a youngster in an alcohol and drug abuse program or a halfway house. At $13,500, the Job Corps was a far less expensive investment for taxpayers, and the youngsters were learning self respect and job skills so they could become a productive, and tax-paying, member of society.

The real issues were then and are now: What are the values of the society, and where do we want to spend our money? Drastic cuts in basic social and human service programs exact social and human costs, and they also appear as direct financial costs to taxpayers at future times in different ledgers.

Reagan's reduction of human and social services did not promote better family life; they destabilized it. They did not reduce alcoholism; they increased it. They did not increase respect for the law; they weakened it.

Politics in the eighties under Reagan reached a level of abstractness removed from the circumstances of ordinary Americans. When a sane and civilized family runs into tough financial times, two things happen. The one thing that they do is to assure that those members of the family—or society—who are least able to fend for themselves are given the protection and minimum amenities necessary for survival. The one thing that they do not do is to allow those who have more than enough and are enjoying luxuries to continue to hoard. There are certain natural principles of behavior, of caring and decency, that have prior claim over untested game plans of economic theorists or politicians on the make. And it wasn't only politicians on the make. It was a time when Wall St. hucksters could appear on campuses and tell budding MBAs that greed is good.

As the Reagan era closed, pundits of type and tube gushed over Reagan's ability, as the Great Communicator, to manipulate the American public, and the pundits themselves. At that time, I came across a poem by a 17-year-old in the Job Corps. The youngster, from Appalachia, got it right. Perhaps a bit awkwardly, but with keen insight, he wrote:

> Ronald Reagan took an axe,
> to make inflation bygone.
> He gave the budget 40 whacks,
> and sent the guns to Tehran.
> While militarism and space go on apace,
> each funded in entirety.
> Matters of poverty and race,
> are of the chopped variety.
> For each man kills the things
> he knows not of.
> Farewell oh Great Society.

The economic policies of Reagan and Bush I during the 80s were failures—a fool's paradise built on the sands of borrowed time and borrowed money. The consequences were a staggering debt, industrial decline, shrinking wages, two painful recessions, increased poverty and structural unemployment. Their reckless spending and borrowing—combined with de-industrialization, deregulation and privatization—brought us to the brink of economic deprivation and social depression.

In 1992, the nation elected Bill Clinton. The Clinton administration presided over the longest peacetime economic expansion in our history. The national debt was reduced dramatically, the industrial sector boomed, wages grew and more Americans found jobs. Clinton helped the middle class and working poor by increasing the benefit levels and eligibility for the Earned Income Tax Credit. He restored tax progressivity and fairness, with higher rates on the wealthiest taxpayers. And he fought to increase the minimum wage, to get family-leave legislation and to protect the environment. Clinton served two terms; but he was on the defensive for six of those years, because Republicans gained control of Congress. After the eight prosperous Clinton years, the nation elected George W. Bush and returned to the "trickle-down" economic and social policies of Reagan.

Thomas Jefferson warned us that we could be free or ignorant, but not both. We have not taken that warning to heart. We did not have a serious national debate about the Bush administration's economic and social policies. And, thanks to the Tea Party and the mass media, we did not have a serious debate over Obama's policies.

Obama's critics—in the media, the Republican Party and to some extent the American public—are behaving like we live in the unreal world of television commercials; where a problem gets resolved in 30 seconds. You buy a new car and mysteriously, the guy or gal of your dreams suddenly appears. You switch stock brokerage firms, and you suddenly make a boodle of money. You take a pill, and all your sexual problems are resolved. All of this happens at the snap of a finger. In the real world, especially politics, nothing works that way.

As a frame of reference, we should remind ourselves that the American public had the patience and the wisdom to give Franklin Delano Roosevelt four terms in office, and thirteen years to get out of the Depression that Herbert Hoover and the Republicans had created for the country in the late 1920s and early 30s. I am not suggesting that it will take us that long, or that we should let Obama off the hook. What I am suggesting is that we exercise some reason, patience and wisdom. The economic and social problems that we confront as a nation are like cancer of the body politic. There are no quick or painless fixes. I am reminded of an admonition from the Old Testament prophet Isaiah: "Judge us not by the heights we have achieved but the depths from which we have come." Considering the absolutely dire circumstances of the economy and the total opposition of the Republicans, Obama has done an exceptional job.

The GOP Congressional leadership wants to return to the same failed policies of Reagan and Bush. What Obama understood—and what the Republican leadership does not—is that although the economic difficulties facing our nation are complex, they cannot be used as an excuse for reneging on our national social and moral commitments. National issues— such as health care, consumer affairs, the banking system, the environment, Medicare, home foreclosures civil rights and Social Security—require national policy, oversight and programs. They should not be ignored, or turned over to the states or the private sector. The issue is not public versus private or federal versus state; rather, it is the diminution or avoidance of any national standards of responsibility and accountability. To deflect, suspend, or fragment responsibility and accountability suggests that we are either renouncing or failing to assert our moral purpose as a nation. Worse, the Republican leadership, then and now, seems to be denying that this moral purpose exists.

The Reagan and Bush administration's efforts to turn over to the states more program responsibility with less money ended up destroying existing national support systems that were effective and had a proven capacity to deliver services using local implementation capabilities. These systems were replaced with an inequitable system run by the states, which historically have a poor track record. State-run systems are typically restrictively financed, more bureaucratic, and less accountable (one need only look to the crisis in Flint), and they are subject to intense local, political, and financial pressures.

The last point is extremely important: Effective and efficient use of limited federal funds was being sacrificed to conflicting political interests in each state. Instead of the more efficient government that Reagan and Bush promised, we have instead fifty bureaucratic and anachronistic messes: government by locals special interest lobbyists. And the Republican Party is trying to do the same thing with Obama's health-care reform.

The ideological implications behind thirty-five years of Reagan's and Bush's economic policies and those of GOP leadership today are disturbing. They depart from the genuine conservative leadership that has played such an important role in American history. Historically, conservatives have not promised lower taxes and economic privatism. Traditionally, conservative leaders have focused primarily on the underlying problems of the human community—issues of leadership, equality of opportunity, continuity and order, the obligations of the strong to the weak, and the safeguards needed to keep the privileged from abusing their power.

I am well aware that it is quite unfashionable in these days of Tea Party revolts and anti-government slogans to speak of more qualitative initiatives from government. Yet, if government is to do its job, we must do ours. A good part of the job is confronting reality. And that reality is that our nation is facing a brutal political struggle for control over the levers of power.

Not only did Obama face the political challenge of repairing our struggling economy and strengthening our social structure, he had to also overcome the hostile attacks and raw power of an unholy alliance—the Republican Party, the Tea Party, the editorial page of the Wall St. Journal, Fox News, the brothers Koch, Rush Limbaugh, Bill O'Reilly, Glenn Beck. This juggernaut has unlimited amounts of private corporate cash to oppose Obama's, and the Democrat's, policies, thanks to the Roberts-led reactionary 5-4 Supreme Court decision in the Citizens United case. And they were determined to bust Obama. The stakes are very high in this struggle; as it gets to the core issue of the very role of government in a democracy. The right wing, Axis-of Greed cannot be allowed to destroy the safety net that protects the economic security of 95 percent of Americans. This safety net prevents our nation from being turned into a "banana republic," where a plutocracy pulls all the strings. And the rising plutocracy has been adept at pulling the strings.

Wealthy conservatives reacted with a vengeance to the activism of the 60s and 70s, and to resulting federal legislation providing for economic, environmental, and social justice. Here's a thumbnail sketch of how the Orwellian process works. The rich conservatives plow money into scores of Washington think-tanks like the Heritage Foundation and the American Enterprise Institute. The think-tanks employ academic and scholarly guns-for-hire who produce ideologically-driven position papers, with an intellectual aura, usually attacking social programs, public interest and accountability, government, taxes and the "liberal" media—conforming to the prescribed positions of their wealthy benefactors. These papers then work their way into the mass media as objective analysis and get headlined by Fox News.

Next in the process are the public relations hacks for the Republican Party, who boil down these position papers into simple talking points for GOP leaders and spokespersons who then mouth this pablum for the evening news and 24/7 cable network, as well as talk radio. And that's how processed propaganda becomes acceptable and eventually turns into widely cited clichés and slogans. It's misinformation run amok.

The practice continues right up to the present. An example is Americans for Prosperity, bankrolled by the billionaires Charles and David Koch of Koch Industries. Americans for Prosperity provides organizational and training support for the Tea Party. All those noisy and hostile attacks on Democrats in 2009 at local town meetings over their support for health care legislation were not as spontaneous and grass roots as it appeared on the TV news. Those attacks were systematically organized and choreographed performances.

This is a short version of how conservative ideas and money laundering scams work. For a more comprehensive version I highly recommend reading Jane Mayer's exceptional and enlightening article, "Covert Operations" in the May 30, 2010 issue of The New Yorker.

By no coincidence, the Tea Party and the Freedom Caucus are most vocal in opposing, and supporting, the very same issues as do the Kochs—like abolishing the federal departments of Education, Commerce and Energy; as well as phasing out Medicare, Medicaid, and the progressive income tax and replacing it with a 23 percent sale tax, which is about the most regressive tax there is.

There is an almost Zen perfection to the wrong-headedness of Trump and Tea Party activists. They do not seem to understand that the central issue is not "small government" versus "big government"; but rather "good government" versus "bad government." No Republican president in their lifetime has provided less government. Nor do the activists seem to understand that they are being conned by the Kochs, in that they are voting against their own economic and social self-interests by supporting an oppositional agenda that favors billionaires.

Volunteers face a critical choice. You can work with public interest, non-profit advocacy organizations that represent your concerns as well as the public good. Or you can do nothing and allow well-heeled organizations and institutions that are fronting for powerful vested, special and moneyed interests pull the strings and run the show.

The naked truth is that the Republican Party—represented most clearly by its candidates for president in 2016—is pandering to, colluding with and exploiting the most regressive and antisocial tendencies in our national character. It is undermining trust in the ability of the one force—government—that has the potential to balance, secure, and protect the freedoms and liberties of all our people and to balance public and private interests. A vital and healthy federal government is indispensable to the well-being and sovereignty of a self-governing people. That is, after all, what democracy is all about. Without this protection, whole segments of our society—especially those who can least afford it—will give up hope and will become more frustrated and alienated, and this can only serve to further polarize our discourse and undermine the very social fabric of all our communities.

Abraham Lincoln was a Republican who advocated the opposite of the contemporary notion of private interest for selfish personal gain being peddled by the Republican Party. Lincoln reminded us that our primary task as a nation should be to continually teach and re-teach American political and social history. He was deeply concerned lest we forget the pain and struggle that are so much a part of our unique historical experience. For Lincoln, there was no higher calling than that of striving to preserve a public liberty that would promote the common good.

Our political and civic history provides us with a commonsense vision of the American promise—one that the founding fathers and Lincoln understood—that calls for justice, freedom, equality, and opportunity. We may forget or we may deny our historical legacy, but we cannot change it. The uniqueness of our nation is that the "noble experiment" was a quest to enhance the human condition, enrich democratic values, ensure the general welfare, endure against adversity, provide economic opportunity, and preserve our natural resources. Hopefully, in 2017, Hillary Clinton, Tim Kaine, and Bernie Sanders will provide the leadership that will promote these principles and values.

American Values, Citizenship, and Civic Engagement[1]

The Dilemma

As the new decade began it became clear that a substantial majority of Americans believed our society to be in serious trouble. Most Americans think their future will be worse, not better, than their past. Most Americans think their children's prospects are worse, not better, than their own.

Though this new pessimism has many sources, the most prominent cause is certainly anxiety about the economy. Public opinion

---

[1] Author's note: This chapter updates, edits, and revises a section of the *Final Report* by the National Advisory Council on Economic Opportunity, Washington, D.C. (I was Chairman of the Council at the time of the Report.)

surveys indicate that economic issues are dominating public consciousness. There is concern about recession and unemployment,
particularly of youth, minorities and blue collar workers. There
is concern about energy. But above all there is genuine fear over
unchecked deficits, debt and deflation. They undermine security
about the future, create doubt and suspicion of our fellow citizens
and undercut the commitments that make democracy possible.

In these conditions the economic sector becomes a microcosm
of the whole society. Doubts and anxieties about our institutions
that have been fed by global warming environmental degradation, the Iraq and Afghan wars and are deepened by our apparent
inability to deal with severe economic difficulties. The "moral malaise" to which President Carter pointed back in 1980 is perhaps
more evident in our economic institutions than anywhere else in
our public life.

Moreover, in our present state of economic uncertainty there
has been a tendency for public action to degenerate into the nar-
rowest pursuit of private interest. The more affluent seek to ease
the strain by redistributing income from the middle class to themselves through their ability dominate the political system and curry
favor with huge campaign contributions on the federal and state
levels. Economic stringency and rising rates of unemployment for
those below the median income are defended as "acceptable costs"
that will among other things "improve labor discipline." There are
those who would use our present economic troubles to institution-
alize a kind of socio-economic triage.

Meanwhile 44 million Americans are poor and another 55 million are near poor, so almost one-third of our citizens are materi-
ally deprived. Those least able to defend themselves economically
suffer the most from the maldistribution of wealth. The cost is high
not only in material deprivation but also in political withdrawal;
for poverty is not a condition for effective citizenship.

The historian Sam Bass Warner, Jr., wrote that we are on "the
eve of the collapse of the national private economy." In the winter of

2008-2009 we came close to that collapse. Indeed, much of the private economy survives only because of direct or indirect subsidization (contracts, tariffs, investment, protectionist trade agreements and tax benefits) by the Federal government, that most ironic form of "welfare." It was the federal government that rescued major banks, AIG and GM among others.

The economy is a central sector of our social fabric, closely bound up with all our other institutions. It is not working very well and it is working much less well for some than for others. Thus we must also ask what kind of social and political problems does the economy give rise to, and how can these be dealt with.

In addition, we must pose the question, how can America, in the economic arena, enhance democratic citizenship. The best way to begin to seek answers to these crucial problems is to look at our present in the context of our past, to seriously consider the history of our nation and seek out what the American democratic tradition has to say about economic institutions and how that tradition can be adapted to our present needs.

The Economy in a Democracy

In *Democracy in America*, perhaps the wisest book ever written about America, Alexis de Tocqueville argued 180 years ago that though the physical circumstances of our country contribute to our public happiness, the laws contribute more than the physical circumstances, and the mores more than the laws. We were fortunate indeed to inherit from the founders of our republic a constitutional and legal order that has proven sound and flexible. But the origin, interpretation and perpetuation of that order are dependent on the mores embedded in society. A society with different mores would long since have eroded and subverted our constitutional and legal order. De Tocqueville defines "mores" as "habits of the heart," "the sum of moral and intellectual dispositions of men in society." The mores include the opinions and practices that create the moral fabric of a society. They are rooted in our religious tradition, our long experience of political participation and our economic life. If we are to better understand the appropriate role of economic institutions in the American tradition, then we must consider relationships of economic, political and religious ideas and practices as well as the tensions that have developed among them.

Since colonial times, Americans have had a genuine desire to create a decent society for all. That concern was expressed in the idea of a covenant, so important to our Puritan ancestors, and reaffirmed in the Declaration of Independence with its pledge of "our lives, our fortunes and our sacred honor" for the common good. But we have also shown a vigorous individualism. The individual with his needs, desires and interests, particularly economic interests, was seen as almost the only good, and whatever social arrangements were necessary were to be worked out by contracts that maximized the interests of individuals. Our covenant heritage provided the context within which a contract could work, for only with the fundamental trust that the covenant fosters will contracts be honored. The American Constitution was hammered out in major part as an instrument that could balance the various conflicting interests threatening the stability of the nation, and use the energy of those interests to offset and check one another.

The idea was that an approximate equality of economic conditions was essential to the operation of free institutions, because economic equality and also economic independence is necessary for the creation of enlightened citizens. Alexander Hamilton expressed the common view when he said, "In the general course of human nature, a power over man's subsistence amounts to a power over his will." Concentration of economic power, therefore, would create a degree of dependence for many that would be incompatible with their role as free citizens. Hamilton felt pessimistic that such concentrations of wealth could be avoided and so predicted the republican institutions in America would survive but briefly: "As riches increase and accumulate in few hands; as luxury prevails in society; virtue will be in a greater degree considered as only a graceful appendage of wealth, and the tendency of things will be to depart from the republican standard."

Thomas Jefferson, characteristically, was more optimistic about the possible social and economic basis for American free institutions. For all the differences between them the founders of the republic had a fairly clear understanding of the interaction of economics, politics and religion in a republic. Great wealth and extreme poverty alike were to be avoided. They undermined morality and piety, so important for the social climate of free institutions, and they produced tyrannical attitudes on the one hand, and subservient ones on the other, that were equally incompatible with active citizenship.

De Tocqueville, writing about America in the 1830's, continued to raise the social and political issues that were of such concern to our founders. He worried lest too great a concern with economic prosperity undermine our free institutions by drawing men's attention too exclusively to their private and selfish interests. Like Jefferson he thought public participation was the best school of democratic citizenship. Like our founders, he believed that economic independence and social cooperation could go hand in hand in America. As de Tocqueville wrote:

> The free institutions of the United States and the political rights enjoyed there provide a thousand continual reminders to every citizen that he lives in society. At first it is of necessity that men attend to the public interest, afterwards by choice. What had become calculation becomes instinct. By dint of working for the good of his fellow citizens, he in the end acquires a habit and taste for serving them.

Citizen Participation

De Tocqueville, then, in ways consistent with the beliefs of Jefferson and John Adams, argued that the key to American democracy was active civic associations. He observed that only through active involvement in common concerns could the citizen overcome the sense of relative isolation and powerlessness that was a part of the insecurity of life in an increasingly commercial society. Associations, along with decentralized, local administration, were to mediate between the individual and the centralized state, providing forums in which opinion could be publicly and intelligently discussed and the subtle habits of public initiative and responsibility learned and passed on. Associational life, in de Tocqueville's thinking, was the best bulwark against the condition he feared most: the mass society of mutually antagonistic individuals who, once alienated, became prey to despotism.

What de Tocqueville sought, then, was a modern version of classic political democracy. He thought social differentiation inescapable, since the division of labor creates differences among groups in the goals they seek to attain. Democratic politics must seek to coordinate—and adjust—these differentiations in the interest of equity and concern for the liberty of all.

A vital democracy, then, requires a complex effort to achieve a political community through balancing the relationships among the administrative organization of the state, the individual citizen and the associations that come between individual and state. By association individuals become citizens and thereby acquire a sense of personal connection and significance that is unavailable to the depoliticized, purely private person. Through mutual deliberation and joint initiative, moral relationships of trust and mutual aid are established and come to embody the meaning of citizenship for the individual.

Politics in the genuinely associational sense is substantially more than the pursuit of self-interest, since it involves sharing responsibility for acts that create a quality of life quite different from the mere sum of individual satisfactions. De Tocqueville hoped that civic participation could make the individual an active, politically aware subject rather than a passive object of state control. For de Tocqueville, lack of participation, no matter what its material effects, was humanly degrading and finally a manifestation of despotism. In this he was restating the traditional, and basic, civic republican notion that human dignity requires the freedom that exists and grows only in a context of active civic community.

The Individual and the Community

In de Tocqueville's America, as for most Americans throughout the nineteenth century, the basic unit of association and the practical foundation of both individual dignity and participation was the local community. There a civic culture of individual initiative was nurtured through custom and personal ties inculcated by widely shared religious and moral values. Concern for economic betterment was strong but it operated within the context of a still functional covenant concern for the welfare of the neighbor. In the town the competitive individualism stirred by commerce was balanced and humanized through the restraining influences of a fundamentally egalitarian ethic of community responsibility. These autonomous small-scale communities were dominated by an active middle class, the traditional citizens of a free republic, whose members shared similar economic and social positions and whose ranks the less affluent segments of the population aspired to enter, and often succeeded. Most men were self-employed and many who worked for others were saving capital to launch themselves on enterprises of their own. Westward expansion, as de Tocqueville noted, reproduced this pattern of a decentralized, egalitarian democracy across our continent. American citizenship was anchored in the institutions of the face-to-face community—the neighborliness—of the town. Such communities provided the social basis of the new Republican Party in the 1850's and Abraham Lincoln was perhaps their noblest representative.

Undemocratic America

De Tocqueville carefully noted two forms of socioeconomic organization that differed profoundly from this form of civilization—which he considered basic to American democracy—and threatened its continued existence. One was the slave society of the South, which not only treated blacks inhumanly but also, as de Tocqueville in ways quite similar to Jefferson noted, degraded whites as well, reducing them to something considerably less than autonomous, responsible citizens.

The second ominous social form was the industrial factories, evident at first in the Northeast, which concentrated great numbers of poor and dependent workers in the new burgeoning mill towns. Here de Tocqueville feared a new form of authoritarianism was arising that made petty despots out of owners and managers and reduced workers to substandard conditions incompatible with full democratic citizenship. Ironically, the traumatic civil war that destroyed slavery enormously furthered the growth of the industrial structures that so profoundly threatened the original American pattern of decentralized democratic communities.

A National Economy

By the end of the nineteenth century the new economic conditions fatally unbalanced the community pattern of American life. New technologies, particularly in transportation, communications and manufacturing, pulled the many quasi-autonomous local societies into a vast national market. Problems arising in this increasingly centralized and economically integrated society required the growth of the structures of central government, and steadily sapped the ability of local associations to deal with local problems. Under these conditions the very meaning of the traditional idea of American citizenship was called into question.

This shift in emphasis had a profound effect on the role of the individual in society. One response was to adapt to the new structures of centralized economic power by choosing a career whose rewards are wealth and power rather than a calling that provided status and meaning within a community of complementary callings. This shift was becoming evident by the mid-nineteenth century but has progressed enormously in the twentieth, and is now dominant. Virtually all Americans depend directly or indirectly for livelihood, information and, often, ideas and opinions, on great centralized and technologized organizations, and they identify themselves more by professional prestige and privilege than by community ties. The increasing uniformity of national life has developed concomitantly with the rise of a national pattern of social inequality that has replaced the more immediately perceived differentiations of local community.

In modern American experience, constraints and social discipline such as tax paying, company loyalties and professional commonality have been increasingly justified because they are instrumental to individual security and advancement. Some measure of equality of opportunity seemed the appropriate and "American" way to democratize this new national society, but the focus has been on private, economic betterment, not on the quality of shared, public life.

These tendencies, which bear an all too close resemblance to de Tocqueville's fear that an exclusive concern with material betterment would lead America away from free citizenship and toward a form of what he called "soft despotism," have not gone unopposed. Some forms of opposition, like the efforts of the late-nineteenth-century Populists and, later, the Progressives, to defend the integrity of the local community, have failed, though even in failure they have presented examples of a citizenry that will not passively accept its fate.

Democracy at Work

Other efforts to control the most exploitative tendencies of the industrial sector, such as the enactment of health and safety laws and the regulation of working hours and minimum wages, have been more successful. The growth of labor unions has brought some sense of citizenship rights into the workplace. The tendencies toward despotism inherent in profit-oriented bureaucratic corporations have been muted at the bargaining table where wages, hours and working conditions as well as grievance procedures have all become subject to quasi-political negotiation. This has not, with minor exceptions, given the worker a say in the direction of the corporation that employs him, but it has given him some sense of active participation in the conditions of his employment and some protection against any tendency of his employers to disregard his needs.

In our recent history, significant social movements such as the Civil Rights movement or the movement to oppose the Vietnam War have continued to have an impact on public policy. Such movements have mobilized large coalitions of people, motivated by a combination of self-interest and a great deal of disinterested civic concern, to a degree of participation in the political process not common in day-to-day political life. That such movements can still make a difference in our society, even though not as quickly or as completely as some would desire, is evidence that the civic republican spirit is still present among us.

Diluted Principles

Although the spirit of republican citizenship and the social conditions that support it are by no means gone from American life, alarming danger signals are visible. The belief in the individual as a self-interested "economic animal" is certainly not new in our history, but it is less and less tempered by the covenant values based in local communities and religious mores. Now, shorn of many of the nurturant values of traditional civic association, the ethos of self-advancement as an exclusive strategy has been able to run rampant with fewer constraints. The result has been a definition of personal worth almost exclusively in terms of competitive success, measured by status and advancement in large organizations. The ideals of loyalty and service based on personal trust and commitment have faltered in this atmosphere.

Even when the national economy was rapidly expanding and the hope of significant self-advancement was realistic, the social consequences were often what we have recently heard described as "moral malaise." Inability to commit oneself to or believe in anything that transcends one's private interests leads to a less positive commitment to family and community and a negative self-absorption and greed. These very same traits put the nation at the edge of financial bankruptcy in 2008- 2009.

Unfortunately, the difficulties arising from too exclusive a concern with self-betterment have of late been enormously compounded by the gradually dawning knowledge that the cup of plenty is not inexhaustible. Material blessings were never shared equitably in America, but while the economy was growing everyone could look forward to more. However, if wealth is not going to grow or is going to grow much more slowly, and our values have become focused on self-interest, then we are on the verge of the war of all against all, as each interest group strives to get to the well first before it dries up.

The Role of Government

We have for a long time turned, not unwisely, to government to regulate the quest for economic aggrandizement. The ideology of radical individualism, with its notion that the pursuit of self-interest is the best incentive for a free society, has always required a mediator who will guarantee at least minimal conditions of fairness in the race for material goods. Government has been that mediator and has become increasingly active in that role in recent decades. While privileged individuals and groups have often viewed the role of government as intrusive and even destructive, less privileged groups have found in government a protector against the worst consequences of being crushed by the inequities of our competitive economy. Social programs, with all their inadequacies, and affirmative action have brought a measure of justice to people (women and minorities) who have been deprived and/or handicapped by poverty and prejudice. Perhaps it is a sign of the times that such minimal and basic human programs are viewed by the privileged as programs designed to victimize *them*.

Our present danger does not come from government as such, or from self-seeking individuals either, for that matter. The danger to our democratic institutions comes rather from the declining effectiveness of the intervening structures—the variety of civic associations—that serve to mediate between individual and state. It is those intermediate structures that encourage citizenship and provide the best defense against despotism, soft or hard. Without them the government, even when acting benevolently, may encourage a dependence and a lack of civic concern that play into the hands of authoritarianism. The danger increases when the economic pie is shrinking or growing slowly and erratically, when the privileged are talking about "social discipline" while the deprived feel existent inequalities more keenly.

In the meantime, public cynicism about the modern American notion of pursuit of economic self-interest in the context of free enterprise, tempered by a degree of expert bureaucratic fine-tuning by the Federal Government, is growing. The failures of conventional economics (particularly in the past decade) to meet certain problems—unemployment, underemployment, slow economic growth and national concern about the energy crisis—have engendered widespread public disillusionment in government and business corporations alike. One form of this disillusionment is a growing cynicism and a tendency to "look out for number one," together with a deepening fear of one's fellow citizens. Such sentiments as these, republican theorists warn, are the preconditions of despotism.

Volunteerism and Civic Engagement

But another response to the failures of the recent pattern of American political and economic life is to look to the possibility of the revival or our democratic civic culture and social structures, and above all the intermediate local and neighborhood associations that nurture them. There are many who view the present necessity—to rethink the notion that quantitative, undifferentiated economic development is the answer to all our problems—as a genuine opportunity to recover aspects of our public life that could never be fully absorbed into that pattern They view the present challenge not with dismay but rather as a stimulus to become our true selves as a democratic society.

On both the right and left of the political spectrum there is much talk of intermediate structures. Some use the language of participatory public life simply as a means to attack the growth of "big government" without a reasonable assessment of the social benefits government confers; one that *no other structure* in our society can presently provide. For such critics the ideal intermediate structure is the business corporation, which they believe should be freed from "government interference." (This seems to be the role of the Tea Party, which has been co-opted by corporate America to blame government for our problems)

Others who talk about intermediate structures view business corporations as massive structures of bureaucratic power, largely unresponsive to citizen needs, and certainly not forums for civic participation and democratic debate. Or else they see business corporations as needing drastic reform before they can function as truly representative intermediate structures. At any rate, however important it may be to nurture religious, ethnic, neighborhood and other forms of civic association, it is the economic institutions that are the key to present difficulties, and it is a new way of linking our economic life with our democratic values that is the key to their solution.

Let us consider the relevance of the early American pattern to our present situation. The founders saw occupation and economic condition as closely linked to the religious, social and political bases of a free society. They feared excessive wealth, excessive poverty and lack of independence in one's occupation. They thought self-employment the best guarantee of good citizenship, which would then lead to civic cooperation in the local community, particularly when nurtured by the religious and moral ideal of the covenant.

Our present circumstances—massive economic inter-dependence, employment mostly in large organizations and the near disappearance of the self-employed farmer, merchant and artisan—would seem so far from the vision of the founders as to have no connection with it. But if we consider the intentions and purposes of the founders, and not the economic conditions they found close at hand, then we might understand how their vision and wisdom could apply to our present situation.

If the intention of the founders was to create independent citizens who could then cooperate together in civic associations so as to produce a democratic society conducive to the dignity of all, we must consider how we might attain the same ends under conditions of our present political economy. A renewed citizenship must build upon our still living traditions of volunteerism, civic engagement and cooperation wherever they may be found, but it cannot take the older forms and resources for granted. Contemporary citizenship requires a moral commitment as well as an

institutional basis appropriate to our interdependent, occupation-
ally segmented national society. And because professionalism and
occupational identification have become so crucial to contemporary society and personal identity, a renewed civic identity must
be institutionalized in the workplace as well as the community at
large if we want to avoid the classic war of "all against all."

Private/Public Enterprise

If we would recover again the social and personal commitment
to free institutions that is the life-blood of a democratic society,
then we must bring the public democratic ethos into the sphere
of economic life. To view economic institutions as "private" made
sense when most Americans spent their lives on family farms or in
family firms. But today when most American men and a rapidly increasing proportion of American women spend much of their lives
in large economic structures that are for most purposes "public"
except that the profits they make go to institutional and individual
"private" stockholders—it becomes imperative to bring the forms
of citizenship and of civic association more centrally into the economic sphere. There is no simple formula for achieving that end;
it certainly does not require "nationalization," which, by bringing
vast economic bureaucracies under the domination of the Federal
Government, would make the democratization of economic life
even more difficult. What we need is a series of experiments with
new forms of autonomous or semiautonomous "public enterprise"
as well as reformed versions of "private enterprise" as we pursue,
with circumspection, our aim of a healthy economy that is responsive to democratic values.

If the profit imperative creates problems even under "normal"
conditions of economic growth, its consequences become severe
under conditions or economic stringency. The experimentation
and free-wheeling nature of a period of growth begins to close
down because everything must be justified in terms of the bottom
line. Social purposes and human needs—perhaps even the survival

of some individuals—that cannot be translated into a short-term prospect of profitability are necessarily ignored. This is especially true if we analyze the impact of past inflations on wage-earners in the basic necessities: health, energy, housing and food. It is under these conditions that a new, more public and more civic purpose must be injected into the economy and the language of "economic democracy" comes into play.

The Dynamics of Bureaucracy

The profit imperative and the bureaucratic form of social organization often combine in an unfortunate way. The profit imperative itself can become a kind of tyrannical command that limits the options even of top management. Concerns for the humanization of the work process or more vigorous corporate social responsibility may have to be shelved under pressure to show profitability. Unfortunately, it is not true that all good things are "good business." If they were, our economy and our society would not be suffering their present difficulties. In any case it seems clear that a broadening of the purposes of economic organization to include a greater range of social responsibilities than the obligation to show a profit goes hand in hand with a concern to make the internal operation of economic organization more genuinely responsive to human needs.

Non-Profit Corporations and Cooperatives

This is not the place to more than hint at the possibilities for transforming our economy into a more democratic and socially responsible one. Clearly we have only begun to realize the values of consumer, publicly owned, or cooperative forms of economic non-profit enterprise. Where there is expert assistance and capital available, a variety of small-scale economic non-profit enterprises can be organized as self-help development efforts. Such ventures make excellent sense in economically depressed areas; they provide multiple opportunities for those otherwise excluded from employment. In addition to fostering the self-respect that comes from steady employment, the owners of a cooperative enterprise receive an education in the democratic process when they choose their board of directors and participate in a variety of functions in running their own business. Further, the cooperative is not tempted to drain the profits away from its own community as a branch of a large firm would do. Profits are ploughed back into local expansion, the proliferation of other cooperatives and, often, some forms of local social services, such as day-care centers, health clinics and credit unions.

The non-profit corporation has already proved its usefulness in the form of Community Economic Development Corporations (CDCs). By combining profitable or at least viable economic undertakings with a variety of community services, the non-profit corporation has many of the advantages of the cooperative on a larger scale. Undoubtedly we have only begun to realize the potential in a variety of forms public enterprise can take. The Tennessee Valley Authority, for all the opposition it has generated, stands as a reasonably successful venture in public enterprise. As economic difficulties beset some of out largest corporations, experiments with mixed public/private enterprise might be contemplated.

Of course, all these forms of experimentation are dependent on a climate of financial and government support. There should be ways to make tax savings available to corporations that can show a consistent record of public responsibility at the cost of their own reduced profitability. A program of government grants might be made available to support innovative efforts to create energy efficient businesses, to democratize the workplace, humanize work or heighten community responsibility Particularly in a situation of little or no economic growth, the emphasis must shift from quantitative expansion to qualitative improvement.

Even though the past failure of public courage may be discouraging, there are still some aspects of our present situation that could lead to a reinvigoration of our mores and a new sense of the importance of the covenant model. The greatest opportunity exists in the growing realization that endless—and mindless—economic growth is not the answer to all our problems, even if it were possible. And we are only beginning to comprehend some of the inherent brutalities of an over-technologized society. If the rise of industrial capitalism, for all the material benefits it has conferred, also lies at the root of many of our problems, then the faltering of the economy that has become evident since the 1970's, and that shows no early sign of change, may provide an occasion for some profound reflections about the direction of America in the decades ahead. If serious Americans in large numbers realize that the cause of our difficulties is not "big government" but, rather, a way of life that worships wealth and power, that makes economic profit the arbiter of all human values and that delivers us into the tyranny of the bottom line, then it may be possible to re-examine our present institutions and the values they embody.

A democratization of our economic institutions, by whatever name, is a key to the revitalization of our mores and our public life. Clearly the fusion of economic and governmental bureaucracies into a kind of superburearcracy is not the answer, but would only compound the causes of our difficulty. The crisis in confidence that has overtaken our present system of bureaucratic capitalism can lead to a new shared public interest in our economic life.

We must develop the conditions for a new, shared public interest through a movement for the reform of economic life. The process needs to invite the enclaves of neighborly cooperation out from their present defensive position on the peripheries of our public life to join in a larger effort to transform the mainstream institutions into vehicles for and expressions of citizen concern and positive values. This necessitates a process of moral education at the same time it attempts to restructure institutions. The effects of such a positive movement, already beginning in many areas, would be to revitalize the principle of civic association, to strengthen the intermediate structures that make it possible for individual citizens to maintain their independence and to make their voices heard, and, thus, to reinforce the vitality of our free institutions generally. Moving into a world of little or no economic growth, without such a process of democratic character and values, would only precipitate no-win Hobbesian struggles among groups wanting to profit at one another's expense—a struggle already too evident in our present politics of special interests.

But a healthy shift in the organization of our economic life, with all it would entail in our society, cannot be expected as a result of mere technocratic or organizational manipulation. So great a change, overcoming not only entrenched power but entrenched ways of thinking, could be brought about only by a change in social or moral consciousness. We are, like it or not, going to face a world of increasing scarcity and simplicity, voluntary or involuntary. We can enter that world with bitterness and antagonism, with a concern to protect ourselves and our families whatever the consequences to others. Or we can enter with a keen sense of freedom, justice, opportunity and community; bequeathed to us by our founding fathers.

To come to terms with what has happened to us in the last century in a way that allows us to regain the moral meaning and the public participation that characterized our formative period—that seems the only way to create a livable society in the decades ahead. There are no easy formulas as to how to attain that goal. A great deal of creative experimentation and a variety of types of organization that will explore different possibilities are surely needed. But only the presence of a new sense of moral commitment and human sensibility can provide the time and space for such experimentation.

Summary

It would seem clear that though the rise of corporate capitalism has brought Americans many good things, it has also disrupted our traditional social system while finally creating enormous economic problems that it cannot seem to solve. The national private economy has not only created problems but has, through its enormous political influence, involved government and massive government spending in ways that have been self-serving and thus compounded those problems.

Ever since World War II, high-technology and service industries have boomed in the "sun belt" with the help of massive military orders and huge Federal underwriting for infra-structure. During the same years the industrial cities of the Northeast and Midwest have been allowed to deteriorate. The housing bust is yet another example. Profits have been enormous, but the human costs have been very high. It has been suggested that this unbalanced pattern of growth and stagnation will exact enormous sums in taxpayers' money in the decades ahead. Just reflect on the Wall St. and banking bailouts. It could have been avoided if the public interest had been given greater consideration in the planning of a healthy and balanced national economy; as well as providing appropriate regulatory oversight and accountability.

Another example of the disastrous consequences of economic decisions made solely on the basis of profitability is the proliferation of energy-consuming, pollution-creating automobile and truck transportation at the expense of rapid transit and railroad systems, especially since World War II. Due to the power of automobile and oil lobbies, billions have been spent in Federal highway programs while railroad and mass transit supports have been attacked as "wasteful." Dependence in initially cheap foreign oil, which was part of this transportation package, has proved to be not only an economic time-bomb but an international political disaster that has made our national interest highly vulnerable.

Stephen A. Marglin, Professor of Economics at Harvard University, recently wrote:

> The real issue of the next decade is not planning, but what kind of planning. If planning is to be democratic in process and end product, the entire structure of the capitalist economy must be overhauled to become significantly more participatory, from the shop floor to the corporate board room.
>
> Either our dominant economic institution, the corporation will come to reflect democratic ideals, or the polity will come increasingly to incorporate the notion of the divine right of capital.
>
> My own position is clear. Authoritarian capitalism is no longer a vehicle of human progress, but an obstacle. By contrast, democracy, extended to our economic institutions, has a rich and glorious future.

Professor Marglin, as our historical review has shown, sets the issue in terms thoroughly consonant with our American democratic tradition.

In dealing with our economic problems then, we must not be oriented to technical efficiency alone; that could produce an authoritarian solution. The economy is part—a central part—of our entire social system. That means that the criterion of success cannot be cost-accounting alone. The human implications of various forms of organization must always be considered. Above all, the economy must reinforce, not undermine, that structure of intermediate voluntary associations upon which the vitality of our democracy rests. Only an economy that can provide security, dignity, equality of opportunity and participation to all our citizens will be a democratic economy.

We have in America the human and natural resources as well as the cultural and spiritual values to surmount the present challenges; to reinvigorate our democratic life and to revitalize our communities. That is the challenge of this decade.

The Value of Service

Nearly fifty years ago when President John F. Kennedy launched the Peace Corps he articulated a memorable and oft-quoted challenge: "Ask not what your country can do for you; ask what you can do for your country." This quote signaled a new, and hopeful, direction in American political and cultural life. The country was in transition, moving away from a difficult and trying period: the pain of the Great Depression; World War II; the Korean War; the threat of mutual nuclear destruction during the height of the Cold War; and the repression and cynicism of the McCarthy period.

And Americans, young and old, responded to the call by joining the Peace Corps, Volunteers

In Service to America (VISTA), The Teacher Corps, and soon after, the War on Poverty. It was a time of idealism, hope and promise. More recently, Americans responded with the same spirit and enthusiasm to other crises such as 9/11, Hurricane Katrina, the earthquake in Haiti and the BP oil spill in the Gulf of Mexico.

Indeed, volunteerism has a long and honored tradition in the history of our nation. The traditions of community service and citizen participation have been at the heart of American civic culture since the nation was founded. Whether through town hall meetings, the local school board, a political party, a hospital auxiliary, or one of our innumerable other national and local organizations, Americans have felt and acted on the need to give something back to their communities. Since the events of September 11, 2001 and in the midst of our nation's severe economic decline, this need has become more urgent as Americans have become more introspective and more patriotic, and more anxious. Patriotism and anxiety have taken many different forms, but one thing is clear: our concern for our country, our communities, our families, and our neighbors has become more acute and our need to contribute more urgent.

The response to 9/11 was probably the most vivid example with firefighters, police officers, and rescue teams leading the way after September 11, many thousands of ordinary citizens—ironworkers, teachers, public health clinicians, professionals, businesspeople, and school-children—volunteered to go to Ground Zero or offered their support from a distance. Everything from blankets to blood, peanut butter to poetry, arrived in New York City by the bale, the gallon, the barrel, and the ream. Americans didn't wait until New Years Day to make resolutions; in mid-September, many resolved to be more caring and giving.

If once again, our nation is in a crisis of major proportion. The Great Recession has hit our country like a steamroller and some economists are predicting that the present level of unemployment could continue for several years. In cities and towns across the nation, and particularly in America's industrial heartland, factories are closing and Main Street stores are being boarded up. Families are experiencing loss of homes, health insurance and unemployment benefits as well increases in bankruptcies, divorce, alcoholism and drug problems. And most of all fear and anxiety is undermining family stability.

How we respond to these crises as individuals, families, communities and as a nation is absolutely critical. One of the main purposes of this book is to help harness the compassion, energy and concern of those who want to serve their communities in creative, constructive and useful ways. So, if volunteering is one of those things you've been meaning to do all along but just haven't gotten around to, or if you're just curious about what's out there, this book can help you take the next step. It is designed to help you decide that you can make a contribution to the well-being of your community. It will help to answer the why, the how, the what, and the when. Why is community service important? How can you get in touch with a group that promotes the values and goals that you believe in? What specific volunteer activities match up with your skills and experiences? When is a good time to volunteer?

Each of the organizations profiled in this book has been selected because of its commitment to educational, social, economic, environmental, and community development goals. Some have been in existence for many decades; others are fairly new. Most are national organizations, and some are local prototypes, but all have a solid track record of delivering services that are useful and meaningful. Before you select an organization to volunteer for, ask yourself a few questions:

- How much time do you want to serve?
- What kind of service fits your personality?

- What neighborhood and community do you want to work in?
- Which target population do you want to work with?
- What skills do you have to offer?
- What would you like to gain from the experience?

Historically, our greatest strength as a nation has been to be there for one another. Citizen participation is part of our birthright. As Thomas Paine put it, "The highest calling of every individual in a democratic society is that of citizen!" Accidents of nature and abstract notions of improvement do not make our communities better or healthier places in which to live and work. They get better because people like you decide that they want to make a difference.

Volunteering is not a conservative or liberal, Democratic or Republican issue: caring and compassion simply help to define us as being human. Volunteering not only helps communities but it helps individuals volunteers to integrate their own idealism and realism in a healthy way. An idealist without a healthy dose of realism tends to become a naive romantic. A realist without ideals tends to become a cynic. Community service helps you put your ideals to work in a comprehensive approach to complex problems. I've seen it happen time and again with my students and with VISTA and AmeriCorps volunteers.

Volunteering is very much a two-way street. It is about giving *and* receiving, and the receiving can be nourishing for the heart

and mind. The very act of serving taps into a wellspring of empathy and generosity that is both personally gratifying and energizing. Again and again, former volunteers describe their experiences with words like these: *adventure, growth, human connection, exciting, spiritual, maturing, learning,* and *enjoyable.*

I have seen this in action, first-hand, for the past ten years, since I decided to give the students in each of my classes, mostly university seniors, the choice between a midsemester exam or sixteen hours of community service. The students unanimously chose service, though most of them didn't know what was in store for them. They had a choice of over eighty different activities organized by the Public Service Center at the University of California, Berkeley.

Here's what one student wrote about this experience:

Before I started volunteering, I had very different expectations about the [after-school] program. I thought it would be very sports-oriented with little academic emphasis. Luckily, my expectations proved false. The program—for fourth and fifth-graders at the Thousand Oaks/Franklin Elementary School—has a set schedule for each grade. The students rotate between free play, sports, library study time, circle time, and arts and crafts.

It was in the library that I saw how truly behind these children are in mathematics, reading, and grammar. In addition, I never expected to see the immense poverty that these children experience or to be so emotionally affected by it. Last week I learned that one of my favorite children is homeless. It seems so silly to be reprimanding him for not doing his homework and not putting the effort at school. This seems so trivial compared to the real-life horrors that he must experience. Although I had my expectations, never did I anticipate the emotional attachment that I now share with these children. I find myself yearning to become a teacher, which was a career I never thought about before this program. I know that as these children grow, they will probably forget about me; but I know I will never forget them. I have truly changed and matured as a result of them.

A second student wrote:

Before I started tutoring I was really scared, because I didn't know what tutors did in junior high schools. I was afraid of not being able to explain things so that kids could understand. I thought I might lose patience quickly with kids who were slower in understanding and for whom I would have to repeatedly state the same thing. I was concerned that the kids would resent me or not respect me because I wasn't the teacher and was closer to their age. And finally, I thought they wouldn't like me; the first day I even had trouble introducing myself because of this initial uncertainty.

Contrary to these preliminary fears, however, tutoring at Willard *has been a life-changing experience for me*. I've found that I have more patience working with kids than I've ever had in any other area of my life. I work hard to come up with lots of examples when the kids I'm working with don't understand. We relate well to one another because they know that I'm there to help them. It's been the joy of my semester to work with these students, who I really appreciate.

These comments were typical of the experiences of nearly all the students. Their testimony is consistent with the more formal academic research and evaluations, which tell us that service-learning clearly enriches and enhances the individual volunteer in multiple ways.

At the university level we know that service-learning contributes to a student's critical thinking, creative imagination, and moral intelligence.

And for the past fifteen years there has also been a substantial body of research with respect to the impact of service-learning in K-12 schools—primarily in the 10th and 11th grades. It is uniformly positive

What better way for students to understand early on, the connection between ideas and behavior, between the values and ideals that people hold and the ethical consequences of those beliefs, than integrating civics, American history and social studies with quality service-learning.

Recent studies in K-12 schools across the country have demonstrated that:

- Service-learning has a positive effect on the personal development of young people
- Students who participate in service-learning are less likely to engage in "risk" behavior
- Service-learning helps develop students' sense of civic and social responsibility and their citizenship skills
- Service-learning helps students acquire academic skills and knowledge
- Students who participate in service-learning are more engaged in their studies and more motivated to learn
- Service-learning helps students to become more knowledgeable and realistic about careers
- Service-learning results in greater mutual respect between teachers and students as well as improving the overall school climate.

What is interesting is that the students today are having the same responses as I did during my own community service forty-five hears ago, when I taught in Harlem during the early years of the War on Poverty and VISTA.

My students now, and I back then, confronted the complexities of the everyday worlds of individuals and communities quite different from our own. We were forced to deal with difficult social and economic realities. It was an eye-opener to learn about the inequities and injustices of our society, to see first hand the painful struggles of children who did not have the educational, social, or economic opportunities that we took for granted. This experience was humbling, and it broke down my insularity, for which I'm truly grateful. Margaret Mead called this "heart-learning."

Community service also taught me an important lesson about our society: ethical values and healthy communities are not inherited; they are either recreated through action by each generation, or they are not. That is what makes AmeriCorps, VISTA, and other forms of community service unique and valuable. They help us to regenerate our best values and principles as individuals and as a society. From Plato to the present, civic virtue has been at the core of civilized behavior. My experience as a teacher and with service-learning has taught me that moral and ethical values cannot survive from one generation to the next if the only preservatives are academic texts or research studies. Real-life experience is the crucible for shaping values. Out of it develop an intuition and a living memory that are the seeds of a humane and just society.

The task of passing along to the young our best civic traditions has been made more difficult in the past thirty years by the steady shift of emphasis away from qualitative values (civility, cooperation, and the public interest) to quantitative ones(competition, making it, and privatism) as well as the demoralizing pursuit of mindless consumerism and trivia force-fed us by the mass media. Just about every parent and teacher I know has, in one way or another, expressed the concern that they cannot compete with the marketing techniques of the mass media, particularly television. They are worried about the potential consequences of the growing acquisitiveness, the indulgence, and the self-centeredness of children. I hear this from conservatives, liberals, and moderates. Small wonder. The average eighteen year old in the United States has seen more than 380,000 television commercials. We haven't begun to comprehend the inherent brutality of this media saturation on our children's psyches.

Materialism and assumptions of entitlement breed boredom, cynicism, drug abuse, and crime for kicks. Passivity, isolation, and depression come with television and on-line addiction. Ignorance, fear, and prejudice come from insularity and exclusivity. A national and local effort to promote community service by young people is the best antidote to these social ills. It's also important for parents to volunteer because in the same way children develop good reading habits, they learn by the example set by adults.

I have devoted a good deal of space to why it's important for young people, as well as their parents, to volunteer and participate in the civic life of their communities. Now I'd like to focus on the role of the not-so-young: seniors, boomers and pre-boomers who are retired, semi-retired or thinking of retiring. And I'll do so by sharing a story told to me by the late Senator Jack Gordon, an old friend and former President Pro-Tem of the Florida Senate. Jack was an outstanding legislator and had an inquiring mind. He thought that there was a meaningful inter-relationship between the health and well-being of seniors—an important constituency—and their active participation in the life of their community. So, one day he decided to launch a pilot project to test this hypothesis and he helped to raise the money to initiate a unique undertaking.

Miami Beach was part of his district and he knew that there were many retirees who resided there who were musicians. They were "snowbirds", like many other residents, who came from northern climates to vacation in the winter and eventually decided to live there permanently. So he put a call out; and they responded— cellists, oboists, cymbalists, pianists, trumpeters, drummers, flutists, and what have you—from the symphonies, philharmonics, orchestras and ensembles of Boston, Buffalo, Chicago, Cleveland, Detroit, Philadelphia and beyond. They practiced and practiced and then performed at free public concerts. There was one caveat however; each individual had to do a before and after—to record the number or times they visited their doctors and how much medication they took before they participated and then keep a weekly record after they began rehearsing and performing. The results bore out Gordon's hunch. Astoundingly, the number of the visits to a doctor were reduced by 70% and the amount of medication reduced by 64%. A word to the wise is sufficient. My advice to all you retirees is simple: KEEP ACTIVE and do so with the kind of rewarding efforts make you feel needed and useful.

You don't have to volunteer more than a few hours a week. If you're an architect work with Habitat for Humanity; an accountant, help low income people with their income taxes; a teacher, work with disadvantaged kids in a reading program or a literacy program for immigrants; a dentist, doctor, nurse or psychologist, volunteer at a community health center (my own dentist, when he announced his retirement to me also said he was going to volunteer two days a week at a clinic for migrant workers) ... You can figure out what makes sense for yourself; there are plenty of opportunities listed in the book. But keep in mind that it will be good for your health and vitality. Stay young at heart!!!

In summary, the goals of service are inclusive and nourishing; they seek to honor diversity, protect the environment, and enrich our nation's educational, social and economic policies so that they enhance human dignity. On a personal level, volunteering—the very act of caring and doing—makes a substantial difference in our individual lives because it nourishes the moral intelligence required for critical judgment and mature behavior.

Dr. Seuss reminded us in *The Lorax* that nothing is going to get better unless someone like you cared enough to pitch in and make it happen.

Throughout our history we have responded to crises with introspection, generosity, and caring. Now is not the time to push the snooze button and be complacent. Just as we mobilized our capacities to confront hardship in the past, we must take action and confront our present economic and social problems. In the real world, we know that taking ordinary initiatives can make a difference. It is within our power to move beyond this economic crisis and to create new opportunities. What it comes down to is assuming personal responsibility. If we decide to become involved in voluntary efforts, we can restore idealism, realism, responsiveness, and vitality to our institutions and communities.

PART TWO

STORIES TO INSPIRE, BOOKS TO CONSIDER

Any level of community involvement—whether a daily commitment or simply starting a book club in your neighborhood, as described in this section—is good for you, vital to those being served, and healthy for your communities and our nation. There is a postscript to this story that is worth thinking about. It is that in my fifteen years of working with volunteers has confirmed what my intuition told me: that volunteering for community service could well be the quickest, most rewarding and least expensive way of gaining self-esteem. ★

Volunteer Stories

Community service makes an enormous impact on peoples' lives—both the volunteer and the recipient. As I said at the beginning of this book, I've never seen anything like the power of public service to bring an extraordinary sense of self-esteem to a person. ★

A CHANGE IN WORLDVIEW

My parents volunteered. After a great tornado devastated parts of Lubock, Texas, my hometown, my father, a dry land wheat farmer, went to the bank and took out $500. Then he went alone to the poorest section of town hit by the storm, helped each family dig out, left $20 for groceries, and moved on to the next house. Even as a teenager, I admired my mother's involvements, which included serving on the library board and the board of Faith City Mission while supporting international initiatives such as Frank Laubach's literacy program Each One Teach One. One parent responded "hands on" to immediate needs; the other addressed systemic change. In my involvements since, I have tried to keep an eye on both.

One weekend early in college, at the University of Texas I went on a service trip to Monterrey, Mexico, where we built a basketball court for a church camp. During my senior year a group of us traveled only a few blocks away to East Austin where we spent Friday and Saturday nights in the basement of an African-American Church, doing carpentry during the day to help an elderly woman get her house back up to codes after a fire. The Friday night before we got to work, an economics professor led a discussion in the basement of that church. He asked if we knew why poor people sometimes drove big cars, then explained that cars can be easily repossessed, while loans for home repairs cannot. With that simple insight, my world-view shifted on its axis.

From these two experiences I realized one doesn't have to go very far or stay very long for a life to be changed. Later, when students stepped forward who wanted to do it, I helped them organize an Alternative Spring Break program that became a template for similar programs at universities all over the country and led to many service-learning courses at my own, Vanderbilt University.

A year after I graduated from college, I had to choose between going to Mississippi for Freedom Summer or learning German and French to prepare for a PhD program. My head eventually followed my heart and I chose the academy. Over the years, however, I have found plenty of opportunities for activism: helping create a Women's Studies program; organizing a faculty march against apartheid in South Africa; supporting a major lawsuit that sought gender equity at my university. For a scholarly article I spent a summer researching the history of civil disobedience. Much later I chose to practice it with two hundred other members of Soulforce in protest against the anti-gay policies of one of the mainline churches. That led to a day in the Cleveland city jail in good company that included the Rev. James Lawson and Arun Gandhi, grandson of Mahatma Gandhi.

I do what I do out of gratitude and responsibility—grateful for those who brought us this far, responsible for those yet to come.

—Susan Wiltshire, formerly Chair of the Classics Department at Vanderbilt

--------------------------------- ★ ---------------------------------

VISTA TO POLITICS

When I left New York City in 1966 to serve as a Volunteer In Service To America (VISTA) in Eagle Pass, Texas, I had no idea that I would wind up staying in Texas, pursuing graduate degrees in both social work and law at the University of Texas and, ultimately, serving as a long-standing member of the Texas House of Representatives. As I look back at my career, I realize that everything I've done is directly related to the community organizing skills I developed as a "front-line warrior" in Lyndon B. Johnson's War on Poverty.

Working at the grassroots level as a VISTA volunteer, trying to implement the policy of "eliminating the paradox of poverty in the midst of plenty in this nation," was always a challenge. We started preschool programs and teen clubs, laid the groundwork for a legal aid program, tried to get water and sewers to a barrio called Seco Mines, and organized neighborhood councils to advocate on behalf of low-income families.

While we didn't eliminate poverty, we did succeed in developing local leadership and maximizing the involvement of poor people in decision-making processes that directly affected their lives. Through community action programs, we gave people opportunities in education, job training and economic development. We helped them learn to negotiate the system. It was an exciting era in the history of this country, and it put me on a path to public service as well as advocacy for the needs of low-income and vulnerable populations.

After graduate school, I ran a legislative internship program as staff counsel for a state senator who'd been one of my supervisors in VISTA. I developed legislation that enhanced protective services for elderly people and abused children. I drafted an anti-hazing bill. I helped the senator become a champion for dropout prevention. I used my training in social work and the law to address, at the state level, many of the same issues we'd focused on during the War on Poverty.

In 1990, I was approached by a group of people who thought I should run for a seat in the Texas House of Representatives, against a three-term incumbent who'd never lost. I told them that as a native New Yorker and ex-

VISTA volunteer, I wouldn't have a chance. They convinced me that if I used my organizing skills to put together an effective campaign, I might win.

The incumbent had the money, but I had dedicated volunteers and a strong organization. We won, and I took the oath of office in January 1991 and have been reelected nine times. My focus in the House has always been on health, human services, housing, domestic violence, discrimination, and social justice. I work on issues that affect the elderly, people with disabilities, children, minorities, women, and all vulnerable populations. I take pride in what I do, face new challenges every day, and sleep well knowing that I'm working on behalf of people who occasionally need assistance from their government or laws passed that will protect and enhance their rights and dignity.

—Elliott Naishat

NURTURING INTERESTS

When I was eight years old, I volunteered for the Weinberg Nature Center and Kerr Riding Stables in Scarsdale, New York. I would like to think that I was precocious in my social consciousness, but in fact I was just looking for a way to access my greatest loves: nature, small creatures and horses. At both the nature center and the barn I had the lowliest of jobs. I cleaned the tanks and the stalls. But this meant that I got to handle the animals. I studied the snakes, salamanders and toads. I picked the horses hooves, removed the burrs from their tails, and saddled them for lessons and pony rides. After some time at the stables, I was allowed to exercise the ponies. And at the nature center, I soon was allowed to lead nature walks and talks.

I entered Dartmouth College at 16 years old, and majored in English. After graduation, I found a job in New York City writing adv for Redbook Magazine and, after earning a Master's Degree in from Columbia University, I worked my way up the corporate l become a Managing Director for an investment bank. In my l after a cancer scare that required a bone transplant, I left my c job to focus on starting a family. Once my daughters were in joined a small group of other motivated parents who ran the sc auction, and other fund-raising events. That wasn't very insp then I volunteered to train the horses and officers for the moun rangers who protected the New York City parklands, and disco a hidden world of nature in the Big Apple.

I chose my volunteer jobs because I loved what I got to do. I had chosen my business career because I was good at it and could make money, but not because it was how I wanted to spend my life. Work was interesting enough, and I kept getting promoted. But it took the threat of my illness to force me to consider how my values were important enough to make them my life's work.

So I turned my volunteering into a career. I became the Director of the Park Rangers, accepting a salary a fraction of my corporate pay. But as a public servant, my rewards far exceeded anything I had received before. I started free public canoe and camping programs, opened nature centers and challenge courses, created The Natural Classroom programs that bring inner city school children into the parks, even reintroduced the Bald Eagle to Manhattan. I also volunteered as a Board Member of the city's animal shelters. Today, as the Executive Director of the Horticultural Society of New York, I run social service programs in prisons, supportive housing and public schools that teach the benefits of gardening and fresh vegetables. I build community gardens and urban farms. And I just volunteered to help start New York City's first Farm School. My older daughter is in AmeriCorps working for the volunteer organization, New York Cares, and my younger daughter just started volunteering at a small museum. Their values are guiding them, and volunteering is their pathway. I guess it runs in the family now.

—Sara Hobel

THE TOUGHEST JOB YOU'LL EVER LOVE

Growing up on my family ranch near Mokelumne Hill, a small community in California's Mother Lode country, I quickly learned about community service from my parents. They were constantly involved in the PTA, Boy Scouts, and local community clubs. Having only five kids in my eighth grade class and three rooms in the school that my great-grandfather helped build in the 1890's made it clear that if something was to get done, we all had to help. On my way to becoming an Eagle Scout, we had the annual duty of cleaning two historic gold rush cemeteries. Service often meant hard work.

But the real lesson in service was taught to me in 1965 by my girlfriend at the University of California, Berkeley (CAL) where I had some success as a football player. In our senior year, I asked her to marry me. She replied, "I would love to marry you, but you're heading for the NFL, and I am going into the Peace Corps."

She became committed to the cause following President John F. Kennedy's commencement speech at Memorial Stadium at CAL. She heard his call to service and decided then and there to join the Peace Corps. I joined her.

September of 1966, nine months into our marriage, we arrived in Metu, a village in southwestern Ethiopia. 30 kilometers from the grass airstrip and an endless muddy road, we found our new home: tin roof, dirt floor, wattle walls, outhouse out back, and unlimited opportunity to serve. Teaching seventh and eighth grade students and women's family health education, digging wells, offering small pox vaccinations, building remote schools, setting up coffee co-ops—every day filled with helping the community, building friendships, and setting the pace for a life of service. As the Peace Corps motto goes, "It's the toughest job you'll ever love."

We witnessed good people needlessly suffer and die in Ethiopia. Returning to America, we experienced culture shock at Harvard Business School. Upon graduation, Patti and I returned to California with a sense of purpose. We decided that a career in public service, committed to policies that open doors and lift people out of poverty, would be a much more fulfilling life than being a banker.

Patti followed her heart and set out to fulfill JFK's call to service. She returned to Ethiopia in 1996 as the Associate Director of the Peace Corps, restarting the long dormant program in that country to give a new generation the chance to serve.

We decided to go to Africa 45 years ago. After serving as an Assemblymember, State Senator, California Insurance Commissioner, Deputy Secretary of the U.S. Interior Department, California Lieutenant Governor, and now a member of Congress we are not about to slow down. It has been a marvelous journey, and it's not over yet.

—**John Garamandi**

A PROFOUND IMPACT

I was born and raised in Seattle and I received my bachelor's degree in Community, Environment and Planning from the University of Washington. My first experience volunteering was at the Washington Park Arboretum when I was 16. I spent my Saturday mornings at their greenhouse organizing plants for weekend sales, gathering soil, repotting trees and getting dirty. Ten years later I found myself living in a rural West African village as a Peace Corps Volunteer in Ghana.

The two years I spent living in the village of Apimsu were some of the most remarkable years of my life so far. Like many other 20-somethings with a bachelor's degree I was trying to find my place in the working world. Joining the Peace Corps seemed like a great way to gain more international experience and expand upon my life skills while doing something that would make a difference. Soon after my arrival in Ghana I realized that not only was I contributing to the local community, but it was also having a profound impact on me.

As the only American within a 10-mile radius, I lived in a village of about 300 and worked with a local farmer's organization to improve sustainable farming practices. I made friends in the community, learned how to wash my clothes by hand, eat local foods, and live a completely different lifestyle than the one I had known in at home. I quickly overcame the challenges I had initially anticipated, and the new cultural norms I had adopted became second nature. Through these experiences I gained a strong sense of self-assurance and independence. I felt that if I could do *this*, I could do anything.

I finished my Peace Corps service nearly two years ago but the impact it had on me still resonates. My experiences working with local communities in Ghana have honed my desire to work towards bettering communities here in my own country. I have returned to school, pursuing a master's degree in City Planning, where I will be working on urban issues relating to housing and community and economic development. While I have yet to determine my future career, my desire to learn about foreign lands and different cultures and my interest in helping underserved populations will always be a compelling force in my life.

—Casey Rogers

---------------------------------- ★ ----------------------------------

HEALING AND SERVING

Fortunately, my parents honored community service and taught by example. My first volunteer experience was in the Charity Hospital Record Room in New Orleans during a summer when I was 15 years old. The year was 1973! It was an eye-opening experience. It introduced me to the reality of long standing racial discrimination. I initially was allowed to eat lunch in an air-conditioned dining room with the full time workers until they realized that I was a person of color. I was mistaken for a Native American because of my skin hue and almost black braids. After that realization, I was relegated to eating in a dusty corner of the record room with other African Americans. This experience strengthened my resolve and desire to want to leave the South, and pursue a meaningful profession that

I had some passion for, and persevere. This incident brought to light the painful reality of the pervasive inequalities that existed throughout the fabric of American life; even after the Civil Rights Acts of the 1960's.

Next, I volunteered at a mental health institution when I was 19 years old —as an undergraduate majoring in anthropology—during summer break at Yale. I wanted to learn more about mental illness as a result of this opportunity. After medical school at the University of Pennsylvania I learned that health care is a business and that providing quality and safe care can be a challenge even when the financial resources are abundant.

I am sure that all my experiences have shaped my life in ways that cannot really be explained or measured. I have worked with homeless populations in Chicago during my internship and with HIV infected patients in San Francisco, when physicians and the medical community did not know very much about the disease and were just speculating about risk factors and its etiology. I have also worked closely with developmentally challenged populations including people with spina bifida.

I found my place in society and my passion by being a physician...a healer. Despite the difficulties my profession is experiencing today there is something quite remarkable about being a physician. Now I work with an underserved population because I realize that this provides a real opportunity to change some of the many health inequalities that are still present in American society. And I feel an incredible encompassing sensitivity for those marginalized in our society: the developmentally challenged, the mentally ill, the homeless and persons of color from all walks of life. Healing and serving the community go hand in hand; and I am grateful to be doing both.

—**Julie Claire Morial MD MPH**

---------------------------------- ★ ----------------------------------

AN AGENT FOR CHANGE

I grew up going to a Presbyterian church in Tucson, Arizona, that was led by a minister who was a great believer in the church's role in seeking "social justice", especially for those who were in poverty and discriminated against. My mother was a great believer in the "Golden Rule" and it was the dominant principle of ethical behavior of my childhood. The church 'youth group' (early teen years) had an activity in which we went outside of town to some of the surrounding farms to work/play with the children of the migrant farm workers (almost all of Mexican descent) whose parents were in the fields, and who lived in "substandard housing" (rundown shacks). Few spoke any English, but we were able to have a lot of fun with them and of course, we suburban middle-class white kids got a lot more out of it than they did. This was probably the first time I ever realized how well-off I lived , and how many opportunities I had that others did not.

When I was still in high school in Tucson, John F. Kennedy was elected President, and my dad took me to hear one of the first Peace Corps Volunteers (PCVs) speak to a Rotary Club meeting. I was fascinated by their world. I then went to Occidental College in Los Angeles and studied political science and international relations while increasing my understanding of the world 'out there'. President Kennedy's assassination, while I was at college, made a huge impression on me. I decided to join the Peace Corps, after obtaining an MA in International Relations at John's Hopkins.

I learned a lot more during 2 years in Bolivia than I did during two years in graduate school; working with impoverished Aymara Indians on the Altiplano of Bolivia (in the Andes) in a 'community development' program, which was intended to help the *campesinos* organize in their communities and mobilize to access resources. Their most pressing needs related to getting/keeping their kids in school and earning a bit more income for their families. I was able to initiate several projects with the local teachers to improve the local primary school, and to develop several income-earning projects (sheep-shearing to 'commercialize' wool, and chicken-raising for egg/meat production). While it was sometimes difficult to adjust one's expectations about "saving the world" to a level that reflected the realities these *campesinos* faced daily, it was gratifying to feel that at least you were having a positive impact on the lives of a few families, one day at a time.

The Peace Corps experience reflected the fundamental values I had acquired earlier in my life. While one individual may only be able to make a modest difference in the lives of others, if you can find a way to make your difference strategically, it can create the "ripple" that Bobby Kennedy spoke about.

The experience of two years on the Bolivia Altiplano clearly guided the direction of my professional career. I returned to the U.S. determined to become "an agent for change" and became involved in legal assistance work. Then, after working for a law firm in Washington, DC, I realized that corporate legal work was not what I wanted to do with my career, and left the firm. I found an opportunity to return to work in international development and accepted a position as a Foreign Service Officer in the U.S. Agency for International Development. I knew that I had finally found the right place to serve, and a place where I could make a major contribution to addressing the needs of people affected by poverty and social exclusion. I worked in Haiti, Morocco, Nepal, Guatemala and South Africa over a period of almost 24 years In August, 2009 I was appointed by the White House to be the new Chief of Staff at the Peace Corps, a wonderful way to complete the circle of my career. I feel very much at home doing the community development work that has been consistent with my values since an early age.

—**William Stacy Rhodes**

------------------------------- ★ -------------------------------

TREATING CHILDREN WITH DIGNITY

In 1972 I was working for the New York State Council on the Arts when my first baby arrived and I decided I would be a temporary stay-at-home mom. Soon after I received a call from a family friend who was the chairman of the board of the Northside Center of Child Development He wanted to tell me about the work of the organization.

When we got together he told me about Drs., Mamie and Kenneth Clark. He told me of how Kenneth was an influential and pioneering civil rights leader and how both were preeminent psychologists. He also told me about how Mamie had developed the "doll study" which was when a child chose the favored white doll over the black doll. In 1954 the Supreme Court cited the doll study when they decided the Brown vs. Board Education ruling declaring segregation in public schools to be unequal and unconstitutional. The Clarks founded the Northside Center for Children in 1946, which was in Central and East Harlem. It was a very difficult time. There was poverty, violence, drugs, failing schools, and sub-standard housing.

A few weeks later I met with Mamie. She was soft spoken and very convincing. She was in the midst of moving the Center to Fifth Avenue at 110th Street. We spoke about what would be happening in the new space and she invited me to visit when it opened. A month later Mamie invited me to come over. I was awed when I arrived. They had done a great job: the halls were painted bright colors there were wonderful paintings on the walls children and some from important painters, that the children could enjoy. She said that she and Kenneth were very excited about all of the new programs: the therapy, the outpatient clinic, the remedial program , six school classes for children who could not learn in large classes, and a library. A library that was full, from the floor to the ceiling!!

I know very well that there was no other library in any other mental health center at that time, and even few today. But beyond all the programs what was perhaps the most important to the Clarks was being certain that all their children would be treated with have dignity; and that they could be certain that the children would develop self-esteem. I left Northside awestruck by what they did and what help it would provide to the children and their families. A few weeks later I was asked if I would join the board . I was stunned but replied that I would be certainly honored. I was the youngest member and quite shy at board meetings. The other members were people I admired and they were all kind and helpful to me.

I spent a lot of time at Northside; working with the staff; being with the children; planning events; meeting with foundations; finding new members for the Board; reaching out to others , speaking to and inviting people to the center.

I have been on the board for 38 years, 18 of which I have been chair and I have loved it all. It has opened my eyes and taught me so many important lessons about education, psychology, race and class. And it changed my life more than I ever could have imagined.

—Susan Patricof

BECOMING AN ADVOCATE

When the Peace Corps first started I was working for the Bank of Boston, learning Spanish for an assignment in Buenos Aires. Its building there had been under siege with tar bombs, and I was to develop a community program to present a more benign image of the bank. However, just as I was to leave for Argentina, the bank told me that it had solved its problem—with a new solvent that dissolved the tar. That was the jolt that changed my "career". If the bank felt that my job could be replaced with a solvent, my wife Polly and I decided that we would join the Peace Corps and we were assigned to Caracas, Venezuela.

While at first I may have worried about what would happen to my "professional" career (my expensive college and B-school education), I soon realized that banking was not for me. I had no further use for my Brooks Brothers suits. In the Peace Corps the job was to organize the very poor to address issues related to their community infrastructure and gain access to healthy food and clean water. As my focus changed, I began to believe I could change the world, one barrio at a time.

After returning to U.S. and working in the South for Civil Rights and the War on Poverty, I got worked for George McGovern's presidential campaign and realized that what I really wanted to do required political power.

While my wife worked in a Family Planning Program, I ran for office to be a Maine State Senator as a Democrat—in a district of 20 coastal towns whose voter registration ran to 12 to 1 Republican. Based on my Peace Corps and McGovern experience, I mounted a door-to-door canvass against an incumbent of 22 years and I won. But getting elected did not change much. I refocused again as an advocate; gathering signatures for three statewide referendums. While I lost two—one to establish a public power agency and another to elect the Public Utility Commissioners—these campaigns were responsible for the creation of the permanent office of the Public Advocate and significantly changed the way utility rates were set. And, I won one, defeating what the telephone company then called "Local Measured Service". And my wife Polly won five terms in the Maine House of Representatives and sponsored successful legislation including the state's first seat belt law. Later, through all of these victories and losses, we realized that while we didn't change the world the way we first thought we would, we did change it. And all the effort was well worth it.

—Bruce Reeves

THE "LEMON LAW"

Growing up in North Canton, Ohio, I watched my mother devote years to creating new opportunities for young women, by volunteering with the League of Women Voters as well as my father spending hours after a long day's work, volunteering at the YMCA to train youngsters in gymnastics. I suppose it was in my genes that I would value civic engagement and volunteering. But I never would have predicted how I would end up following in their footsteps.

Years later, after majoring in English at Case Western Reserve University; while I was teaching at a university and married to a Navy Judge Advocate General (JAG) officer; an auto dealer in Lemon Grove, CA kept our car for repairs for three months. After repeatedly claiming it would be ready "tomorrow," he admitted he hadn't ordered all the parts, and threatened if we complained he would put bad parts in the car. Desperate for transportation, I started to picket. The dealer tried to have me arrested. But the police refused, and when they would drive by, they gave me thumbs up.

Others began to tell me their auto horror stories. I learned that many people who bought brand new cars suffered due to serious—often life-threatening—defects that kept their vehicles in the repair shop for months—while they had to keep making payments for a car they couldn't drive. I organized protests, generated news coverage, and drafted California's auto "lemon law." Five months later, toward the end of summer, the Admiral of the Sixth Fleet invited us onboard his ship. He said he'd heard I was giving a certain dealer a hard time. I feared he would pressure me to stop picketing. Instead he declared, "Those dealers have been ripping off my sailors for years. It harms morale, readiness and our ability to accomplish our mission. If that dealer hasn't settled with you by the end of September, you get me his coordinates."

Soon afterward, we won and I founded a non-profit consumer group. Assemblywoman Sally Tanner agreed to author the lemon law bill. We fought the powerful auto lobby for three years. Until then, auto manufacturers were allowed a "reasonable number" of repair attempts before they had to buy back a lemon. But there was no definition of what is "reasonable." Ford testified they should be allowed to have 30 tries. The lemon law established a legal presumption that four tries, or a total of 30 days out of service, is enough to trigger a refund. California's law became the model for similar laws in all 50 states.

Since then, for over 30 years (the first 14 as an unpaid volunteer), I've worked to improve protections for consumers and promote auto safety. Auto manufacturers and dealers tend to think of consumers as suckers. The most important lesson I learned is that in a democracy, when we organize, for the public good, we can lick them.

—Rosemary Shahan, President of Consumers
for Auto Reliability and Safety (CARS)

★

THINK BIG. CREATE A SIMPLE PLAN. GET STARTED.

I tell everyone that I am a selfish person. Every day I try to help others. My joy abounds. It began at an early age. In the 6th grade, we had a competition to collect food for the poor. This planted the service seed. In 1965, after Yale where I majored in American Studies, I had the privilege of working for U.S. Senator Robert Kennedy in Bedford-Stuyvesant revitalizing one of America's poorest communities. A key issue was business ownership for minorities. Imagine. In 1968 in New York City, the banks did not lend $1 million to minority businesses.

In 1967, as a volunteer, while working full time, I began linking minority businesses to skilled financial professionals. By the end of 1969, we had enlisted over 3,000 volunteers and the New York banks were lending over $50 million annually to minorities. This was a major pioneering effort. A handful of us across the country changed national lending practices.

Again as a volunteer, in 1972, I founded the Jefferson Awards with Jacqueline Kennedy Onassis and U.S. Senator Robert Taft, Jr. For over 35 years as a volunteer, we built the Jefferson Awards into the nation's premier award system for community and public service, and today, we are enlisting over 1 million young Americans into student-led service projects.

The early volunteering efforts led to a full-fledged public service career. Looking back, I'm proudest that I have had the privilege of dreaming up and running a program for each of the past seven U.S. Presidents from Richard Nixon through George W. Bush. The greatest NDC impact was with President Carter. Vision. Think big. Create a simple plan. Get started. In the 1960's and 1970's the nation focused on Fortune 500 companies.

We saw small business as the major job creator—especially in low-income communities. The banks had the money. They weren't lending in inner cities because government was "bureaucratic." No city employee could read a financial statement. NDC had a staff of six. We promised President Carter that we would combine the efforts of the above partners and do $1 billion of small business financing in 48 months in 65 cities. We surpassed the $1 billion goal in 22 months. Our system was generating $1 billion per year. Basically, NDS and a handful of others, changed the direction of economic development in our nation.

My message for any young reader: start with your passion. Volunteer. Think Big. Create a Simple Plan. Get Started. You too can create a program for the President of the United States. And possibly craft a joyous and meaningful career.

**—Sam Beard, President of the Jefferson Awards
and Chairman of the Development Council**

PROMOTING HUMAN DIGNITY AND SELF-RESPECT

For the past 38 years, I have directed the Federation of Child Care Centers of Alabama, dedicated to high quality child care and the empowerment of grassroots leaders who work together to sustain the programs in service of families. From 1968 to 1970 I spent three summers with American Friends Service Committee Community Services Program for youth in Brandon, Vermont, Roxbury, MA and

Luna Pier, Michigan. I did this as a consequence of a life-changing experience I had three years earlier. As a 10th grader I was among the first African Americans to integrate the all white high school in Wetumpka, Alabama. Coming from a large, rural and economically poor family, I thought I knew hardships, but nothing could compare to the firebombing of our family home. That left the ten of us living in a two room shack for 15 months. The response of people who placed their lives at risk to help my family was my very first awareness of the value of service to others.

I spent a summer of service in Luna Pier, a town nestled on the banks of Lake Erie between Toledo and Detroit. Its lush fields of tomatoes, beans and corn drew migrant workers during the picking season. Our project was to convert an abandoned Catholic school into a health clinic and way-station for the migrant Latino families. Recalling my own time in the crowded shack, without personal belongings, without privacy, I was humbled to see the families who had no home for themselves and their children, and had all types of medical conditions that had not been treated. Their resolve to cope with these challenges inspired me in my life's work.

In each of these summer situations, as one of a handful of youth of color among the group of 15 predominantly upper class whites, I had to balance my own discomforts and sense of racial and class issues, with keeping our service mission to be the primary focus. We all had to learn to live and work together to provide the best service to those we were there to assist. My biases and those of my peers had to be confronted and dealt with for the larger good. I identified with and remembered what it was like to be on the receiving end of help; and the pride that comes from doing for oneself. Promoting human dignity and self respect became the centerpiece that I took from these experiences and carried into my professional life. They remain a passion of mine today. It is not enough to give service, but to provide service in a way that fosters self-empowerment and independence that really counts.

—**Sophia Bracy Harris**

★

A SENSE OF SOMETHING LARGER

I was 19 years old and a sophomore at Yale; looking for something to do that was more concrete, useful, and valuable to society than just demonstrating. I reasoned that food, clothing, shelter and jobs were as basic and concrete as it got, and began to talk with my friends who were working on these issues in adjoining neighborhoods in New Haven. I then found a group of architecture and planning students working on creating a sweat equity housing project. Though I knew little about the machinations of housing, I did know how to speak Spanish and I was a friendly guy, so I became the community outreach person for this VISTA project.

There were two other major volunteer experiences that shaped my life. The first was at a bilingual community newspaper. I had been in San Francisco about a year, and had no connections to other Latinos. During that time, there had been a series of arson fires in the barrio near my apartment. Those fires culminated in a horrific hotel fire that I witnessed. I wanted to explain how these fires served a larger negative purpose of pushing poor people out of their barrio. I approached a local community newspaper about writing an analysis of the consequences of the fires. They published my article and became especially interested in me, when they found out I had "basic journalism" experience from high school; like writing, editing, layout, and photography. Within 18 months, I became editor and business manager of the paper.

My other major experience as a volunteer was a founding member of a pioneering bilingual mental health clinic. I had been working as an organizer and activist in community development for several years. A psychology professor I was working with suggested that I help establish one of the first bilingual and bicultural mental health clinics in the California. I developed and implement political and clinical strategies in order to win funding and then to sustain this new institution. This year the clinic is celebrating its 33rd anniversary

The newspaper opened the door to a community that embraced me and gave me the sense of something larger than me, something that I was responsible to and something that would sustain me. And the clinic gave me deep insight in the role of health in a community and what it takes to build and nurture a community's institutional asset. The work I did as a volunteer at this clinic became the major focus of my career and the foundation of my efforts to create healthy communities from California to the deep South; where I now work.

—Juan Cruz

★

A LIFELONG VOLUNTEER PATH

My first memorable volunteer experience was with my sister, Joan, canvassing neighborhoods for Senator George McGovern's presidential campaign in 1972. She was 16 and I was 12, and most people who answered their door assumed we were selling Girl Scout cookies. I enjoyed watching the Democratic Conventions and was inspired by the messages of compassion and service. We grew up in Wisconsin, known for its progressive political history, and my father prided himself on pegging Nixon long before Watergate. He also worked with the Peace Corps and Father Groppi (a peace activist) in Milwaukee. My paternal grandmother also helped found a community center and camp for inner-city children. Social activism was a natural family fit.

This early experience carried over into my career choice to become a lawyer, which led me to Washington, DC for law school. I was the student director for the Consumer Protection Clinic at George Washington University Law School, a program that helped consumers mediate solutions to complaints they had against local businesses. Very often we could find a resolution acceptable to both parties, with little rancor involved. This was far from the confrontational role for lawyers we read about in class, and it helped us see the possibilities of approaching problems with a goal toward equitable solutions rather than "winning."

While at law school, and living in Washington, I realized that politics—in the broadest sense of the word—can impede progress. Direct service, on the other hand, is only limited by time and resources. I volunteered for My Sister's Place, a shelter for battered women and their children, as a way to provide a concrete benefit to the community I lived in. The level of abuse these women suffered was unimaginable. The contribution made as a volunteer paled in comparison to the sacrifices they made on a daily basis just to make a better life for themselves and their children.

I'm now a few decades out of law school and have spent my entire career working for non-profits, mostly with a focus on consumer protection. Sometimes it feels like a lifelong volunteer path, which is exactly how I wanted it to be when I graduated. Social progress is really the story of individuals, together or alone, choosing to act for the public interest.

—Laura Polacheck, Advocacy Director (for Utah)
for the American Association of Retired Persons in Salt Lake City

------------------------------ ★ ------------------------------

THE VALUE OF ENGAGED PARTICIPATION

I began to do volunteer work in high school. I found that I enjoyed teaching younger kids, and that I could see the effects of my efforts very readily. This was true whether I was teaching swimming in the summer or tutoring math during the school year. As a tutor I found a sense of purpose and satisfaction. The purpose was very clear—someone had trouble reading, or calculating, or overcoming fear of the water—and the satisfaction came from the tangible results one could see almost immediately.

At Berner High School in Massapequa Park (Long Island, New York) I organized a tutoring service that helped out at the nearby elementary school. I did this through our chapter of the National Honor Society. As I recall, the Honor Society up to that point had had no other function but to recognize the academic achievements of its members, and I developed the tutoring program to connect the group to something useful—to do what we would today call service. It was great fun, and I think we did some good.

I then worked in a psychiatric ward while a first year student at Wesleyan University. This was an extraordinarily important experience for me. At the time I thought that mental illness was a myth, and that the patients were only part of an oppressed group waiting to be liberated from the shackles of convention. After working with some people who were suffering greatly, and who were sometimes deeply disturbed, I realized that learning about pathology from books was not enough. My respect for the patients grew as I came to know them and not just think of them as facets of an ideological apparatus.

Like many volunteers, I learned that "giving back" is immensely satisfying, and that by engaging in the life of a community one enhances one's own life. I got to know some amazing people—as co-workers, and as friends. I also learned a lot about organizations and about how successful institutions can function in relation to their neighborhoods, regions and the country as a whole. In a word, I learned more about the value of engaged participation.

I have been an active proponent of community partnerships throughout my professional life. At Scripps College in Claremont, California (where I began my career as a professor) many of my students became active volunteers, especially around women's issues. At the Getty Research Institute, I led a staff deeply committed to working in parts of Los Angeles that were typically underserved by the Getty (and many other cultural organizations). They studied and stimulated participation in the arts in a robust way. As president of California College of the Arts (2000-2007) and at Wesleyan University, I have supported service learning, community partnerships and the development of an ethos of engagement as a crucial part of our educational experience.

I believe that only an engaged university can be a great university, and that belief was formed through my own efforts as a volunteer.

—Michael Roth, President of Wesleyan University

---------------------------------- ★ ----------------------------------

MORE THAN AN EXTRACURRICULAR ACTIVITY

My first experience with public service was on the receiving end, at the age of ten, when our house burned down in the Oakland hills fire. Fortunately for my family, we had a safety net: insurance to help us rebuild what we lost, the kindness of family and friends to house us for those few months when we— along with thousands of others—were without shelter; and services from the Red Cross. This experience inspired me to get involved with community work in high school, working with the Red Cross and running an arts program at a homeless shelter. I also founded the Human Rights Club at my high school. Initially, the club focused on international violations of human rights. With time, our focus expanded to include local issues, recognizing that human rights violations exist abroad as well as in our own backyards.

However, it wasn't until college that I realized public service was more than an extracurricular activity and that it would strongly influence my studies and career. As an undergraduate at Stanford University, I majored in Urban Studies with a focus on community organization. Then, upon graduation, I applied for the AmeriCorps-VISTA program. Through VISTA, I worked with Habitat for Humanity in New York City, advocating for policies to increase affordable housing. While my daily work focused on program planning and policy, I was most moved by my interactions with community members. I remember working side-by-side with family partners on the weekends to help them finish their homes and proudly witnessing the moment they families received the keys to their hard-earned, finished homes.

These experiences shaped my professional career, inspiring me to develop professional skill sets around policy analysis and research. So, I went graduate school to get my master's in community economic development and housing at UCLA's Urban Planning department. I have now come full circle, working again in the nonprofit sector for a leading advocacy organization, the Los Angeles Alliance for a New Economy, where we promote a new economic approach based on good jobs, thriving communities and a healthy environment. As a Policy Analyst, I work with environmental, community, labor, faith, and community groups, advocating for systemic change; recognizing that policy is most effective when applied and combined with coalition building, strategic communications and thorough research. I feel very fortunate to a career rooted in public service; and my dedication to this field is reinforced by the times of growth and victories—from building four new units of affordable housing to major policy wins, and by working with the ιlented and motivated individuals I've met ong the way.

—Sabrina Bornstein

MOMENTS OF "RIGHTNESS"

Kindness, connection, giving: to see these elements in motion is to enter a rarefied space. Sincere gestures of interest—be they simple nods of understanding or the running of a soup kitchen—grant us moments of, well, "rightness." In committing to a lifestyle of volunteering, we answer both philosophical riddles of meaning and sociological calls to community change.

I didn't always recognize this. Growing up in St. Joseph Michigan, I was an egotistic athlete whose primary ambition, like many kids, was the cultivation of my own image. My bemused mother, however, was well beyond such concerns. Although raised in suburban wealth she was never drawn to superficial attention or her own mother's country club pressures. Her discomfort with self-absorption or pretention of any sort is neither dramatic nor forced. When she began opening our home to the gang kids from across the river in Benton Harbor, I was embarrassed, even ashamed. These were kids who grew up in crack houses, they dressed and spoke with rough edges. To my mother, they were simply human beings with a common need to be someone's priority. She would listen to them, feed them, house them. More often than not, this was all that was needed to change their lives, and hence—one person at a time—the nature of our socially and racially divided towns. Week after week, year after year, she was the odd "white woman" attending the graduations, deliveries, weddings and funerals of the gang kids from across the bridge. In volunteering to help those in the forgotten parts of a forgotten community, she understood the power of giving, of transcending the self.

Such wisdom comes to us in mysterious ways. What my mother seemed to know intuitively about volunteering, I discovered in stages. My first act of volunteering occurred in college. I had always been interested with military history and often volunteered to read to the veterans at a hospital that rarely saw visitors. Most recently, I have been volunteering with a group called "Birthday Wishes." We work with a shelter for homeless (and often fatherless) families. Our role is to organize birthday parties for children who otherwise have no access to the cakes, candles and gifts that all boys and girls deserve. The genuine pleasure I've seen in these children for even the simplest gift or moment of attention humbles me, and I can say without exaggeration that I have received much more from them than anything I have given.

At some point in each of our journeys, we start to feel the value of service, the pleasure of connecting and engaging. Volunteering begins the moment we understand the power of stepping momentarily outside of our own interests to honor another's. What concerns me today, and what prompted my launching of the Emerson Circle, is a visceral sense that the conditions of our times (social, economic, and civic) are sliding away from generosity and connection and tilting more toward self interest and disconnection. There is, I feel, something uniquely toxic about the modern era and its endemic "me-first-ness." Our new media—its tweets, friend requests, chat rooms etc—offer tremendous access to others, but at what expense, at what diluted valuation? We come away from such experiences diverted but internally malnourished—for there is little substance in such empty lands of form. Whether channel surfing or net surfing, bonus seeking or bond selling, we seem to be falling deeper and faster into ourselves and further from our relations to each other.

Over 500 million of us are social networking, spending 700 billion minutes a month (!) on facebook alone. Imagine what could be achieved if just 1% of this online time was diverted to volunteering? When I consider this faith in technology, I think immediately of St. Exupery's observation that today we are capable of manufacturing 5000 pianos a day, but incapable of creating a single worthy pianist...

I harbor no illusions that anything I do in my acts of volunteering or in my personal connections at the Emerson Circle will, of themselves, reverse the direction of this largely (but not entirely) shallow river. Instead, I put my faith in the example of my mother and her rough-edged gang kids, the books read aloud to forgotten war heroes in veterans' hospitals or the smiling birthday girl at the shelter in Boston. Stepping away from all the noise and headlines, we can discover a space for ourselves and others where one person, one smile, one connection, and one kind gesture at a time, we finish each day a little better than it began. That, at least, is what volunteering has confirmed for me.

—Mathew Piepenbury, founder and director of the Emerson Circle

------------------------------ ★ ------------------------------

EXPLORING WHAT IT MEANS TO SERVE

I come from a long line of preachers and teachers so I probably learned about the value of service at a very early age. My first memory of deliberately volunteering to take action was my first year in college at Lewis and Clark, in Portland, Oregon when I volunteered to be an ESL tutor for homeless Latino men. I was touched by the men's life stories and within weeks started organizing other college students to lobby the city for more services for the homeless and to stop police raids on encampments of people without homes. It was a powerful learning experience that expanded my sense of community, and taught me how important it is to be involved in addressing systemic, structural issues that create inequity. My service with the Latino community inspired me to bring Cesar Chavez to speak on my campus, and my experiences organizing my peers inspired me to start the Community Service Office at Lewis and Clark.

Those experiences ultimately led to my current career. For the past ten years, I have been the Director of the Public Service Center at the University of California, Berkeley. Last year, over 6,500 CAL students volunteered to work with 270 local community-based organizations and schools. In addition, we recruited, trained and placed 170 AmeriCorps volunteers.

It has been an incredible experience to work with others to not only create opportunities for students to learn the value of service, but to work on creating a culture where everyone is exploring what it means to serve— every day and from every department. I thoroughly enjoy teaching students that meaningful service does not only take place when we go off campus and volunteer for three hours; but that service can also means deliberately choosing a research project that may benefit others; being involved in shaping local public policy; and choosing to live our lives in intentional ways that serve the common good.

I love helping others realize that service is not just about the act of serving, though that act alone is very important. It is also about being willing to touch and to be touched, and it is about the experience of belonging. Volunteering is about experiencing genuine connection with others and the world around us, and using our gifts to create a world that is better for all of us.

**—Megan Voorhees, Director of the Public Service
Center at the University of California, Berkeley**

★

THE BEST LEARNING OPPORTUNITIES

Volunteer work, over many years, has brought me some of the richest, most rewarding experiences in my life. Also, I have discovered some of the best learning opportunities that have literally opened up the world. It started in grade school in Peoria Heights, Il., where Dominican nuns sent me and all of my classmates who would "volunteer", out into the neighborhoods, selling Christmas Cards to raise money for the "pagan babies" of the world. I had no clear idea of what a "pagan baby" was, but my fourth grade teacher assured me that "these are very poor children in all remote parts of the world who are far less fortunate than you or me. They don't have enough food or clothing or books for school." I decided right then that one day, I would go to see these pagan children for myself, to see what might be done directly.

Next came Troop 28, Boy Scouts of America and food drives for poor folks right in our own community. In college, at Northwestern University I joined with a campus group which traveled by bus, two nights a week to tutor school kids on Chicago's south and southwest neighborhoods. My eyes were opened to harsh poverty, and deprivation, but also children, ever so eager to learn, and curious youngsters, who wanted to be "better at math and reading, but we also want to learn about white college students, like you."

Medical School at Northwestern opened yet new opportunities to go to the neighborhood health centers for clinical work. At that time I discovered an opportunity to develop, on my own, a transitional program for women who were being paroled from the Ill. State Prison for Women at Dwight, Ill. This program would have its base at St. Leonard's House, a halfway house for (up to that time,) men only, who likewise had recently been paroled from the state prison system. I was able to get supervision and support from "volunteer" faculty at my school, and also from the Episcopal Diocese of Chicago. The program became so popular with group therapy meetings for the women to "process" the transitional experience from prison to the work-a-day world, the men demanded a "program like you do for the women, for us!" Recently, I discovered that "the program" has evolved into a meeting center for "Friends Outside", a national volunteer program for assisting incarcerated individuals who want a job and support after leaving prison.

After graduation from med school and internship, I "turned down" a U.S, Navy commission, entered the U.S Public Health Service, and "volunteered" to serve with the Peace Corps. I became a Staff Physician in Malawi, where I worked with a fantastic group of volunteers in the Malawi Health program. There the work was treating patients with tuberculosis. We also developed maternal and child health clinics, many of which were still functioning after 40 years. Perhaps best known is the Malawi Children's Village, just outside of

Mangoche, Malawi. This "Village for children" started up as a clinic, evolved into an orphanage, that included a primary school, next a secondary school and finally a technical trade school and on-the-job learning in agriculture, computer technology, seamstress work and yes, teaching and now, complete with an Alumni Organization!

Nearly all of my adult life I have been a volunteer of one sort or another. I volunteered to stay on with Peace Corps and became Chief Medical Officer, participating in the development of programs all over the world. I also founded, a migrant health program in Fort Lupton, Colorado. This program continues from humble beginnings, as "Plan de Salud del Valle". Which has grown into a large, multi- specialty health center for migrant farm workers, with a number of satellite clinics near Denver.

Upon reflection I realize that I found the "pagan babies" of my childhood wonderment in all parts of the world and right here at home. Three years ago, I was afforded an opportunity to do a tutorial for six resident physicians in psychiatry at The Royal School of Medicine in Phnom Penh, Cambodia. This was the first group of psychiatrists to complete tanning in Cambodia, since the restoration of the medical school after the end of the Khmer regime. Six graduating resident physicians in psychiatry raised the national number of psychiatrists in Cambodia (a country of fifteen million people) from twelve to eighteen! Two years ago, I went back to Malawi, where I will continue to be involved with the Malawi Children's village. This past year I am involved in relief efforts in Haiti, where I have spent three weeks on two trips, developing a health clinic and community education center in Marie Gracier, about fifteen miles from Port au Prince.

It is extremely gratifying to give to and work with others. But I now find this volunteer work to be truly self-serving. Selfishness binds up the body of altruism. Nothing has been better.

—**Dr. Tom Powers**

---------------------------------- ★ ----------------------------------

A FIRE IN THE BELLY

I am a white woman, 64, retired and disabled; the only thing about me that hasn't aged is the fire in my belly for equality. What stirred it? A summer job teaching "ecology" took me to Nevada, home of philanthropist and environmentalist, Maya Miller. In 1971, Maya introduced me to southern Nevada's emerging champion for the rights of poor people, Ms. Ruby Duncan. Our rapport was instantaneous, and I agreed to volunteer in her fight against the indignities being imposed on poor women and their children by the agencies designated to "help" impoverished Nevada families. Ms. Duncan and the women had to march, sit-in, and go to court before a federal judge ruled that Nevada's welfare director had "run roughshod over the rights of poor people."

As a VISTA volunteer with Clark County Welfare Rights (CCWRO), I worked at every imaginable task: driving families to health screening appointments, publishing a "know your rights" newspaper, running a food bank, and much more. We wrote demand letters, petitions, and legislative testimony and organized protests by families desperate for food stamps to replace awful USDA farm subsidy commodity foods—moldy cheese, weevil-ridden flour and rodent-infested peanut butter, distributed to the poor. The David-and-Goliath nature of CCWRO's struggles impelled me to law school.

I returned to CCWRO, as a lawyer for the group's newly created community development corporation, (Operation Life), which shaped the entirety of my professional career. Topping the list was the a realization that "uneducated" people are capable of brilliance. In pursuit of social justice, there is no substitute for local "hands on" experience, wisdom and integrity. I learned that grassroots leadership holds the key to social change. People find ways to get things done, at times because of school-learning, but also, in spite of it.

Schooling gave me tools to help my community; and we know that education is a lifeline out of poverty. But anomalies sometimes teach us the most. This past weekend, I attended the ribbon-cutting ceremony in Las Vegas for the Ruby Duncan Elementary School. In the sweetness of the moment, a huge crowd assembled to honor this extraordinary woman, mother of seven, herself a high school dropout who overcame illiteracy—she once told me—by reading the Congressional Record. She told the audience how she made certain all her children graduated; she exhorted parents to be activists, their children's first teachers. As her strong voice rose, I heard the brilliance, courage, common sense and compassion that drew me to her cause 40 years ago! What want-ad could I have possibly answered that would have shown me all this? Volunteering allowed me to choose the people who would enhance my life. In giving, we often get far more than we give.

—Martine Makower

★

THE MOTIVATION FOR RIGHT ACTION

"White boy can jump!" I heard this through the fence at West 4th Street, the legendary and tumultuous basketball fishbowl on 6th Avenue in Greenwich Village. Son of a Holocaust survivor, I was bred to be a warrior. I didn't jump better than others, but I always wanted the ball more than anyone else. I went to Stanford on a tennis scholarship, but for three decades I ate, slept, and dreamt basketball.

The 70's was breakout time for the women's movement. Every Saturday morning for five years, from nine to noon, I held a free open gym session for women who wanted to learn how to play basketball. It was my way of combining the deep love of the game with the need to actively participate in the most important social movement of my early adulthood.

For the past ten years on my own time, I have run a community garden at the college I work for. In the spring and fall I head out there at the end of the workday. In summer I use my break time. It requires building and maintaining sheds, deer fencing, benches, raised beds, soil, compost, walkways. I get help from students, but the heavy lifting often falls on my shoulders. My dad asks me from time to time, "Now tell me again why you volunteer most of your free time to the college you work for when you could be growing a beautiful garden at your own home?"

I don't really believe in "service". I think we are all just going about our business trying to make the world the way we want it. I like to play. I like being in a world full of flowers and vegetables. I like work. I want other to people to like and want and need these things too. I consider my volunteer efforts invitations to participate in the world with me. My mom had a knack for making everyone she came into contact with feel as if they were the most special person on the planet. From her I learned that everyone's contribution to the party counts.

For the past thirteen years I've run a program at Bard College called the Trustee Leader Scholars. I give stipends to students who design and run social action programs based on their own compelling interests. Since Katrina, over 600 Bard students have traveled to New Orleans. Many of them are now professional educators in a rebuilt neighborhood called Broadmoor. Other students raised the funds for and built a primary school in a small Ghanaian village. One student started a prison education program, and the college, having hired this former student, now grants degrees in NY State prisons. This summer I traveled to the West Bank with twenty students where we built a children's library and ran a summer camp. Ultimately I want my students to leave the college informed, humble, capable, and carrying a quiet and potent sense that what they do matters and the motivation for right action needs to come from within themselves.

—Paul Marienthal, Associate Dean of Student Affairs & Director of the Trustee Leader Scholar program at Bard College

THE STRUGGLE FOR EQUAL JUSTICE

In 1966 I was the assistant chaplain at a prep school in New Jersey, and hoping to capture the attention of the boys at one of the required chapel services, I invited seminary classmates to come from New York to present a folk music program. They did, and in their presentation they talked about their volunteer work the previous summer in a Student Interracial Ministry project in Southwest Georgia. After the service, they urged me to go with them the next summer, and I did.

I was born and raised a white person in the segregated South. I attended Washington and Lee, an all male segregated university that had disaffiliated its student Christian association from the YMCA because of the national organization's integrationist policies. Thanks to the influence of a new young religion professor at that university, however, I did go to Union Theological Seminary in New York, and it was there that Charles Sherrod of SNCC came for a sabbatical year and to recruit volunteers for his Southwest Georgia Project.

My stay in Baker County, Georgia was brief. I taught that summer in a Head Start Program and I worked with black farmers trying to get a fair shake on peanut allotments from the U. S. Department of Agriculture. For the first time, I tried to read and interpret federal regulations. I watched lawyer C.B. King and the law student volunteers with him try to bring justice to that land. I thought they were more effective than I was, so, three years later I enrolled in law school in the South because that was where I wanted to live and work for civil rights and the poor.

During my first year at Vanderbilt Law School I applied for a summer job with the Law Students' Civil

Rights Research Council. When I did not hear from them, I offered to work for free, but still no response. Finally, I gave up and applied for a summer clerk position at the new legal aid office in Nashville. They gave me a job and paid me, and I stayed 37 years. Friends and colleagues helped build the organization and expand its services over the years. It became, in time, the Legal Aid Society of Middle Tennessee and the Cumberlands. I recently retired after 31 years as Executive Director. The volunteer experience in Southwest Georgia focused my faith and gave me a rewarding vocation. Prior to that summer, I had been mostly a spectator of the struggle for equal justice. With that volunteer experience, I was inspired to try to do more.

—**Ashley Wilshire**

THE SOCIAL IMPLICATIONS OF DESIGN

I have a vivid memory of being pushed in a stroller by my mother in what I remember to be a Heart Health Awareness walk in my hometown of Moss Point, Mississippi. It was more fun for me than anything, but most importantly it set the stage for my community involvement. I participated in my first self-initiated volunteer project in the 1st grade when I asked my mother to sign me up for the St. Jude Math-a-thon. I didn't have a complete grasp on what cancer or leukemia was at the time. All I knew was that kids like me were very sick and I could raise money (by doing math problems) to help make them better.

At Howard University while studying architecture, I participated in a program called School Building Week. The program included a student design competition. The students I worked with were in middle school and students were challenged to design a new school facility that fostered leaning and was environmentally friendly and technologically advanced. As a mentor, my primary "job" was to educate them on architectural principles and guide them through the design process. I visited the students a couple time a week during the Spring semester and helped the them prepare for their final presentation.

After the first year I realized that the students needed more than my explaining principles of architecture. Most of the students had heard of architecture and engineering but did not think those were careers that Black people were able to do. For the next three years, I augmented the program to include conversations about career opportunities, attending college and becoming activists in their community.

MAKE A DIFFERENCE

Because of my volunteer service activities, I developed values with a strong community focus. It's a necessary part of my life, as an individual, to be involved in my community in some capacity. As a Black female, it is even more important to me to be an example and a source of encouragement for other young people. I understand that I am able to do the things I do because someone helped and encouraged me. Now, it is my obligation to help and encourage others.

I believe it was no accident that I chose the professions of architecture and city planning. These two professions have a tremendous impact on our physical and mental wellness as well as how we participate in our communities. In architecture school, I was always more interested in the social implications of design and how to bring good design to underrepresented communities that are usually neglected. I'm convinced this will remain my focus in the future.

—Anna McCorvey

---------------------------------- ★ ----------------------------------

PART THREE

ON YOUR

OWN

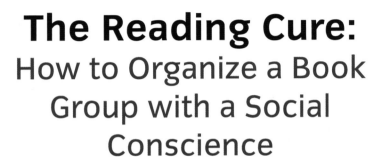

The Reading Cure:
How to Organize a Book Group with a Social Conscience

If, for whatever reason, you do not want to volunteer to do community service there is one other important role you can perform in your neighborhood or community. It is to help organize—with friends, neighbors or colleagues—a socially conscious book group. This chapter lists all the essential elements that go into setting one up. ★

MAKE A DIFFERENCE

It also has a suggested reading list of novels that deal with social, environmental, political and economic justice. And, if you are willing to volunteer for community service you might very well want to read some of the books recommended as, quite often, volunteers are not familiar with the issues and problems facing neighborhoods or groups different than their own.

> In a democratic society, where every individual opinion counts, [literature's] incomparable ability to instruct, to make alternatives intellectually and emotionally clear, to spotlight falsehood, insincerity, and foolishness—[literature's] incomparable ability, that is, to make us understand—ought to be a force bringing people together, breaking down the barriers of prejudice and ignorance, and holding up ideals worth pursuing. Literature in America does fulfill these obligations.

The novelist John Gardner wrote these words in his essay collection On Moral Fiction, and he is absolutely correct. Novels offer genuine hope for learning how to handle our daily personal problems – and those political issues of our communities and our country—in a moral and human way. They can help us to understand the relationship between our inner lives and the outer world, and the balance between thinking, feeling, and acting. They can give us awareness of place, time, and condition—about ourselves and about others. As our great Nobel Prize winner William Faulkner said, the best literature is far more true than any journalism.

Throughout history, the imaginations of young people have been fired by characters that function as role models. Yet when we look around us today, we find role models who are less than healthy and truths that are far from self-evident. We find troubling and false symbols of success, fantasy, or celebrity. All the while, we are surrounded by a technology of speed and efficiency that neither questions its means nor knows its ends. In the past thirty years, mass-marketing and advertising techniques have created an entirely new moral climate in America. The superficiality, the alienation, the escapism, and the hollowness are a result of a steady bombardment of confusing and deadening messages designed to reduce us to passive consumers. And we have paid a heavy price: a sharp decline in both civic participation and meaningful public discourse. We have become serious about frivolous issues and frivolous about serious ones.

How curious: while people around the world are risking their lives for American democratic ideals, we're voting in underwhelming numbers and telling pollsters that we're alienated from our political system. For the past thirty years, the acquisition of more and more material goods has become our highest form of endeavor. Terminal consumerism has become a way of life. However, as novelist John Nichols puts it, "Thirty-six flavors doth not a democracy make." How has it come to pass that our founding fathers gave us a land of political and economic opportunity, and we have become a nation of political and economic opportunists? As we have come to worship the idols of power, money, and success, we have neglected the core political principles of justice, equality, community, and democracy.

POLITICS AND THE MEDIA

The decline in our political culture has occurred in direct proportion to the increase in TV-driven soft news, celebrity scandal-mongering, and superficial political coverage. Every day the electronic media feverishly compete to hype news into entertainment. And when they get a Michael Jackson, Mark Sanford, Elliot Spitzer or O.J. trial or scandal—especially if it has a sex angle—they stage extravaganzas that would make Barnum and Bailey blush.

With the attention span of viewers decreasing with each generation, and with the networks and cables competing for a large audience, what counts is who can make the fastest and the most enjoyable images. Faster images may tickle the pleasure centers of viewers and achieve higher ratings and more money for media owners, but they make America stupid. TV news turns democracy into "duh-mocracy." Television actress Kristen Johnson put it this way: "TV can really suck the brain right out of your body." And suck the life out of our democracy.

Politics has become a business-game of manipulating symbols and perpetuating myths to conform to the media's mass-marketing techniques and needs. As with so many other aspects of modern living, the process itself has become kingmaker. The process is politics as entertainment—a curious combination of hype and palliative. We know our dependence on mindless, endless, irrelevant TV commercials—and evening news sound bites—creates the illusion that we are learning something. But we are not. In the process we lose our freedom to make genuine choices based on coherent, rational ideas. As T.S. Eliot asked, "Where is the wisdom in knowledge? Where is the knowledge in information?" We might add, where is the knowledge in a 30-second decontextualized political news sound bite? Hype has impoverished our political debate. It has undermined the very idea that political discourse can be educational and edifying—or that national public policy can grow out of reflective discussion and shared political values. This MacNews approach has undercut our moral values and civic traditions. We have sought simplistic answers to complex problems without even beginning to comprehend the consequences of our loss. We desperately need a common-sense prescription for change. My practical and modest solution is a four-step remedy for reviving our ailing civic culture:

1. Pull the plug on television news and stick with serious print media.
2. Get active in the organizations and political campaigns that support the same issues and causes you do.
3. Read good political novels.
4. Organize a political reading group.

The last two steps may seem tangential, but they are indispensable to the cure. A good novel serves as a conscience and a guide to action. It revives passionate and thoughtful political debate, providing in-depth exploration of values and political problems marginalized by the media circus.

ORGANIZING A BOOK GROUP

The number of book clubs and reading groups is growing across the country. Individual readers, booksellers, and librarians are organizing new groups and facilitating the introduction of new members into ongoing groups in record numbers. These active readers are following in the American historical tradition of the women's literary discussion groups of the colonial era, the literary and study clubs of the late 1800s "progressive era," and the Great Books groups of the mid-1900s. So, if you're interested in a stimulating, pleasurable and democracy-building literary exercise, why not organize a reading group yourself? Here are some basic guidelines.

The Logistics: Who and When

Look for eight to twelve people who are thoughtful, interesting, and curious. If they already enjoy reading, so much the better. A group needs people who can articulate their ideas and who are good listeners. Those who are enthusiastic, sensitive, and have a sense of humor are a real plus to any discussion. Start with your friends, relatives, and acquaintances who enjoy reading. Ask them to make suggestions. Branch out to those at work and your social, professional, or neighborhood organizations. Put up a sign in your local bookstore or advertise in a community newspaper. Although groups may be homogeneous, such as those composed of women—which are a majority of existing groups—some of the most successful groups are quite diverse. They have men and women, a variety of cultural backgrounds, and a wide range of ages. While some groups shy away from structure, most groups do have rules. You might consider adopting guidelines that address issues related to attendance and tardiness, the presence of children and animals, and methods for accepting new members and choosing appropriate books.

Most groups also have facilitators. The facilitator is often the group member who suggested the book, but it could be any participant or a professional leader hired by the group. One good way to find a facilitator is to make inquiries or put up an ad at your local university, community college, or high school. A good facilitator encourages active participation and listening, and ensures that each member is listened to and respected. He or she influences the ambience by making members comfortable in voicing unpopular opinions. By keeping the discussion on track and making sure no one dominates, the facilitator provides the background for a successful discussion.

The goal for facilitation is to encourage the flow of discussion as subtly as possible, in the style of a free-flowing, informed, spirited direction, while assisting the group to move from one topic to another in a timely manner. There is no formula for assuring lively and insightful discussion, but each member of the group might think about the following issues while reading the book: What do you think is the central theme? What are the underlying themes? Did the author raise any emotional conflicts you may have had … or resolve any? Did the author challenge any political, economic, social, or cultural beliefs that you may have held with regard to race, sex, gender, class, or ethnicity?

The Books

Finding appropriate books can be challenging. Many reading groups adopt an annual reading list, while others select books a month or two in advance. Suggestions come from the group's members, their friends, librarians, and booksellers.

One process for book selection that works well is to designate one person each month to bring a selection of books and introduce them to the group. Anyone who has read the books can veto them. The group then narrows the selection down to three, and votes. As a reading group participant, you will find yourself involved in a perpetual search for stimulating books. So I've provided a balanced list of fifty novels by contemporary authors that I believe will enliven the mind and nourish the soul. The novels I recommend are a healthy antidote to living in Entertainment Nation—and reflect that the best in our character is carried in our literature.

We depend on our fiction for metaphoric news of who we are, or who we think we ought to be. The writers of today's political and social realism are doing no less than reminding us of our true, traditional American values—the hope, the promises, and the dreams. When we read these novels, we learn about who we are as individuals and as a nation. They inform us, as no other medium does, about the state of our national politics and character—of the difference between what we say we are and how we actually behave. They offer us crucial insights into the moral, social, and emotional conflicts that are taking place in communities across America. We need such exploration today more than ever.

MAKE A DIFFERENCE

Dorothy Allison, *Bastard Out of Carolina* (Dutton). An unsparing, passionate, and gritty work about a young girl growing up in poverty. Resonates with integrity and empathy.

Lisa Alther, *Original Sins* (Knopf). Set in the South, this intelligent and absorbing story details the challenges, dreams, and follies of the 1960s. Transcends the differences between races in an insightful and generous manner.

Harriette Arnow, *The Dollmaker* (Avon). A family moves from the hills of Kentucky to industrial Detroit. This epic novel tests the strength of the human heart against the bitterest odds.

James Baldwin, *Another Country* (Dell). A magnificent, tumultuous, and disturbing work about racism that rings with authenticity.

Russell Banks, *Continental Drift* (Ballantine). An absorbing story about a frost-belt family that moves to Florida to find the good life. Instead, they find a nightmare.

Charles Baxter, *Shadow Play* (Norton). The assistant city manager of a small, depressed town in Michigan sees his life fall apart when the chemical plant he lured to town turns out to be an environmental disaster.

Saul Bellow, *Herzog* (Penguin). Keen insights into what it takes to maintain one's individuality and civility while corporations dominate our culture and politics, and critical thinking gives way to the demands of social conformism and consumerism.

Wendell Berry, *The Memory of Old Jack* (Harvest). Remarkable and graceful; explores the life of an aging Appalachian farmer amid America's changing values.

Dorothy Bryant, *Confessions of Madame Psyche* (Ata). The twentieth century as experienced by a Chinese American woman. This moving account of Mei-li Murrow's saga is a metaphor for California's and our nation's multicultural experience.

Sandra Cisneros, *The House on Mango Street* (Knopf). A poignant coming-of-age novel, with unforgettable characters, set in the Latino section of Chicago.

E. L. Doctorow, *The Book of Daniel* (Plume). The most important political novel about the Cold War, the arms race, Red-baiting, and McCarthyism.

Michael Dorris, *A Yellow Raft in Blue Water* (Warner). Compassionate and psychologically complex, this novel spans three generations of Native American women in the Pacific Northwest—on and off the reservation—who share a fierce independence and a love of family.

Ralph Ellison, *Invisible Man* (Vintage). A powerful classic about race, individuality, and identity. A Southern black man moves to New York and learns the many ways whites are unable to see him.

Gretel Ehrlich, *Heart Mountain* (Penguin). Explores the experience of Japanese Americans exiled to a World War II relocation camp in Wyoming, and their relationship with local ranchers.

Louise Erdrich, *Love Medicine* (Harper Perennial). Presents stunning and haunting insight into life for Native Americans today.

Denise Giardina, *The Unquiet Earth* (Ivy). From the devastation of the Depression to the hope of the War on Poverty, a moving story of a West Virginia community's struggle for survival.

Kaye Gibbons, *Ellen Foster* (Algonquin). An exhilarating and endearing tale of an eleven-year-old orphan who calls herself "old Ellen," and who moves from one woebegone situation to another with spirit and determination.

Davis Grubb, *Shadow of My Brother* (Zebra). Perfectly paced; a dramatic tale of a Tennessee town in the 1950s caught in a moral crisis over racial violence.

Ernest Hebert, *The Dogs of March* (New England Press). Brilliant, sensitive, and funny. Captures what it was like to be unemployed in the 1980s. Set in New England, it's the American dream gone belly-up.

Ursula Hegi, *Stones from the River* (Scribner). In a small German town, the ordinary and secret lives of people and their relationship to politics disclose the quandaries and conflicts that allowed the greatest crime of the twentieth century.

Linda Hogan, *Mean Spirit* (Ivy). A magical and compelling story about whites robbing the Osage Indian tribe of their oil wealth in Oklahoma.

John Irving, *The Cider House Rules* (Bantam). A fine writer brings his incisive storytelling gifts to fruition with this excellent novel about choice, class, and Yankee common sense.

Arturo Islas, *The Rain God* (Avon). A Southwestern classic set in a fictional small town on the Texas-Mexico border. Examines the spirit of Mexican American life—faith, family, and culture—and how it conflicts with the Anglo drive to "make it."

William Kennedy, *Ironweed* (Penguin). A Pulitzer Prize winner's shrewd study of the diceyness of fate. This modern Dante's *Inferno* about life on skid row is especially poignant as homelessness continues to cast a shadow across our land.

MAKE A DIFFERENCE

Susan Kidd, *The Secret Life of Bees* (Penguin). A stunning and lush story of race and gender set in South Carolina. In the struggle between bigotry and love, the latter wins out.

Barbara Kingsolver, *Animal Dreams* (Harper Perennial). A wonderful tale of multiculturalism in Arizona. Explores themes of authenticity, community, integrity, and truth.

Maxine Hong Kingston, *The Woman Warrior: Memories of a Girlhood Among Ghosts* (Vintage). A brilliant portrayal of the Chinese American experience. Kingston's account of growing up Asian and poor adds a cultural richness to the landscape.

Ella Leffland, *Rumors of Peace* (Harper Perennial). A fierce California girl comes of age during World War II, making her own sense of racism, Nazism, the bombings of Pearl Harbor and Hiroshima, and the coming of peace.

Alan Lightman, *The Diagnosis* (Vintage). A Kafkaesque tale that questions America's compulsive love affair with modern technology, efficiency, speed, money, and "making it."

Thomas Mallon, *Henry and Clara* (Ticknor & Fields). Clara and Henry, the young couple in the box with Lincoln when he was shot, are the focus of this riveting account of the political and cultural conflicts of the Civil War era.

Carson McCullers, *The Heart is a Lonely Hunter* (Bantam). This enduring masterpiece, set in small-town Georgia, is a compassionate study of how people confront the problems of poverty, race, class, and gender—and how they handle the conflicts of the human condition.

Toni Morrison, *Beloved* (Plume). Winner of a Pulitzer Prize, this is a powerful story of the legacy of slavery. The central theme, the relationship between slave and master, illuminates the tragic complications underlying our historical experience.

Bharai Mukherjee, *The Middleman* (Fawcett). Winner of the National Book Critics Circle Award, this is a profound, intelligent, and often funny book about recent immigrants to America and their struggle to survive.

Faye Ng, *Bone* (Harper Perennial). In a clear and emotionally powerful novel, Ng takes us into the heart and inner secrets of a family in San Francisco's Chinatown.

John Nichols, *The Milagro Beanfield War* (Ballantine). Reveals how the economic and political "shell game" is being run on ordinary Americans. Part of the author's New Mexico trilogy, it is a contemporary *Grapes of Wrath*, leavened with Mark Twain's down-home humor.

Joyce Carol Oates, *Them* (Vanguard). A poignant account of the hopes, strategies, and chaos of urban community organizing during the time of the 1960s riots.

Tillie Olsen, *Yonnondio* (Laurel). A remarkable, poetic, and timeless book about a young family's struggle to overcome poverty during the Great Depression.

Ruth. Ozeki, *My Year of Meats* (Penguin). A feisty Japanese American filmmaker takes on the beef industry, chemical corporations, and commercial advertising. Muckraking, witty and provocative.

Jayne Anne Phillips, *Machine Dreams* (Dutton). A chronicle of middle-American family life, from the Depression to Vietnam, about identity, shifting values, and the ironies of a rapidly changing America.

Marge Piercy, *Gone to Soldiers* (Fawcett). A sweeping epic about women's lives during World War II that seamlessly blends political, social, and economic issues on the home front.

Chaim Potok, *Davita's Harp* (Fawcett). A compassionate coming-of-age novel about a young girl in 1930s New York developing a social, moral, and political consciousness.

E. Annie Proulx, *Postcards* (Collier). Winner of the PEN/Faulkner Award. A remarkable story of the struggle of New England farmers to confront the loss of home and place in economic hard times.

Philip Roth, *American Pastoral* (Vintage). An unsparing story of the political excesses of the 1960s. How youthful idealism led to romantic, out-of-control, anti-liberal activism, which in turn laid the groundwork for the reactionary policies of Nixon and Reagan.

Richard Russo, *Empire Falls* (Vintage). A passionate and rich examination of the working-class heart of small-town America, and the consequences of inequitable distribution of wealth in a deindustrialized society.

May Sarton, *Kinds of Love* (Norton). Three generations celebrate the American bicentennial in a small New Hampshire town. About truth, honesty, integrity—all those traditional virtues that have become unfashionable.

Danzy Senna, *Caucasia* (Riverhead). Birdie Lee's black father flees in the seventies, and her white, activist mother is forced to take the girl underground, where Birdie copes with adolescence and the complexities of her racial identity.

Mary Lee Settle, *The Scapegoat* (Ballantine). A stirring account of a historic strike in the coal fields, depicting a real-life struggle between immigrants

(Italian, Greek, Polish, and Slavic, among others) and robber barons. You won't find this in most history texts.

Jane Smiley, *Moo* (Random House). The financial, academic, sexual, and political scandals of a Midwest university are laid bare in this satire of higher education.

John Steinbeck, *The Grapes of Wrath* (Penguin). This classic novel of farmers forced to move West during the Great Depression electrified the nation and reminded us of our historical commitment to compassion, opportunity, and social justice.

Kurt Vonnegut, *Jailbird* (Dell). Hilarious tale about Nixon's social policies of "benign neglect" and the Watergate era. An unflinching mix of wit, politics, and class that should be required reading.

Alice Walker, *Meridian* (Fawcett). A powerful novel about civil rights activism in the South of the 1960s. Warm, generous, and complex, it challenges each of us to examine what it is to become a decent, responsible, and honorable person.

PART FOUR

SPECTATOR

BECOMES

PARTICIPANT

Each of the organizations profiled in this section has been selected because of its commitment to educational, social, economic, environmental, and community development goals. Some have been in existence for many decades; others are fairly new. Most are national organizations, and some are local prototypes, but all have a solid track record of delivering services that are useful and meaningful. ★

Organizations by Interest

You probably have skills you can share, or interests you can pursue by volunteering. If you're an architect work with Habitat for Humanity; an accountant, help low income people with their income taxes; a teacher, work with disadvantaged kids in a reading program or a literacy program for immigrants; a dentist, doctor, nurse or psychologist, volunteer at a community health center. ★

CHILDREN

4-H

4-H (which stands for "head, heart, hands, and health") is the largest out of school youth organization in the country with the involvement of over six million children between the ages of 8-19. The education program offers practical life skills in areas such as nutrition, safety, communication, science, and technology, amongst others. Youth members can join a 4-H club, attend a camp, or participate in school-based or after-school programs. Though recognized in 1902, the foundation for 4-H began in the late 1800's.

Volunteer Opportunities

The 4-H community includes over 500,000 volunteers who lead children in a wide array of hands-on activities and help coordinate community clubs. Adult volunteers can also teach a special skill or plan local and national events that help 4-H educate children with their "learn-by-doing" approach. 4-H clubs are organized under county extension offices.

Contact Information

Headquarters: 1400 Independence Avenue, S.W., Stop 2225 Washington, D.C. 20250-2225 (202) 401-4114

www.4-h.org or national4-hheadquarters.gov 4hhq@nifa.usda.gov

BIG BROTHERS BIG SISTERS OF AMERICA (BBBSA)

For more than 100 years, Big Brothers Big Sisters has operated under the belief that inherent in every child is the ability to succeed and thrive in life. Most children served by Big Brothers Big Sisters are in single-parent and low-income families or households where a parent is incarcerated. As the nation's largest donor and volunteer supported mentoring network, Big Brothers Big Sisters makes meaningful, monitored matches between adult volunteers ("Bigs") and children ("Littles").

Headquartered in Philadelphia with a network of nearly 400 agencies across the country, Big Brothers Big Sisters serves more than 255,000 children. Established in 1904.

MAKE A DIFFERENCE

CHILDREN

Volunteer Opportunities

Big Brothers Big Sisters provides community-based and school-based mentoring. To become a Big Brother or Big Sister, please contact the Big Brothers Big Sisters agency in your area. While they are affiliated with Big Brothers Big Sisters of America, each is its own agency with its own board of directors and the requirements vary slightly.

The simplest way to contact Big Brothers Big Sisters is to visit its website, BigBrothersBigSisters.org, to enter one's zip code. Contact information on a local agency will be provided.

Contact Information
Headquarters: 230 North Thirteenth Street Philadelphia, PA 19107

(215) 567-7000
www.bbbs.org

★

CHILDREN NOW

This national, nonpartisan organization focuses on children's interests, especially in the areas of health care and education, and how the media is influential in both matters. In 2004, Children Now had a notable victory as one of the leaders in a campaign that influenced the Federal Communications Committee to protect children from certain forms of advertising and to provide more educational television programming. Established in 1988.

Volunteer Opportunities

Internships are available in Oakland and Sacramento for undergraduate and graduate students. There is a required commitment of a minimum of 16 hours per week for a period of at least 10 weeks. Depending on the policy area, duties can include researching policy and budget proposals, drafting fact sheets, and preparing for meetings and events; researching and summarizing reports and scholarly articles on a range of topics related to key children's issues; updating online data tools and assisting with report releases; and assisting staff with general administrative work, preparing legislative briefing binders, organizing meetings, recording minutes, and attending legislative hearings and policy discussions.

When applying, make sure to include your interest in the following policy areas: education (early learning, K-12 and afterschool), health, and media.

Desired Skills:

- Interest in and familiarity with policies affecting children and their families, particularly in health, education, and/or media
- Strong analytic, research and writing skills
- Demonstrated organizational and time-management skills, preferably developed in an office
- Demonstrated ability to work independently and as a member of a team

To apply, submit a resume, cover letter, and 1-2 page writing sample (excerpts are fine) in Microsoft Word. The organization asks that applicants include their names in the file name for all documents (e.g., g.smith – resume).

In addition to outlining applicant's qualifications, cover letters should clearly indicate the following:

- Preferred policy area
- Preferred dates
- Hours available per week

Resumes should include the name, title, and contact information for at least two references.

Contract Information:

Headquarters: 1212 Broadway, 5th
  Floor
Oakland, CA 94612
(510) 763-2444

www.childrennow.org
info@childrennow.org
jobs@childrennow.org

CHILDREN'S DEFENSE FUND (CDF)

CDF implements their "Leave No Child Behind" motto by advocating for children nation-wide, especially minorities and those living in poverty or with disabilities. Ensuring children have access to quality health care, early education and faith, are several of CDF's priorities. Protection from abuse and neglect is also championed. Established in 1973.

Volunteer Opportunities

CDF asks that people interested in supporting the organization's mission visit its website, www.childrensdefense.org, to sign up to receive email updates about upcoming volunteer opportunities and ways to take action to improve the lives of children.

MAKE A DIFFERENCE

CHILDREN

Contact Information

Headquarters: 25 E Street N.W.
Washington, D.C. 20001
(800) CDF-1200 (800-233-1200)

www.childrensdefense.org
cdfinfo@childrensdefense.org

COURT APPOINTED SPECIAL ADVOCATES (CASA)

The mission of CASA is to provide volunteers advocates for neglected and abused children in court. In an effort to prevent children in foster care from getting lost in the legal maze, CASA educates and prepares regular citizens to study cases, conduct interviews, and write written reports that help children get placed into safe and permanent homes. Established in 1977.

Volunteer Opportunities

CASA offers volunteers 30 hours of training prior to service followed by 12 additional hours a year midst-service. Volunteers are expected to research the background of assigned cases, represent the best interests of children in the courtroom, and ensure cases are brought to quick and appropriate conclusions. Most cases last about a year and a half and typical time commitment for volunteers is between 10-20 hours a week. The volunteer stays on each case until it is closed and the child is placed in a safe and permanent home.

Contact Information

Headquarters: 100 West Harrison
North Tower, Suite 500
Seattle, WA 98119

(800) 628-3233
www.casaforchildren.org

IRIDESCENT

Iridescent is a science-education non-profit organization that brings cutting-edge science to underserved communities. Iridescent's unique approach is to empower engineers and scientists to communicate their expertise and passion to children through exciting, inquiry-based programs. In addition, Iridescent invites parents to learn alongside their children and participate in Family Science Courses.

Iridescent has been in operation for 4 years and has trained over 300 engineers to impact almost 4,800 underserved children and parents in three major cities: Los Angeles, San Francisco and more recently, New York.

CHILDREN

Volunteer Opportunities

Opportunities are available in New York City, Los Angeles, and San Francisco. Engineers interested in volunteering can attend Engineer Training (Engineers As Teachers), a rigorous, 16-week training program in NYC and L.A. that enables participants to serve as role models and provide meaningful science learning experiences to the public. The engineers develop their public speaking and leadership skills and a deeper understanding of their own field while communicating complex concepts to large, diverse audiences. Engineers also volunteer significant amounts of time to the Family Science Courses (80-100 hours during four months) and become regular, long-term volunteers. Additionally, volunteer engineers can commit for a short, one-time teaching commitment via Iridescent's four-hour quick trainings (also offered in NYC and L.A.).

For all other supporting positions—Spanish translation (live and remote), Program Directors (individuals who evaluate the engineers' teaching) and other opportunities—Iridescent posts these on volunteermatch.org, idealist. org, and on its website. The organization follows-up with a volunteer orientation, held the first Saturday of every month from 10am-1pm.

Contact Information

(310) 309-0766
www.iridescentlearning.org

Info@IridescentLearning.org

KABOOM!

KaBOOM! is dedicated to the construction of local playspaces for children while also increasing community engagement. The organization leads community-build projects for playgrounds and also strives to increase public awareness about the benefits of play. One of their objectives is to supply do-it-yourself resources that include an online community, grants, publications, and training, for communities that wish to plan a new playspace on their own. Established in 1996.

Volunteer Opportunities

Since many KaBOOM!-led builds are quickly staffed with volunteers, the organization encourages interested parties to check Kaboom.org for other projects occurring in their area. Many of these opportunities are posted on the website by community-based organizations not affiliated with KaBOOM!

Contact Information
4455 Connecticut Ave. NW
Suite B100
Washington, D.C. 20008

(202) 659-0215
www.Kaboom.org

★

MAKE-A-WISH FOUNDATION

Make-A-Wish Foundation allows children with life-threatening illnesses the opportunity to experience one of their wishes come true. Examples of popular wishes include visiting a theme park, meeting a movie star, or receiving a coveted gift. Established in 1980.

Volunteer Opportunities

With the assistance of nearly 25,000 volunteers, the charity is able to a grant a wish every 40 minutes. Opportunities vary by local chapters but volunteers are strongly needed for wish granting, fundraising, special events, general administration, language translation, and several other areas.

Contact Information
Headquarters: 4742 N. 24th St.,
Suite 400
Phoenix, AZ 85016-4862

(602) 279-WISH (9474) or (800) 722-
WISH (9474)
www.wish.org

★

STANDUP FOR KIDS

The mission of StandUP For Kids is to help homeless kids, children living on the street, and at-risk youth. Efforts are carried out by volunteers who walk the streets to find and reach out to those without stabile homes. StandUP For Kids offers necessities such as food and hygiene products, as well as education programs and job training. Established in 1990.

Volunteer Opportunities

Contact a local chapter to learn about counselor positions. Volunteers can also help with advocacy, development, job training assistance, tutoring, marketing, grant writing and graphic design.

Contact Information
Headquarters: 83 Walton Street,
Suite 100
Atlanta, Georgia 30303

(800) 365-4KID
www.standupforkids.org
staff@standupforkids.org

★

CIVIL RIGHTS

ASIAN AMERICANS FOR COMMUNITY OUTREACH (AACO)

AACO is a local volunteer-run organization dedicated to bringing together young Asian American professionals and students in order to serve their communities. Its members work to enrich the community at large by participating in social events such as charity fundraisers. But the organization's purpose is to also promote the awareness of social and political issues relevant to Asian Americans. Established in 1994.

Volunteer Opportunities

AACO offers volunteers the ability to serve at single day events in the San Francisco Bay area. In the past, volunteers had prepared and served food in a soup kitchen, taken pledge calls at a radio fundraiser, and performed security at the Northern California Cherry Blossom Festival.

Contact Information:

www.aaco-sf.org
info@aaco-sf.org

DISABILITY RIGHTS EDUCATION AND DEFENSE FUND (DREDF)

DREDF strives to advance the civil and human rights of people living with disabilities through many means, including legal advocacy, public policy and legislative development. The fund, which is directed by individuals with disabilities and the parents of children with disabilities, offers training and education to multiple groups of people and has run a disability rights legal clinic for over 15 years. Established in 1979.

Volunteer Opportunities

Primary volunteer opportunities are for law students, but DREDF has recently added undergraduate internships in Berkeley.

The Disability Rights Internship for undergraduates is structured to provide interns with an overview of disability rights issues in education, transportation, employment, housing and physical access. The Intern works with the Children and Family Advocacy, ADA Technical Assistance and Public Policy

Programs and will leave with legal, practical advocacy skills and knowledge of political and grassroots organizing. Duties assigned after initial training are likely to include:

- Coordination in parent advocacy trainings and workshops with DREDF Parent Advocates
- Assisting with legislative advocacy including research for potential legislation; assisting in grassroots networking and education
- Assisting with social media and Internet advocacy
- Providing research and assistance to policy analysts on disability issues
- Updating DREDF's press and photo archives
- Participating as member of DREDF staff, including development activities; attend staff meetings if possible

DREDF also offers field placement internships and possible summer positions for law students. Academic term internships generally involve a commitment of 8 to 16 hours per week. Summer internships generally involve a 40-hour per week commitment for at least 5 weeks, and preferably 8-10 weeks. Individuals with disabilities, minority, and women candidates are especially encouraged to apply.

Interns work on a variety of litigation projects under the supervision of DREDF attorneys, including disability rights class-action and individual cases in the areas of employment, access to government programs and activities, architectural access, housing, and educational entitlements of children with disabilities. Projects include researching legal issues, drafting documents for discovery (e.g. interrogatories, requests for admissions, and requests for production of documents), and drafting legal motions and pleadings. Interns will have direct contact with clients, and the opportunity to observe or participate in meetings, depositions, and court proceedings related to litigation on which they are working.

With the close supervision of attorneys, interns may also respond to telephone inquiries about disability discrimination or special education issues that callers with disabilities or parents of children with disabilities are facing, and may provide informal advocacy on clients' behalf. Interns are also invited and encouraged to join DREDF staff in attending disability community events and meetings that occur during their period of internship.

Interested candidates may submit cover letter, resume and references to Attn: Law Student Internships by mail, e-mail (hmin@dredf.org) or fax.

Contact Information

2212 Sixth Street
Berkeley, CA 94710
(800) 348-4232 or (510) 644-2555

www.dredf.org
info@dredf.org

INDIAN LAW RESOURCE CENTER

Preserving Indian and other Native nations and tribes is the principle objective of the Indian Law Resource Center. The center works on a range of issues to protect the human rights, lands, culture, and resources of indigenous communities in the United States and throughout the Americas. Legal assistance is offered to help these efforts and a current project includes providing human rights training to U.S. tribal leaders. Established in 1978 by American Indians who direct the center to this day.

Volunteer opportunities

The Indian Law Resource Center does not have a formalized volunteer program, but it does use volunteers sporadically, and mainly in an internship-type arrangement. Its Washington D.C office brings in legal interns throughout the year. In the past it has had administrative and communications/translation internships but these are on an as-needed basis. The center's Montana office also considers applications for legal clerkships throughout the year. The Montana office also coordinates the Center's fellowship program – the Center awards fellowships each year to up to two law students who show particular promise in federal Indian law and/or international indigenous human rights issues.

With the limited number of volunteer opportunities available, the Indian Law Resource Center encourages individuals interested in volunteering to subscribe to its electronic newsletter to stay informed of advocacy activities and educational opportunities.

Contact Information

Headquarters: 602 North Ewing
Street
Helena, MT 59601

(406) 449-2006
www.indianlaw.org
mt@indianlaw.org

CIVIL RIGHTS

MEXICAN AMERICAN LEGAL DEFENSE AND EDUCATIONAL FUND (MALDEF)

Fighting for the legal rights of Latinos in the U.S., MALDEF is often referred to as the "law firm of the Latino community." The fund's goal is to implement programs that will improve Latino communities and achieve socio-economic change. Their approach combines advocacy, educational outreach and litigation strategies. One of their greatest legal achievements was with the U.S. Supreme Court case, Plyler V. Doe, whose conclusion secured free public education to all American children of undocumented immigrant parents. Founded in 1968.

Volunteer Opportunities

Each regional office—San Antonio, Chicago, Atlanta, D.C.—utilizes volunteers differently, but help is often needed in administration and for planning events. Interested volunteers should visit the website and submit an e-mail.

Contact Information

634 S. Spring Street
Los Angeles, CA 90014
(213) 629-2512

www.maldef.org
jobs@maldef.org

NATIONAL ASSOCIATION

FOR THE ADVANCEMENT OF COLORED PEOPLE (NAACP)

Founded February 12, 1909, the NAACP is the nation's oldest, largest and most widely recognized grassroots–based civil rights organization. Its more than half-million members and supporters throughout the United States and the world are the premier advocates for civil rights in their communities, conducting voter mobilization and monitoring equal opportunity in the public and private sectors. The NAACP's principal objective is to ensure the political, educational, social and economic equality of minority group citizens of United States and eliminate race prejudice. The NAACP seeks to remove all barriers of racial discrimination through the democratic processes.

Volunteer Opportunities

Opportunities are available at the local level and vary by location. Visit the organization's website to find the contact information for a local office near you.

Contact Information

Headquarters: 4805 Mt. Hope Drive
Baltimore MD 21215

(877) NAACP-98 or (410) 580-5777
www.naacp.org

CIVIL RIGHTS

NATIONAL COUNCIL OF LA RAZA (NCLR)

With the help of its formal network of nearly 300 affiliates throughout the country, NCLR aims to improve opportunities for Hispanic Americans. The organization supports Hispanic community-based organizations, particularly those serving low-income and disadvantaged Hispanics, by offering assistance in management, program operations, and other areas. The affiliates, in turn, are able to reach millions of Hispanics in 41 states. NCLR also conducts research, policy analysis, and advocacy in areas such as education, employment, immigration and health. Founded in 1968.

Volunteer Opportunities

Volunteers assist with workshops on health, immigration and economy that NCLR organizes for its annual conference. NCLR occasionally uses volunteers to help with publicity during its advocacy day.

Contact Information

Headquarters: Raul Yzaguirre Building
1126 16th Street, N.W.

Washington, DC 20036
(202) 785-1670
www.nclr.org

NATIONAL URBAN LEAGUE

National Urban League has been around for 100 years, working on their mission to improve the standard of living in underserved African American communities. Efforts to accomplish this include a focus on education (access to scholarships and after-care programs), job training, affordable healthcare, and the protection of civil rights for African Americans. The league has more than one hundred local affiliates that pursue this objective and provide direct services. Established in 1910.

Volunteer Opportunities

Volunteers are recognized as a fundamental part of the National Urban League, serving in the New York headquarter and in the league's local offices. Opportunities include fundraising for events, such as the annual Equal Opportunity Day (EOD) Dinner and Annual Conference, mentoring youth, participating in various community projects, and providing support to staff.

Contact Information

Headquarters: 120 Wall Street
New York, NY 10005

(212) 558-5300
www.nul.org

COMMUNITY DEVELOPMENT AND ECONOMIC JUSTICE

AMERICORPS

Each year, AmeriCorps offers 75,000 opportunities for adults of all ages and backgrounds to serve through a network of partnerships with local and national nonprofit groups. AmeriCorps members address critical needs in communities all across America. As an AmeriCorps member, you can:

- Tutor and mentor disadvantaged youth
- Fight illiteracy
- Improve health services
- Build affordable housing
- Teach computer skills
- Clean parks and streams
- Manage or operate after-school programs
- Help communities respond to disasters
- Build organizational capacity

Full-time AmeriCorps members who complete their service earn a Segal AmeriCorps Education Award of $4,725 to pay for college, graduate school, or to pay back qualified student loans; members who serve part-time receive a partial Award. Some AmeriCorps members may also receive a modest living allowance during their term of service.

AmeriCorps is made up of three main programs: AmeriCorps State and National , AmeriCorps VISTA, and AmeriCorps NCCC (National Civilian Community Corps). Established in 1993.

Volunteer Opportunities

The largest of AmeriCorps programs, AmeriCorps State and National provides funds to local and national organizations and agencies committed to using national service to address critical community needs in education, public safety, health and the environment. Each of these organizations and agencies, in turn, uses their AmeriCorps funding to recruit, place, and supervise AmeriCorps members.

AmeriCorps members serve in AmeriCorps State and National projects in every state, U.S. territories, and on tribal reservations. State and National programs are open to U.S. citizens, nationals, or lawful permanent resident aliens age 17 and older. Members may serve full- or part-time over a period not to exceed 12 months.

After successful completion of their term of service, AmeriCorps members earn a Segal AmeriCorps Education Award that can be used to pay for college or graduate school at Title IV schools, or to repay qualified student loans. Full-time AmeriCorps members also receive a modest living allowance, health care benefits, and child care assistance.

AmeriCorps VISTA is the national service program designed specifically to fight poverty. Founded as Volunteers in Service to America in 1965 and incorporated into the AmeriCorps network of programs in 1993, VISTA has been on the front lines in the fight against poverty in America for more than 40 years.

VISTA members commit to serve full-time for a year at a nonprofit organization or local government agency, working to fight illiteracy, improve health services, create businesses, strengthen community groups, and much more.

During your service, you'll also receive a modest living allowance, health care, and other benefits. And, upon completing your service, you can choose to receive either a Segal AmeriCorps Education Award or post-service stipend.

AmeriCorps NCCC (National Civilian Community Corps) is a full-time, team-based residential program for men and women age 18–24. Members are assigned to one of five campuses, located in Denver, Colorado; Sacramento, California; Perry Point, Maryland; Vicksburg, Mississippi; and Vinton, Iowa.

The mission of AmeriCorps NCCC is to strengthen communities and develop leaders through direct, team-based national and community service. In partnership with non-profits—secular and faith based, local municipalities, state governments, federal government, national or state parks, Indian Tribes and schools members complete service projects throughout the region they are assigned.

AmeriCorps NCCC requires an intensive, 10-month commitment. Members serve in teams of eight to twelve and are assigned to projects throughout the region served by their campus. They are trained in CPR, first aid, public safety, and other skills before beginning their first service project.

AmeriCorps NCCC serves communities in every state. Members are based at one of five regional campuses and travel to complete service projects throughout those regions. Sponsoring organizations request the assistance of AmeriCorps NCCC teams by submitting a project application to the regional campus that covers that organization's state. The campuses provide assistance in completing the application, developing a work plan, and preparing the project sponsor for the arrival of the AmeriCorps NCCC team.

AmeriCorps NCCC members receive a living allowance of approximately $4,000 for the 10 months of service (about $200 every two weeks before taxes), housing, meals, limited medical benefits, up to $400 a month for childcare, if necessary, member uniforms, and a Segal AmeriCorps Education Award upon successful completion of the program.

Contact Information
1201 New York Avenue, NW
Washington, DC 20525
(202) 606-5000 or (202) 606-3472 (TTY)

www.americorps.gov
questions@americorps.gov

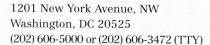

CENTER FOR THIRD WORLD ORGANIZING (CTWO)
CTWO is a training and resource organization that promotes social, economic, and racial justice for people of color, with a focus on the poor. To achieve its objective, CTWO strives to build a network of activists and communities, and provides training for new and experienced organizers. Training sessions include the Movement Activist Apprenticeship Program (MAAP), an 8-week-long intensive program that provides people of color with the opportunity to develop skills and experience in grassroots organizing, and The California Lead Organizer Institute (CLOI), which unites lead organizers who wish to advance their leadership abilities.

Volunteer Opportunities
Volunteer tasks vary by program and range from research to fundraising, to clerical work. Interested individuals can also apply to the organization's Movement Activist Apprenticeship Program (MAAP). MAAP is an eight-week summer internship program for people of color who want to pursue organizing. Participants receive training in CTWO's retreat center in Oakland, CA and are then placed in active campaigns where they become full time community organizers. For details, contact Program Coordinator Araceli Centeno at araceli@ctwo.org or by phone at (510) 355-7583 x13.

Contact Information
1218 E. 21st Street
Oakland, CA 94606

(510) 533-7583
www.ctwo.org

CITY YEAR

City Year, a member of AmeriCorps, unites young people (ages 17-24) of all backgrounds for a year of full-time service, giving them the skills and opportunities to change the world. As tutors, mentors and role models, these young leaders help children stay in school and on track, and transform schools and communities across the United States, as well as through international affiliates in Johannesburg, South Africa and London, England. Established in 1988.

Volunteer Opportunities

There are occasional opportunities during the year for people to join City Year for a day of service, such as painting murals and renovating facilities at a school in which a City Year team is in service year-round.

Contact Information

287 Columbus Avenue
Boston, MA 02116

(617) 927-2500
www.cityyear.org

COMMUNITY ACTION PARTNERSHIP (CAP)

CAP represents the interests of more than a thousand community action agencies that work to eliminate poverty. Community action agencies are nonprofit private and public organizations established under the Economic Opportunity Act of 1964 to fight poverty and make America a better place to live. CAP assists these agencies by sponsoring an annual convention, publishing a quarterly magazine, providing training and technical assistance, and releasing a weekly electronic newsletter. Most recently the federal Office of Community Services in the Department of Health & Human Services designated the Partnership as the lead national non-profit for two working groups: Jobs & Job Creation and Community Economic Development. Established in 1972.

Volunteer Opportunities

Each individual community action agency handles its own volunteers and sets the criteria for recruiting, training and utilizing volunteers so opportunities vary.

Contact Information

1140 Connecticut Avenue NW, Suite 121
Washington, DC 20036
(202) 265-7546

www.communityactionpartnership.com
info@communityactionpartnership.
com

FIELD MOBILIZATION DEPARTMENT OF THE AFL-CIO

The American Federation of Labor and Congress of Industrial Organizations (AFL-CIO) is comprised of 56 national and international labor unions. This department within the AFL-CIO mobilizes members at the state and local levels to support organizing and political action. The department also coordinates the AFL-CIO's Community Services program, which provides training, information and referral services to workers who face economic and other crises. Established in 1955.

Volunteer Opportunities

Contact the organization for details

Contact Information

Headquarters: 815 16th St., N.W. | www.aflcio.org
Washington, D.C. 20006

★

HABITAT FOR HUMANITY

Habitat for Humanity is a nonprofit, ecumenical Christian housing ministry that seeks to eliminate poverty housing and homelessness from the world and to make decent shelter a matter of conscience and action. To accomplish these goals, Habitat invites people of all backgrounds, races and religions to build houses together in partnership with families in need. Through volunteer labor and donations of money and materials, Habitat builds and rehabilitates simple, decent houses alongside its homeowner (partner) families. In addition, the organization monitors public policies related to housing, community and international development, and advocates policy changes that increase access to decent, affordable housing for people around the world. Established in 1976.

Volunteer Opportunities

Local opportunities include working in the office, building on site, or renovating homes. Habitat also offers specific volunteer programs for youth and women. Visit the organization's website to find the nearest Habitat for Humanity in your area and learn of its opportunities.

Volunteers wishing to make a long-term commitment can work at the organization's international headquarters in Americus, GA for two to six months or participate in the Habitat AmeriCorps/VISTA program. Under the program, individuals ages 18 and older live at and work with local Habitat affiliates while earning living allowances and receiving an education award upon completion of service.

International opportunities are also available. Through the organization's Global Village Program, volunteers build decent, affordable housing around the world on short-term volunteer trips. The International Volunteer Program allows participants to spend six to 12 months working in Habitat offices overseas.

Contact Information
Operational Headquarters:
121 Habitat Street
Americus, GA 31709-3498
(800) 422-4828

Administrative Headquarters:
270 Peachtree Street NW
Suite 1300
Atlanta, GA 30303
(800) 422-4828
www.habitat.org

★

NEIGHBOR TO NEIGHBOR (N2N)

Neighbor to Neighbor (N2N) fosters stable housing and promotes housing opportunity through counseling, education, supportive services, and community partnerships for residents of Colorado. Established in 1970.

Volunteer Opportunities

The organization offers opportunities in Northern Colorado for youth, adults, groups, service-learning students, interns, and court-referred volunteers. Online volunteer programs run weekdays during regular business hours but special weekend and evening projects are also available. Areas in need of volunteers include landscaping, fundraising, research, and both office and education support. Opportunities vary by location as follows:

Loveland Office: Volunteers and interns provide information and referral, greeting clients and answering phones, and providing screening for programs.

Murphy Center: Volunteers can help with Spanish translation for housing counseling sessions.

Fort Collins Office: Areas that volunteers can assist with include data entry, outcomes measurement, and mailings.

N2N also owns and manages affordable apartments in scattered-site communities around Larimer County. Volunteer groups can help with landscaping and property improvement projects such as community gardens. Volunteers under the age of 16 must be accompanied with parent and/or guardian for their volunteer shifts. Interested individuals should contact Tracy Schwartz at (970) 488-2369 or tschwartz@n2n.org.

Contact Information

N2N operates in Colorado's Larimer County. The organization's website (www.n2n.org) provides additional contact details.

Two locations in Fort Collins, CO:

1550 Blue Spruce Drive
Fort Collins, CO 80524
(970) 484-7498
242 Conifer Street
Fort Collins, CO 80524

(970) 494-9940
Loveland, CO, location: 565 North Cleveland Avenue
Loveland, CO 80537
(970) 663-4163

VOLUNTEERS IN SERVICE TO AMERICA (AMERICORPS*VISTA)

AmeriCorps VISTA is the national service program designed specifically to fight poverty. Founded as Volunteers in Service to America in 1965 and incorporated into the AmeriCorps network of programs in 1993, VISTA has been on the front lines in the fight against poverty in America for more than 40 years.

Volunteer Opportunities

VISTA members commit to serve full-time for a year at a nonprofit organization or local government agency, working to fight illiteracy, improve health services, create businesses, strengthen community groups, and much more. During service, volunteers receive a modest living allowance, health care, and other benefits. And, upon completing your service, you can choose to receive either a Segal AmeriCorps Education Award or post-service stipend.

See also "AmeriCorps" under Community Development and Economic Justice (p. TK).

Contact Information

1201 New York Avenue, NW
Washington, DC 20525
(800) 942-2677 or 800-833-3722
  (TTY)

www.americorps.gov/about/
  programs/vista.asp
questions@americorps.gov

VOLUNTEERS OF AMERICA

With thousands of human service programs, Volunteers of America helps some of the country's most vulnerable groups and is one of the nation's largest nonprofit providers of quality, affordable housing for low and moderate-income households. Integrating spirituality into their efforts, Volunteers of America is also an interdenominational church and considered an "auxiliary" to the universal Christian church with a special mission of service. Volunteers of America provides services to people of all faiths, and works to better the lives of individuals returning from prison, people living with disabilities, the elderly, the homeless, and at-risk youth, among others. Established in 1896.

Volunteer Opportunities

Volunteers of America has 38 offices across the country, offering many opportunities at the local level. Tasks include delivering Meals on Wheels to clients, providing administrative support, offering professional services (legal, public relations, training, motivational speaking), and managing other volunteers. Volunteering inquiries should be sent to tansmith@voa.org or volunteers@voa.org.

Contact Information

Headquarters: 1660 Duke Street
Alexandria, VA 22314

(800) 899-0087 or (703) 341-5000
www.voa.org

CONSUMER AFFAIRS

AARP

Founded in 1958, AARP is a nonprofit, nonpartisan membership organization that helps people 50 and over improve the quality of their lives. AARP has offices in all 50 states, the District of Columbia, Puerto Rico and the U.S. Virgin Islands. As a social welfare organization, as well as, the nation's largest membership organization for people 50+, AARP is leading a revolution in the way people view and live life.

Volunteer Opportunities

Contact the organization for details.

Contact Information

601 E Street, NW
Washington DC 20049
(888) OUR-AARP (888-687-2277) or
   TTY: (877) 434-7589

www.aarp.org
member@aarp.org

CONSUMERS UNION (CU)

Consumers Union (CU) is an expert, independent, nonprofit organization whose mission is to work for a fair, just, and safe marketplace for all consumers and to empower consumers to protect themselves. CU publishes *Consumer Reports*, one of the top-ten-circulation magazines in the country, and *ConsumerReports.org* in addition to two newsletters, Consumer Reports on Health and Consumer Reports Money Adviser. All of CU's work is informed by the more than 1 million readers who respond to its Annual Ballot & Questionnaire. In 2008, CU also launched several initiatives, including *ConsumerReportsHealth.org* and the Consumer Reports Health Ratings Center, which serve to educate and empower consumers to make more informed health-care decisions and to help change the market. Founded in 1936.

Volunteer Opportunities

Contact the organization for details.

MAKE A DIFFERENCE

Contact Information

101 Truman Avenue
Yonkers, NY 10703-1057

(914) 378-2000
www.consumersunion.org

------------------------------------★------------------------------------

U.S. PUBLIC INTEREST RESEARCH GROUP (U.S. PIRG)

U.S. PIRG, the federation of state Public Interest Research Groups (PIRGs), stands up to powerful special interests on behalf of the American public, working to win concrete results for our health and our well-being. With a strong network of researchers, advocates, organizers and students in state capitols across the country, it takes on the special interests on issues, such as product safety, political corruption, prescription drugs and voting rights, where these interests stand in the way of reform and progress.

Volunteer Opportunities

Each U.S. PIRG internship offers students a structured experience working one-on-one with one of U.S. PIRG's staff of advocates or campaign organizers—the intern's staff mentor. Interns learn basic skills that allow them to analyze issues and articulate solutions to the pressing problems of the day. Interns learn that activism and participation in the democratic process yield results. Though responsibilities vary, most internships include:

- Conducting research into critical public policy problems and preparing investigative reports;
- Coordinating media events, assisting in the preparation of news releases and opinion pieces;
- Working with coalition partners and PIRG offices to coordinate grassroots campaign activities; and
- Monitoring the progress of legislation in Congress and the actions of federal agencies.

Interns may have the opportunity to attend local, regional and national program briefings and trainings where they learn more about public interest issues and gain political skills. Summer interns participate in "brown bag lunch" discussions with leaders within U.S. PIRG and the State PIRGs, as well as leaders within other organizations.

Types of internships available include campaign, legislative, media, and administrative. For more information visit www.uspirg.org or contact Brian Walker, the Internship Coordinator, at (202) 546-9707 or dcinternships@pirg.

org. Although U.S. PIRG internships are unpaid, students may receive academic credit from their college or university.

Internships are also available in the organization's state offices and on college campuses with PIRG student chapters. Other opportunities are listed on the website's Online Action Center and include contacting local representatives.

Contact Information

U.S. PIRG:
44 Winter Street, 4th Floor
Boston, MA 02108
(617) 747-4370

Federal Advocacy Office:
218 D Street SE, 1st Fl.
Washington, DC 20003-1900
(202) 546-9707
www.uspirg.org

EDUCATION

826 NATIONAL

Co-founded by writer Dave Eggers, 826 National is a nonprofit tutoring, writing, and publishing organization with locations in eight cities across the country. Its goal is to assist students ages six to eighteen with their writing skills, and to help teachers get their classes excited about writing. 826 National's work is based on the understanding that great leaps in learning can happen with one-on-one attention, and that strong writing skills are fundamental to future success.

Through volunteer support, each of the eight 826 chapters provides drop-in tutoring, class field trips, writing workshops, and in-schools programs—all free of charge. 826 chapters are especially committed to supporting teachers, publishing student work, and offering services for English language learners.

Volunteer Opportunities

826 centers use volunteers for running its field trips, helping local students learn how to write stories, and assisting student writers during one of the organization's Young Authors' Book Programs.

In addition to support with writing projects, 826 centers depend on its volunteers to help with more specialized tasks—grant writing, event coordination, outreach, website maintenance, training expertise (provided by credentialed-teacher and university-professor volunteers), computer hardware and software support, written and verbal bilingual translations, help with construction projects, book design and layout, marketing expertise, and a variety of other talent-demanding needs at different chapters.

Contact Information

826 Valencia Street
San Francisco, CA 94110
(415) 642-5905 x204

www.826national.org
information@826national.org

Name: Abigail Jacobs

Location: San Francisco, CA

Organization: 826 National (Valencia)

Can you describe what you do as a volunteer for 826 Valencia?

I am a drop-in tutor on Sundays, I teach a few different workshops throughout the year (one coming up is College Essay Writing), and I help with the development committee and in a few other ways here and there.

What inspired you to volunteer?

I was looking for a way to help out in my community. I love to read and write, and I love kids so 826 Valencia seemed like a perfect fit. More importantly is what inspired me to continue volunteering and that is the constant recognition and thanks that I get for everything I do at 826 Valencia. It's an incredible organization and they really know how to keep their volunteers engaged.

Is there a particular memorable moment you can recall as a volunteer at 826 Valencia?

One of my favorite moments was the great personal statement weekend that 826 Valencia hosted for the first time last year. This was a weekend where any high school student who wanted help with their personal statement (college essay) could come and get one-on-one assistance from a tutor. We took over two computer labs at a local high school for the event and we must have helped hundreds of students that weekend. Every one of them left with a better essay than when they walked in. It was really incredible to see the rooms full of tutors and students working in tandem all day long, and the line out the door of students patiently waiting for a tutor's help.

How has volunteering made an impact in your life?

It's had a huge impact. First, and very simply, it has connected me with my community. I've met some incredible people, from the students we work with, to their parents, to the teachers in the classroom, to all the other volunteers and employees of 826 Valencia. It has opened up my eyes to the realities of our public education system and the struggles of teachers, parents and students at underserved schools. And I've learned a lot about myself—how valuable my skills can be and what an impact an hour of my time can make in someone else's life.

What advice would you give to someone who was considering doing volunteer work in their community?

DO IT! Find an organization where your skills will be put to work and appreciated. You won't regret it.

BEHIND THE BOOK

Behind the Book's mission is to excite children and young adults about reading. Working with low-income students in New York City's K-12 public schools, *Behind the Book* brings authors and their books into individual classrooms to build literacy skills and nurture a new generation of book readers. The organization was founded in 2003 by a part-time school librarian.

Volunteer Opportunities

Each of Behind the Book's programs occurs during school hours in a small classroom setting, is taught as part of the class curriculum, incorporates multiple author visits and a writing project, and includes book donations to students and the school library. There are a number of ways you can help as a volunteer:

As a volunteer that helps with author visits in the classroom, you may assist students in crafting stories, writing essays, and/ or producing other projects; or take photographs of the classroom in action which will be posted on the Behind the Book and sponsor web sites

(Note that no previous experience working or volunteering in classrooms is necessary as Behind the Book and school staff are present in the classrooms at all times and will be there to help guide you)

As a volunteer that helps in the office, you may conduct community media outreach and public relations; or extend Behind the Book's community outreach by building classroom/community partnerships, creating relationships with local businesses, and liaising with local political leaders.

If you choose to volunteer in the classroom, please note that each author visit lasts from one-and-a-half to two hours. Typically, volunteers work with the same group of students in the same classroom for three to five author visits, which will be spaced over one to three months. As a volunteer, you will not only experience, but also be integral to, the program from beginning to end.

For volunteer work outside of the classroom, Behind the Book will work with you to establish a schedule of equivalent time.

Interested individuals should contact the organization at volunteer. behindthebook@gmail.com to request a volunteer application. In the body of the email, please identify which volunteer opportunity you are most interested in (classroom or office). You and a member of the Behind the Book team will coordinate an activity that best suits your schedule and abilities.

Contact Information
145 West 96th Street, Suite 1E
New York, NY 10025

(212) 222-3627
www.behindthebook.org

EDUCATORS FOR SOCIAL RESPONSIBILITY (ESR)
The goal of ESR is to improve America's education system by working directly with educators to employ practices that create safe, caring, and equitable schools. ESR provides professional development and training, consultation, and educational resources to adults who teach young people in preschool through high school. The organization's online teacher center offers educators resources on topics ranging from security, conflict resolution, peacemaking, violence prevention, and others. Established in 1982.

EDUCATION

Volunteer Opportunities

ESR occasionally uses volunteers for administrative tasks (which is of great benefit to the small organization). Most of its non-staff positions are filled with paid work study students. ESR is located very close to several universities with schools of education which allows it to offer students an opportunity to work with the organization while in their educational program. Volunteers and work study students engage in research, provide administrative support, and carry out other duties as needed in our fundraising, publications, and professional services departments.

Training is available for all of ESR's work study participants and volunteers in the discrete tasks they're asked to do. Some tasks require a level of prior experience, for example, experience with book design software would be helpful with assisting the organization with a publishing project.

While there is no official time commitment, ESR asks that volunteers be prepared to remain until a discreet project is completed if possible.

Contact Information

23 Garden Street
Cambridge, MA 02138
(617) 492-1764 or (800) 370-2515

www.esrnational.org
educators@esrnational.org

FIRST BOOK

First Book provides new books to children in need addressing one of the most important factors affecting literacy—access to books.

Volunteer Opportunities

Volunteers can serve on First Book Advisory Boards. These are committees of volunteers, representing a community or campus, that come together to raise awareness and funds in order to provide new books to local literacy programs serving children from low-income families. There are more than 270 Advisory Boards nationwide. Visit the organization's website to find an Advisory Board in your community. It is also possible to start an Advisory Board if one does not already exist in your area.

Contact Information

1319 F Street, NW, Suite 1000
Washington DC 20004-1155

(202) 393- 12222
www.firstbook.org

PARENTS FOR PUBLIC SCHOOLS (PPS)

Parents for Public Schools (PPS) is a national organization of community-based chapters working with public school parents and other supporters to improve and strengthen local public schools. Established in 1991.

Volunteer Opportunities

PPS has 15 chapters across the country that work with volunteers. Also, its national office in Mississippi has a state-wide program in place for volunteers. Tasks and projects vary by chapter but may include working in outreach, mentoring programs, arts programs, and in the promotion and marketing of public schools in the community. Individuals not living near a chapter of PPS can contact the organization to learn details on forming a new chapter.

Contact Information

200 North Congress Street, Suite 500
Jackson, MS 39216
(800) 880-1222 or (601) 969-6936

www.parents4publicschools.com
ppschapter@parents4publicschools.org

---★---

PROLITERACY WORLDWIDE, INC.

ProLiteracy was born when two of the leading adult literacy organizations, Literacy Volunteers of America and Laubach Literacy International, merged in August 2002. With the help of their network of organizational and individual members, ProLiteracy is able to promote literacy in all 50 states and the District of Columbia. The organization helps strengthen the programs that are teaching adults to read, write, compute, use technology, and learn English as a new language. ProLiteracy also advocates for public policies and legislation that benefit adult learners and the people and programs that serve them.

Volunteer Opportunities

Most of ProLiteracy's estimated 1,000 local member organizations are heavily dependent on their volunteers. They recruit volunteers to tutor adults, help organize and staff fundraisers, become board members, and assist with administrative tasks. Other opportunities are possible and vary by each individual organization's needs. Volunteers who are interested in becoming adult literacy tutors must complete eighteen hours of training and make a commitment to meet with their student for two hours a week for at least one year. ProLiteracy has a search function on its website to help potential volunteers (and students) find a program in their area.

Contact Information
Headquarters: 1320 Jamesville Ave.
Syracuse, NY 13210
(315) 422-9121 or (888) 528-2224

www.proliteracy.org
info@proliteracy.org

---★---

PUBLICOLOR

Publicolor is a New York City-based not-for-profit that engages at-risk students in their education and empowers them to plan and prepare for college and career. Through its gateway program, Paint Club, Publicolor teaches students the skill of commercial painting, with the belief that transforming environments—such as public schools and community centers—with vibrant colors transforms attitudes and behaviors of the people who use these spaces. In addition, Publicolor provides youth development programs, including weekly career exposure and life skills workshops for middle and high school students, and one-on-one tutoring and mentoring sessions for college students. College scholarships are also offered through the organization. Officially incorporated in 1996.

Volunteer Opportunities

Publicolor does not take on individual volunteers, but it welcomes volunteers (age 13 and up) from corporations, colleges, churches, and established volunteer organizations. Volunteers serve as mentors for students during painting projects and work every Saturday during the academic school year, and Tuesdays through Thursdays during July and August.

Contact Information
149 Madison Ave, Suite 1201
New York, NY 10016
(212) 213-6121

www.publicolor.org
volunteers@publicolor.org

---★---

ROCK 'N' ROLL CAMP FOR GIRLS

The Rock 'n' Roll Camp for Girls builds girls self-esteem through music creation and performance. Providing workshops and technical training, it creates leadership opportunities, cultivates a supportive community of peers and mentors, and encourages social change and the development of life skills. The organization serves girls ages 8-17.

Volunteer Opportunities

Rock 'n' Roll Camp for Girls is almost entirely volunteer-run with summer and year-round camp opportunities available. Positions include helping with Girls Rock Institute, Summer Camp, and Ladies Rock Camp programs; grant writing/research; supporting shifts with the front desk; administrative assistance; procuring a variety of donations; outreach; data entry; gear and music librarian; and store/record label merchandise manager. The Summer Camp program has full and part time positions for female mentor volunteers as college-level intern program coordinators, band coaches, band managers, workshop leaders, and instrument instructors. Male and female volunteer positions are available for roadies/gear management, crafty/food service, maintenance/janitor, publicity/outreach, receptionists and administrative support.

The organization has affiliates in many cities in the U.S.. Visit the Girls Rock Camp Alliance web page (www.girlsrockcampalliance.org) for contact information. Volunteer opportunities vary by location.

Contact Information

P.O. Box 11324
(503) 445-4991

www.girlsrockcamp.org
Get_involved@girlsrockcamp.org

TEACH FOR AMERICA

Teach for America aims to eliminate educational inequity by enlisting recent college graduates to teach in low-income public schools through the country in both rural and urban environments. The organization provides training and support to college graduates to help them become leaders in an effort to expand educational opportunity. Established in 1989.

Volunteer Opportunities

Prospective participants must submit an online application (available at www.teachforamerica.org), and if chosen for the program, attend a rigorous five-week summer training session in one of eight locations (New York, Los Angeles, Philadelphia, Chicago, Atlanta, Houston, Phoenix, and Mississippi Delta) before beginning to teach.

Contact Information
National office:
315 West 36th Street, 7th Floor
New York, NY 10018

(212) 279-2080 or (800) 832-1230
www.teachforamerica.org

EDUCATION

ENVIRONMENT AND SUSTAINABLE COMMUNITIES

AMERICAN RIVERS

American Rivers is a conservation organization that protects and restores America's rivers for the benefit of people, wildlife, and nature. Founded in 1973, American Rivers has more than 65,000 members and supporters, with offices in Washington, DC and nationwide.

Volunteer Opportunities

American Rivers is always looking for volunteer help, which can take many forms. Individuals interesting in helping their community can work with American Rivers to clean-up a local river. American Rivers will provide trash bags, guidance on creating the event, and help promote the event. This can be done whether the person lives near an AR office or not. People can also volunteer to participate in an already established event by visiting the organization's website.

Individuals with less time can volunteer to become an e-activist. These are people who receive action alerts via e-mail when a particular piece of legislation is being introduced. AR needs them to write their congressperson or senator in support of the bill.

In the spring, summer and fall, American Rivers brings on several unpaid interns to learn about the inner workings of an environmental non-profit, including lobbying, communications and conservation work. Housing is not provided.

AR welcomes any interested participants to contact the organization to see if their schedule and skills are a good fit for AR's current needs. Potential volunteers are also encouraged to visit AR's website, friend the organization on Facebook and/or follow it on Twitter. Contact a local office directly for its opportunities.

Contact Information

Headquarters: 1101 14th Street NW
Suite 1400
Washington, DC 20005

(202) 347-7550
www.americanrivers.org
outreach@americanrivers.org

CENTER FOR HEALTH, ENVIRONMENT AND JUSTICE (CHEJ)

The Center for Health, Environment and Justice (CHEJ) is a national environmental organization founded and led by Lois Gibbs, the woman responsible for the relocation of 900 families due to a leaking toxic waste dump in Love Canal, New York. CHEJ is committed to helping communities protect themselves from exposures to dangerous environmental chemicals in the air, water and soil. Since it was founded about 30 years ago, CHEJ has worked with thousands of organizations and groups, providing the research, advice and leadership skills necessary to keep communities and families safe. The organization also builds nationwide collaborative initiatives and advocates for responsible corporate behavior. It has been instrumental in both McDonalds' move from using Styrofoam and Microsoft's move from utilizing PVC plastic in products.

Volunteer Opportunities

Though CHEJ does not have a formal volunteer program in place, it does welcome individuals who wish to support the organization's mission. Volunteers can work in the national office, in CHEJ's regional offices in Albany, NY and Columbus, OH, or remotely in certain cases. Volunteers typically assist with office work and mailings, but web developer help is also needed. Project-based work utilizing the volunteer's specific skills is also a possibility.

Contact Information

P.O. Box 6806
Falls Church, VA 22040-6806
(703) 237-2249

www.chej.org
chej@chej.org

★

COUNCIL FOR RESPONSIBLE GENETICS (CRG)

CRG is a non-profit, non-governmental organization that works through the media and concerned citizens to distribute information and represent the public interest on emerging issues in biotechnology. The organization fosters public debate about the social, ethical and environmental implications of genetic technologies and publishes a bimonthly magazine, *GeneWatch*, on such issues. The publication has covered a broad spectrum of topics, from genetically engineered foods to biological weapons, genetic privacy and discrimination, reproductive technologies, and human cloning. Established in 1983.

Volunteer Opportunities

CRG offers unpaid internship opportunities to qualified undergraduate and graduate students during the summer and the academic year. Interns work with senior staff and board members on individual research, writing or outreach projects in specific program areas.

Internships are available part-time during the school year (September-December, January intersession, and February-May), and part-time or full-time during the summer (June-August). Because the position is unpaid, intern's schedules are flexible. Interns are required to meet with their supervisor on a regular basis during the internship period. Interviews are scheduled by phone or in person at the CRG office in Cambridge, Massachusetts.

Requirements include computer literacy (Mac OS, Microsoft Office), organizational skills, familiarity with internet research, and good academic standing. Interns should be able to work five hours a week at the CRG office in Cambridge, Massachusetts or New York City.

Contact Information

Massachusetts Office:
5 Upland Road, Suite 3
Cambridge MA 02140
(617) 868-0870
crg@gene-watch.org

New York Office:
30 Broad Street, 30th Fl.
New York, NY 10004
(212) 361-6360
www.councilforresponsiblegenetics.
  org

★

EARTH ISLAND INSTITUTE (EII)

EII acts as an umbrella organization, providing support to individual environmental projects by offering a wide range of professional services, from fiscal administration and program management to office space and equipment. EII also publishes a quarterly magazine, Earth Island Journal that offers how-to on environmental activism, hosts an annual awards ceremony through their New Leaders Initiative that highlights the accomplishments of youth working for sustainability, and funds community-based coastal protection and wetland restoration efforts in Southern California. Established in 1982.

Volunteer Opportunities

Opportunities in the Berkeley office range from event assistance to office assistance. Volunteers working on events perform tasks such as greeting guests, sign in, set up, break down, registration, and ushering. For office assistance, volunteers typically proof read, assist with filing, reception, mailings and pre-event coordination.

Earth Island is also a fiscal sponsor for many projects worldwide. Each project has its own volunteers who perform numerous tasks. Some of the many current projects under Earth Island sponsorship include the Global Service Corps, which provides service learning opportunities for adult volunteer participants to live and work on environmental, health and social just projects in developing countries, and Green Café Network, which is dedicated to addressing America's over-consumption by "greening" the coffeehouse industry at the grassroots level.

For more information, contact Claudia West, the Volunteer Manager, at volunteer@earthisland.org.

Contact Information

2150 Allston Way, Suite 460   (510) 859-9100
Berkeley, California 94704-1375   www.earthisland.org

----------------------------★----------------------------

ENVIRONMENT AMERICA

Environment America is a federation of state-based, citizen-funded environmental advocacy organizations. Its professional staff in 29 states and Washington, D.C., combines independent research, practical ideas and tough-minded advocacy to overcome the opposition of powerful special interests and win real results for the environment. Environment America draws on 30 years of success in tackling environmental problems.

Volunteer Opportunities

Contact the organization for details.

Contact Information   **Federal Advocacy Office:**
44 Winter Street, 4th Floor   218 D Street S.E.,
Boston, MA 02108   Washington, DC 20003
(617) 747-4449   (202) 683-1250
                                    www.environmentamerica.org
                                    info@EnvironmentAmerica.org

----------------------------★----------------------------

FRIENDS OF THE EARTH (FOE)

With a network of grassroots groups in 77 countries, FOE supports individuals and organizations who are working to ensure a healthy environment in their communities. Its current campaigns focus on clean energy and solutions to global warming, protecting people from toxic and new, potentially harmful

ENVIRONMENT AND SUSTAINABLE COMMUNITIES

technologies, and promoting low-pollution transportation alternatives. FOE's accomplishments through the years include reforming the World Bank to address environmental and human rights concerns, fostering a debate on global warming, stopping more than 150 destructive damns and water projects worldwide, banning international whaling and winning landmark regulations of strip mines and oil tankers. Established in 1969.

Volunteer Opportunities

Most opportunities for volunteers are not based in an FOE office, but revolve around advocating for environmental causes, sometimes in the comfort of one's home. FOE provides individuals the tools to play an active role in shaping public policies that affect the environment. FOEs website offers instruction on how to support national campaigns, such as The Clean Air Act, by organizing letter-writing campaigns, scheduling meeting with members of congress, and contacting local newspaper editors.

Contact Information

1100 15th Street NW
11th Floor
Washington, DC 20005
(202) 783-7400

311 California Street
Suite 510
San Francisco, CA 94104
(415) 544-0790
Toll Free: (877) 843-8687

GREENPEACE

Greenpeace is an independent campaigning organization that uses peaceful direct action and creative communication to expose global environmental problems and to promote solutions that are essential to a green and peaceful future. Topics of interest include sustainable agriculture, nuclear energy, and global warming. Established in 1971.

Volunteer Opportunities

The organization is looking for people to join its National Activist Network. The Network is an alliance of volunteer leaders who take bold action to protect the planet in coordination with Greenpeace's highest priority campaigns. The Network is made up of Lead Activists who build grassroots power on hundreds of campuses and in thousands of communities nationwide to help Greenpeace save the climate, stop deforestation, fight for the whales... and more.. As part of the Network, you can connect with your own team of grassroots organizers so that you can make a difference in your community. Opportunities are available for people ages 14 on up. Greenpeace asks that interested individuals complete an online contact form.

Internships are also available every spring, summer and fall in a number of cities and in all parts of the Greenpeace organization. Positions range from organization to photography to administration and everything in between. As a Greenpeace intern, you will help promote solutions to the global warming crisis, stop the destruction of the world's last ancient forests, empower consumers and shareholders to hold corporate polluters accountable, and save the whales and other endangered species. Interns participate in trainings such as corporate campaigning, non-violent direct action, media relations, materials production and grassroots outreach. All internships are unpaid, and interns are responsible for covering their own travel and housing. The organization strongly encourages applications from women, people of color, and other under-represented communities.

Contact Information

702 H Street, NW, Suite 300
Washington, D.C. 20001
(202) 462-1177

www.greenpeace.org
info@wdc.greenpeace.org

THE NATURE CONSERVANCY

The Nature Conservancy is an organization that strives to protect ecologically important lands and waters around the world. By partnering with groups such as indigenous communities, businesses, governments and other non-profits, The Nature Conservancy operates more than 100 marine conservation projects globally and addresses threats to preservation that include climate change, fire, and marine ecosystems. Established in 1951.

Volunteer Opportunities

Indoor opportunities are available on weekdays and consist of administrative assistance in one of The Nature Conservancy's offices. Outdoor projects are scheduled on both weekdays and weekends and call on volunteers to perform a range of tasks including trail development and monitoring visitor facilities in preserves. Visit www.nature.org to find opportunities in your area.

Contact Information

Headquarters: 4245 North Fairfax
Drive, Suite 100

Arlington, VA 22203-1606
(703) 841-5300 or (800) 628-6860

PESTICIDE ACTION NETWORK NORTH AMERICA (PANNA)

PANNA links local and international consumer, labor, health, environment and agriculture groups in a global network to fight the proliferation of pesticides. It promotes ecologically sound and socially responsible alternatives to hazardous pesticides and works to ensure that people—as well as the soil, water, and air—are free from pesticides, and that information and resources regarding the issue is available worldwide. Established in 1982.

Volunteer Opportunities

PANNA is looking for volunteers and interns who share a commitment to environmental and social justice issues and a special interest in pesticide reform. Volunteer opportunities depend entirely on the needs of the organization at any given time, whereas interns typically perform tasks such as research, writing, editing and updating webpages, participating in team meetings and programming, data entry and event planning.

Contact Information

49 Powell St., Suite 500
San Francisco, CA 94102

(415) 981-1771
www.panna.org

RAINFOREST ACTION NETWORK (RAN)

RAN seeks to protect rainforests through grassroots organizing, public education, and non-violent action campaigns. It works with environmental and human rights groups in 60 countries to coordinate the role of the U.S. in the security of rainforests and their inhabitants. RAN supports the efforts of activists in rainforest countries, seeks to transform government and corporate policies, and places public pressure on American organizations that refuse to adopt responsible environmental policies. Established in 1985.

Volunteer Opportunities

Contact the organization for details.

Contact Information

Headquarters: 221 Pine Street, 5th
Floor
San Francisco, CA 94104

(415) 398-4404
www.ran.org
rainforest@ran.org

SIERRA CLUB

As one of the oldest and largest grassroots environmental organizations in the U.S., the Sierra Club aims to protect communities, wild places, and the earth. Its current initiatives include increasing sustainable transportation options, limiting greenhouse emissions, decreasing the reliance on coal, strengthening wetlands, forests and barrier islands, and protecting wildlife habitats from climate change. In addition, Sierra Club's mission includes the educating and enlisting of humanity to protect and restore the quality of the natural and human environment. Established in1892.

Volunteer Opportunities

Sierra Club is a volunteer-based organization. Every state, and Puerto Rico, has a Sierra Club chapter which is compromised of local groups. Most major cities have a group, so groups are often the best first interface for potential volunteer.

Sierra Club engages in policy, lobbying and activism, outdoor activities and community service projects. All these areas provide opportunities for volunteers. While there are more volunteer "leadership" opportunities for members, you do not have to be a member to volunteer.

On the local level, there are varying types of opportunities. Most local groups participate in "service outings" which are a combination of an outdoor activity (such as hiking) with a community service (like park maintenance). Sierra Club also has programs to give inner-city youth outdoor experiences and is always looking for volunteers to help. There are even "volunteer vacations" that allow volunteers to travel around the country or around the world and provide service while on the trip.

A particular local policy campaign could be anything from a fight to protect a local wetland from development, lobbying for a new public transit system, clean air laws, or taking on an outdated coal power plant. These kinds of activities need volunteers at all levels, from walking door to door, to creating materials, to showing up at public hearings and voicing your opinion. These campaigns can last as long as a few weeks or years and can vastly vary in scale. Large campaigns will have multiple levels of volunteer involvement and will include trainings for everything from technical environmental policy to organizing tactics and media skills. Sierra Club also participates in local, state and federal elections and looks for volunteers to assist with public education and get-out-the-vote efforts.

In addition, there is an array of online volunteer opportunities which can include sending e-mails to Members of Congress, participating in a phone bank operation from your own home, to writing letters to the editor, and much

ENVIRONMENT AND SUSTAINABLE COMMUNITIES

more. Visit the organization's website for more information on their numerous opportunities.

Contact Information

Headquarters: 85 Second Street, 2nd
    Floor
San Francisco, CA 94105

(415) 977-5500
www.sieraclub.org
information@sierraclub.org

------------------------------★------------------------------

TRUST FOR PUBLIC LAND (TPL)

TPL is a national land conservation organization that preserves natural and historic spaces—such as parks, community gardens, and rural lands—for human enjoyment. TPL's Federal Affairs team works with government and other conservation groups by providing information and guidance about federal policy and funding resources. The organization also helps community groups by identifying lands to be protected, locating funding for conservation projects, offering education and negotiating land transactions. Established in 1972.

Volunteer Opportunities

TPL's regional offices occasionally have volunteer opportunities; details for specific positions are routinely listed on their website. Skills they are usually in-need of include general administration and coordination, research and report writing, marketing, and fundraising. But all interested individuals are encouraged to send a brief cover letter and resume to volunteers@tpl.org, in the hopes that a unique opportunity can be designed around an office's needs and one's skill sets.

Contact Information:

National Office:
116 New Montgomery Street, 4th
    Floor

San Francisco, CA 94105
(415) 495-4014 or (800) 714-LAND
www.tpl.org

------------------------------★------------------------------

WORLD WIDE OPPORTUNITIES ON ORGANIC FARMS (WWOOF)

Operating as an exchange, WWOOF is an international organization that connects people who wish to volunteer on organic farms with farmers looking for help. Established in 1971.

MAKE A DIFFERENCE

Volunteer Opportunities

WWOOF provides its members (membership fee is $30 per year) with listings of volunteer opportunities on farms in the U.S. and around the world that grow food without the use of synthetic or chemical amendments. Volunteers help farmers with a variety of tasks ranging from animal care to gardening for an agreed number of hours per day. Volunteers usually live as part of their host's family and are provided free food and accommodations as well as knowledge about ecological farming practices.

Contact Information

WWOOF USA:
430 Forest Avenue
Laguna Beach, CA 92651

(949) 715-9500
www.wwoofusa.org
info@wwoofusa.org

FREE SPEECH AND GOVERNMENT ACCOUNTABILITY

AMERICAN CIVIL LIBERTIES UNION

The ACLU is the nation's guardian of liberty, working daily in courts, legislatures and communities to defend and preserve the individual rights and liberties that the Constitution and laws of the United States guarantee everyone in this country. These rights include the First Amendment, equal protection under the law, due process, and privacy. The ACLU also works to extend rights to segments of the population that have traditionally been denied their rights, including people of color; women; lesbians, gay men, bisexuals and transgender people; prisoners; and people with disabilities.

Volunteer Opportunities

Interested individuals can check out the ACLU Action Center on the organization's website for downloadable material, action alerts, and for information and suggestions for activists.

Contact Information

125 Broad Street, 18th Floor
New York NY 10004

(212) 549-2500
www.aclu.org

★

COMMON CAUSE

Common Cause operates as a vehicle for citizens to make their voices heard in the political process and to hold their elected leaders accountable to the public interest. The organization remains committed to honest, open and accountable government and serves as a watchdog against corruption and abuse of power. Along with their sister organization, the Common Cause Education Fund, Common Cause employs grassroots organizing, coalition building, research, policy development, public education, lobbying and litigation to win reform at all levels of government. Established in 1970.

Volunteer Opportunities

Common Cause welcomes volunteers to join its "Washington Connection" program at the organization's national headquarters in downtown DC. Volunteers work with Common Cause activists across the country to build grassroots pressure on elected officials on critical issues. Opportunities are also available for individuals who would like to help with administrative tasks in Common Cause's human resources, accounting or membership services departments. Many volunteers work a shift between 10am-4pm on Tuesdays or Wednesdays, but Common Cause also has opportunities after 5pm at certain points during the year. Many of its state offices also welcome volunteers so interested individuals are encouraged to contact their state office directly (information is available on their website) or to contact Betty Brossy at (202) 833-1200.

Contact Information
Headquarters: 1133 19th Street NW, 9th Floor Washington, DC 20036

(202) 833-1200
www.commoncause.org

------------------------------★------------------------------

NATIONAL COALITION AGAINST CENSORSHIP (NCAC)

NCAC opposes the suppression of information and strives to facilitate the creation of a more hospitable environment for free speech and artist freedom. An alliance of 50 literary, artistic, religious, educational, professional, labor, and civil liberties groups, NCAC provides resources and advocacy support to individuals and organizations responding to censorship. Established in 1974.

Volunteer Opportunities

NCAC seeks volunteers and interns with computer skills who are interested in its mission to protect freedom of speech. Most volunteers work out of the organization's New York City office, but location, as well as tasks and time commitment, are discussed with the program's supervisor. Interested individuals are encouraged to email a cover letter and resume to ncac@ncac.org.

Contact Information
275 7th Avenue, #1504
New York, NY 10001
(212) 807 – 6222

www.ncac.org
ncac@ncac.org

------------------------------★------------------------------

PEOPLE FOR THE AMERICAN WAY (PFAW) AND PFAW FOUNDATION

People for the American Way is dedicated to preserving constitution rights, opposing bigotry, and encouraging civic and political participation. Areas of interest include defending public education, religion and reproductive freedom

FREE SPEECH AND GOVERNMENT ACCOUNTABILITY

while challenging censorship and discrimination of all kind. Established in 1980.

Volunteer Opportunities

Interested individuals can join PFAW's e-mail list through its website, to receive updates on ways to get involved.

Contact Information

2000 M Street NW, Suite 400
Washington, D.C. 20036

(202) 467-4999
www.pfaw.org

PROJECT VOTE

Project Vote is a nonpartisan organization that works to increase voting participation amongst low-income, minority, youth and other under-represented groups. Since 1982, Project Vote has helped register more than 5.6 million Americans in low-income and minority communities through programs such as Get-Out-the-Vote. The organization also applies research, legal services and advocacy to ensure that marginalized groups are not prevented from registering and voting. Established in 1982.

Volunteer Opportunities

Contact the organization for details.

Contact Information

737½ 8th St. SE,
Washington DC, 20003

(202) 546-4173 or (800) 546-8683
www.projectvote.org

PUBLIC CITIZEN

Founded by Ralph Nader, Public Citizen represents the consumer public against special interest and corporate lobbyists. Public Citizen describes itself as the "countervailing force to corporate power" and has challenged abusive practices by the pharmaceutical, nuclear and automobile industries. It currently has five policy groups in place: Congress Watch division, the Energy Program, Global Trade Watch division, the Health Research Group, and Litigation Group. Established in 1971.

Volunteer Opportunities

Public Citizen has multiple opportunities available, usually for organized events such as bank protests, or for contacting members of Congress. Interested individuals should sign up at www.citizen.org to receive news on upcoming events.

Contact Information

Main Office:
1600 20th Street, NW
Washington, D.C. 20009

(202) 588-1000
www.citizen.org

------------------------------★------------------------------

THE RUCKUS SOCIETY

The Ruckus Society provides resources to environmental, human rights, and social justice activists and organizations. Through its own training camps or via personalized sessions requested by communities, The Ruckus Society helps people learn the skills they need to practice nonviolent direct action. Material covered includes action planning, media outreach, building leadership and political analysis, and nonviolent philosophy and practice. Established in 1995.

Volunteer Opportunities

Contact the organization for details.

Contact Information

PO Box 28741
Oakland, CA 94604
(510) 931-6339

www.ruckus.org
ruckus@ruckus.org

------------------------------★------------------------------

FREE SPEECH AND GOVERNMENT ACCOUNTABILITY

GAY AND LESBIAN RIGHTS

GAY, LESBIAN AND STRAIGHT EDUCATION NETWORK (GLSEN)

GLSEN works with educators, policy makers, community leaders and students to combat homophobia in the education system. The network strives to protect students from harassment, to empower principals to make their schools safer, and to build the skills of educators to teach respect for all people. Amongst its campaigns, the organization sponsors National Day of Silence, an event that addresses anti-LGBT name-calling and bullying in schools, and the annual No Name-Calling Week which consists of educational activities that provides schools with the tools to eliminate bullying in their communities. Established in 1993.

Volunteer Opportunities

Contact the organization for details.

Contact Information

National Headquarters:
90 Broad Street, 2nd Floor
New York, NY 10004

(212) 727-0135
www.glsen.org
glsen@glsen.org

INTERNATIONAL GAY AND LESBIAN HUMAN RIGHTS COMMISSION (IGLHRC)

IGLHRC advocates for human rights on behalf of people who experience discrimination or abuse on the basis of their sexual orientation, gender identity or expression. IGLHRC works with local activists and partners by monitoring and responding to human rights violations against lesbians, gay men, bisexuals, transgender and intersex people, and others whose identities do not fit the LGBTI paradigm. The commission's goals are to advocate for the elimination of discriminatory laws and practices and to support the implementation of anti-discrimination policies. IGLHRC also strives to reduce family, community and state-sanctioned violence, and to promote economic, social and cultural rights. Established in 1991.

Volunteer Opportunities

Internships are available for undergraduate and graduate students in IGLHRC's New York office as well as in its offices in Cape Town, South Africa and Buenos Aires, Argentina. Interns in the New York office mostly perform research and writing tasks (responsibilities are commonly based on an individual's skills) and are required to commit at least two full days per week. The international offices do not have structured programs but are open to discuss possibilities with potential interns.

Contact Information
80 Maiden Lane, Suite 1505
New York, NY 10038
(212) 430.6054

www.iglhrc.org
iglhrc@iglhrc.org

----------------------------★----------------------------

NATIONAL GAY AND LESBIAN TASK FORCE (NGLTF)
NGLTF works to build the grassroots power of the lesbian, gay, bisexual and transgender (LGBT) community by providing training and support to activists and state and local organizations seeking to advance pro-LGBT politics. NGLTF's Action Fund lobbies to defeat anti-LGBT ballot initiatives and legislation and pass pro-LGBT legislation and other measures. It also analyzes and reports on the positions of candidates for public office on issues of importance to the LGBT community. Established in 1973, the Task Force is the oldest national LGBT organization.

Volunteer Opportunities
There are myriad volunteer opportunities at the Task Force and each of its six offices (D.C., NY, Cambridge, Miami, Minneapolis, and L.A.) utilizes volunteers. Its development team works with volunteers on special events, such as the Winter Party Festival, the Miami Recognition Dinner and the D.C. Recognition Dinner. The Academy for Leadership and Action collaborates with volunteers to train local grassroots activists to work on phone banks, campaigns and fundraising efforts. Volunteers help with NGLTF's public policy and government affairs team on phone banks to call legislators and voters to support efforts to attain LGBT equality. Volunteers also are an important component of the National Conference on LGBT Equality: Creating Change and NGLTF's faith work department, which has training throughout the U.S. and an annual conference of pro-LGBT people of faith. Time commitment is flexible with opportunities available business hours as well as nights and weekends. Volunteers mostly do work around the foundation but occasionally contribute to the Action Fund when it's related to policy or advocacy.

Contact Information
1325 Massachusetts Ave. NW Suite 600
Washington, DC 20005

(202) 393-2241
www.thetaskforce.org
info@thetaskforce.org

----------------------------★----------------------------

HEALTH CARE, HUNGER, AND HOMELESSNESS

BREAD FOR THE WORLD

Bread for the World strives to end hunger in the United States and abroad with its network of individual members, churches and Christian denominations. The organization mobilizes individuals to raise awareness about hunger and poverty and provides tools for advocacy, including tips on media outreach and event organizing. Members write to and meet with members of Congress in an effort to change policies and programs. Its partner organization, Bread for the World Institute, provides education and research, and publishes an annual report on hunger. Established in 1972.

Volunteer Opportunities

The organization encourages those interested in eradicating hunger to write to congress and to engage their local church about supporting Bread for the World's mission. Resources for advocacy and education are provided at www.bread.org.

Contact Information

50 F Street, NW
Suite 500
Washington, DC 20001

(202) 639-9400 or (800) 822-7323
www.bread.org
bread@bread.org

BRIGHT PINK

Bright Pink is a national non-profit organization that provides education and support to young women who are at high risk for breast and ovarian cancer. It arms young women with knowledge and options, and offers companionship and empathy during their journey.

Volunteer Opportunities

Bright Pink depends on its volunteers to help further its mission so there are many ways to get involved. Interested individuals can visit Bright Pink's website to join its network and sign up to volunteer. A Volunteer Coordinator will be in contact with details about a local active chapter or about beginning a new chapter in your area.

In Bright Pink's Chicago Headquarters office, there are monthly volunteer orientations at 6pm on the first Wednesday of each month for new volunteers. For those interested in volunteering in Chicago, attending one of these meetings is mandatory. Email emily@BeBrightPink.org for more information on upcoming orientations and to get involved in the Chicago chapter.

Contact Information

400 N. State Street, Suite 230
Chicago IL, 60654

www.bebrightpink.org
welcome@bebrightpink.org

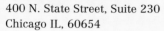

DAILY BREAD

The Daily Bread project is an entirely volunteer-run, grassroots organization in California that picks up nutritious surplus food from local restaurants, bakeries, caterers and markets and brings the food to local free-food kitchens, pantries, and shelters. Established in 1983.

Volunteer Opportunities

Daily Bread offers volunteer opportunities for people who can transport food to recipient organizations. Daytime, evening, weekday and weekend opportunities are available throughout Berkeley, Oakland, and Richmond, CA.

Contact Information

(510) 526-3123

www.facebook.com/pages/Daily-Bread-Berkeley/123947177634828

ELIZABETH GLASER PEDIATRIC AIDS FOUNDATION

In 1994 the Pediatric AIDS Foundation was renamed after Elizabeth Glaser, a pioneer in advocating for the rights of children living with HIV. With a focus on research, the foundation strives to eliminate pediatric AIDS and provides HIV prevention, care and treatment services to women, children and families in 17 countries. Established in 1988.

Volunteer Opportunities

Opportunities mostly consist of helping with events, such as university-run dance marathons.

HEALTH CARE, HUNGER, AND HOMELESSNESS

Contact Information

Washington, D.C.:
1140 Connecticut Avenue NW, Suite 200
Washington, D.C. 20036
(202) 296-9165
www.pedaids.org
info@pedaids.org

Los Angeles, CA:
11150 Santa Monica Blvd., Suite 1050
Los Angeles, CA 90025
(310) 314-1459

FEEDING AMERICA

America's Second Harvest was renamed Feeding America in September 2008. The hunger-relief charity provides food to more than 37 million low-income individuals through its nationwide network of member food banks. Established in 1979.

Volunteer Opportunities

Feeding America has a handful of opportunities at its national office but stresses that more opportunities for volunteering are available at its network of local food banks.

Contact Information

National Office:
35 East Wacker Drive, Suite 2000
Chicago, IL 60601

(800) 771-2303
www.feedingamerica.org

FOOD FIRST

Food First—also known as the Institute for Food and Development Policy— works to eliminate the injustices that cause hunger and poverty. It carries out research, analysis, training, advocacy and education for citizen engagement, believing in one's right to healthy food produced through ecologically sound and sustainable methods. The organization also collaborates with community colleagues and is known for its many publications about hunger and the global food crisis. Established in 1975.

Volunteer Opportunities

Volunteers typically assist with non-research related tasks, such as gardening and envelope stuffing. Food First also has a need for interns who can work at least 15 hours a week for a minimum of 12 weeks. Interns help with research, analysis and writing.

Contact Information

398 60th Street
Oakland, CA 94618
(510) 654-4400

www.foodfirst.org
www.foodfirst@foodfirst.org

---------------------------------★---------------------------------

HOUSING WORKS

Housing Works is the largest community-based AIDS service organization in the United States, as well as the nation's largest minority-controlled AIDS service organization. Since its founding in 1990, it has provided lifesaving services, such as housing, medical and mental health care, meals, job training, drug treatment, HIV prevention education, and social support to more than 20,000 homeless and low-income New Yorkers living with HIV and AIDS. Housing Works operates more than 50 facilities in the five boroughs of New York City, at the state capitol in Albany, NY and in the nation's capitol, Washington, DC.

Housing Works also runs social enterprise businesses that raise millions of dollars every year to help pay for the services that it provides, spread awareness of its mission, and provides jobs to graduates of its Job Training Program. The organization's best-known businesses are Housing Works Thrift Shops, a chain of upscale thrift shops located throughout New York City, and the Housing Works Bookstore Café, a used bookstore, literary hub and concert venue located in downtown Manhattan.

Volunteer Opportunities

The organization considers volunteers to be its backbone. They run the bookstore café and thrift shops, help with annual events, tutor Housing Works' clients, work in outreach and art therapy programs, provide administrative support, and much more.

Contact Information

Headquarters: 57 Willoughby St.,
　2nd Floor
Brooklyn, NY 11201
(347) 473-7400 or TTY: (212) 925-
　9560

www.housingworks.org
volunteer@housingworks.org

---------------------------------★---------------------------------

Name: Catherine Sullivan
Location: New York City
Organization: Housing Works

Can you describe what you do as a volunteer at Housing Works Bookstore Cafe?

I take responsibility for the children's book section of the store. I sort donated books, stock shelves, and assist customers. I train other volunteers to work in the section and do whatever special tasks I'm given by the manager.

What inspired you to volunteer?

Housing Works' mission was very important to me. I lost several friends to AIDS and wanted to do something more than donate money to help deal with the crisis. Providing housing and services for homeless people with AIDS and raising the money to do that by operating thrift stores and a bookstore seemed like a brilliant concept. I have some expertise in children's books, and I thought I would make a useful contribution by volunteering at the bookstore.

Why do you feel it is important to volunteer?

I think there is a tension between individual and community and, in recent times, an unwillingness to acknowledge how interdependent we have become. I think volunteering in some enterprise that strengthens the community is something every citizen should do.

I believe the organization makes a real difference in people's lives—this includes everybody working at Housing Works, from Charles King (President and CEO of Housing Works) to the custodian who cleans the bathrooms. It is a diverse group of people with very different talents working hard, cooperating and supporting each other's efforts to achieve a common objective. I feel proud to be a part of it.

MEN'S HEALTH NETWORK (MHN)

Men's Health Network (MHN) is a national non-profit organization whose mission is to reach men and their families where they live, work, play, and pray with health prevention messages and tools, screening programs, educational materials, advocacy opportunities, and patient navigation.

MHN was founded in 1992 by a group of health professionals and others interested in improving the health and well-being of men, boys and families. Today, MHN has a Board of Advisors totaling over 800 physicians and key thought leaders.

Volunteer Opportunities

Volunteers can participate in local health fairs and screening events, serve on MHN's Speaker's bureau, help with administrative duties in the organization's home office, or serve as advocates for men's health at a local, state and national level.

MHN hosts many community outreach programs throughout the year and volunteers help by registering people for health screenings, passing out health education materials, and—for those volunteers with certain health training—speaking with individuals about their health. The organization also does several mailers every year that volunteers assist with.

Internships include working in legislative advocacy, health outreach, and research. Applications are available for download or to complete online at www.menshealthnetwork.org.

Contact Information

P.O. Box 75972
Washington, D.C. 20013
(202) 543-MHN-1 (6461)

www.menshealthnetwork.org
info@menshealthnetwork.org

★

MENTAL HEALTH AMERICA (MHA)

Formerly known as the National Mental Health Association, MHA is an advocacy organization addressing mental and substance use conditions and their effects nationwide. The nonprofit works to inform, advocate and enable access to quality behavioral health services for all Americans. With over 300 affiliates across the country, MHA practices national and grassroots actions that promote their mission, with an emphasis on recovery from mental and substance use conditions. Established in 1909.

HEALTH CARE, HUNGER, AND HOMELESSNESS

Volunteer Opportunities

The organization's national office is comprised of five basic departments: Affiliate and Consumer Services, Public Policy, Development, Public Education, and Administration. Through these departments, the organization develops and provides support to its 300 plus affiliates and chapters. Mental Health America's affiliates typically use volunteers to a great extent in multiple areas of service and outreach. Tasks include event planning, serving on agency programming committees, providing office staff support on either a special task or on a regular basis.

Mental Health America has internships for one or two semesters for undergrad or graduate students with one of the organization's primary departments at its national office. It also has occasional volunteer support for a specific event or temporary replacement for a staff member.

Volunteer time commitments can run from one hour per month up to 20 hours per week, depending on circumstances.

Contact Information

Headquarters: 2000 N. Beauregard Street, 6th Floor Alexandria, Virginia 22311

(703) 684-7722 *or* (800) 969-6642
www.mentalhealthamerica.net
infoctr@mentalhealthamerica.net

NATIONAL COALITION FOR THE HOMELESS (NCH)

NCH is a national network for advocates, community-based and faith-based service providers, people who have personal experience with homelessness, and others committed to ending homelessness. NCH engages in public education, policy advocacy, and grassroots organizing to carry out its mission. Examples of the coalitions sponsored projects include the "You Don't Need A Home To Vote" voting rights campaign, and The Homeless Challenge Project, an event that asks economically-privileged individuals to spend time on the streets as homeless people for up to 48 hours. Established in 1984.

Volunteer Opportunities

NCH encourages interested people to seek volunteer opportunities at shelters and direct service agencies in their own communities. A partial listing of service providers can be found on the NCH website of local homeless service organizations. The website also provides suggestions for volunteer activities, such as providing professional skills (e.g. catering, plumbing, legal, writing) to a direct service provider, planning a game night, or serving food at a shelter.

Contact Information

2201 P St NW
Washington, DC 20037
(202) 462-4822

www.nationalhomeless.org
info@nationalhomeless.org

-- ★ --

OPERATION ACCESS

Operation Access was founded by two surgeons and a former hospital executive with the goal of providing healthcare to the uninsured. The OA network includes community clinics, medical professionals and medical centers throughout the California Bay Area. OA also supports other communities interested in utilizing its program model or integrating medical volunteerism to improve access to healthcare in the U.S. Established in 1993.

Volunteer Opportunities

Operation Access is a volunteer-driven organization that offers many opportunities. Always in need are surgeons and specialists who can donate their time and expertise. Other medical departments that rely on volunteers include anesthesia, gastroenterology, operating room and sterile processing. Positions are also available for anesthesia providers, nurses, technicians, translators (present desired languages are Spanish, Portuguese, Mandarin, and Cantonese), photographers, and people interested in working on administrative tasks such as fundraising, event planning, communications, and improving the website.

Contact Information

115 Sansome St. Ste. 1205
San Francisco, 94104

(415) 733-0052
www.operationaccess.org

-- ★ --

PLANNED PARENTHOOD FEDERATION OF AMERICA, INC. (PPFA)

Planned Parenthood delivers reproductive health care, sex education, and information to millions of people worldwide. Planned Parenthood also advocates for policies that promote women's health and allow individuals to prevent unintended pregnancies through access to affordable contraception. The organization's 88 locally governed affiliates nationwide operate more than 840 health centers, which reflect the diverse needs of their communities. Established in 1916.

Volunteer Opportunities

Volunteer opportunities and internships vary by location but can include positions in health center patient services, advocacy and public policy, community outreach and education, administrative projects and support, fund raising, social networking, and health center administrative office support. Visit www.plannedparenthood.org to utilize the organization's search engine of opportunities.

Contact Information

New York:
434 West 33rd Street
New York, NY 10001
(212) 541-7800

Washington, D.C.:
1110 Vermont Ave. NW, Suite 300
Washington, D.C. 20005
(202) 973-4800
www.plannedparenthood.org

SHARE OUR STRENGTH (SOS)

Share Our Strength brings together community groups, activists and food programs to combat childhood hunger in America. Through its No Kid Hungry campaign—a national effort to end childhood hunger in America by 2015—Share Our Strength ensures children have access to federal nutrition programs, invests in community organizations fighting hunger, teaches families how to cook healthy meals on a budget, and develops public-private partnerships to end hunger. Established in 1985.

Volunteer Opportunities

Volunteers are needed to assist SOS staff for specific events. Visit its website for current opportunities. SOS also features resources on its website for individuals interested in hosting fundraising bake sales.

Contact Information

1730 M Street NW
Suite 700
Washington, DC 20036

(202) 393-2925 or (800) 969-4767
www.strength.org
info@strength.org

WORLD HUNGER YEAR (WHY)

Founded in 1975 by radio talk show host Bill Ayres and the late singer-song-writer Harry Chapin, WHY is a leader in the fight against hunger and poverty in the United States and around the world. WHY is convinced that solutions to hunger and poverty can be found at the grassroots level. It advances long-term solutions to hunger and poverty by supporting community-based organizations that empower individuals and build self-reliance, i.e., offering job training, education and after school programs; increasing access to housing and healthcare; providing microcredit and entrepreneurial opportunities; teaching people to grow their own food; and assisting small farmers. WHY connects these organizations to funders, media and legislators.

Volunteer Opportunities

WHY often needs people to perform various tasks at its events and in its New York City-based offices. Visit www.whyhunger.org to complete a volunteer form.

Contact Information
505 Eighth Avenue, Suite 2100
New York, NY 10018

(800)-5-HUNGRY
www.whyhunger.org

★

HUMAN RIGHTS

BRENNAN CENTER FOR JUSTICE

The Brennan Center for Justice at New York University School of Law is a nonpartisan public policy and law institute that focuses on the fundamental issues of democracy and justice. Its work ranges from voting rights to campaign finance reform, from racial justice in criminal law to presidential power in the fight against terrorism. A singular institution – part think tank, part public interest law firm, part advocacy group – the Brennan Center combines scholarship, legislative and legal advocacy, and communications to win meaningful, measurable change in the public sector.

Volunteer Opportunities

The Brennan Center offers many opportunities for volunteer lawyers to work with its staff on litigation, policy research, and public advocacy efforts. Although the Center is based in New York, it performs work across the country and is often looking for local counsel in other states and localities.

Inquiries from law students, attorneys, and other persons who would like to participate in the work of the Brennan Center are welcome. The organization encourages individuals to learn from its web site about the activities of its Democracy and Justice programs, and to approach the Center with ideas for becoming involved. Potential participants can submit a resume and cover letter to brennancenterjobs@nyu.edu.

The Center also offers semester-term and summer-term internships and externships for undergraduate, graduate and law students, as well as particular opportunities for NYU School of Law students.

Contact Information

New York:
161 Sixth Avenue, 12th floor
New York NY 10013
(646) 292-8310

Washington, D.C.,
1730 M Street, NW, suite 413
Washington, D.C., 20036
(202) 785-4747
www.brennancenter.org
brennancenter@nyu.edu

CENTER FOR VICTIMS OF TORTURE (CVT)

CVT's mission is to heal the wounds of torture on individuals, their families and their communities and to stop torture worldwide. The organization fulfills its mission by providing services directly to torture survivors, training and providing capacity-building support to professionals and organizations who work with torture survivors and refugees, conducting research on the effects of torture and on effective treatment methods, and by advocating for public policy initiatives worldwide that put an end to the practice of torture. Established in 1985.

Volunteer Opportunities

Examples of opportunities include serving as an English language tutor, providing donation and moving assistance, driving clients to appointments, working as a bus guide, offering graphic and web design support, educating the public, and gardening for CVT's Garden of Healing.

Medical and mental health professionals can volunteer for the Minnesota Asylum Network, a joint project of Advocates for Human Rights, CVT, and Physicians for Human Rights. Volunteers provide expert assessments and testimony in support of asylum seekers. Training is provided for volunteers by The Advocates for Human Rights.

Contact Information

717 E. River Parkway
Minneapolis, MN 55455
(612) 436-4800

www.cvt.org
cvt@cvt.org

------------------------------------ ★ ------------------------------------

GLOBAL EXCHANGE

Global Exchange protects international human rights and works to advance social, environmental and economic justice. Acting in alliance with partner organizations, Global Exchange works on a variety of issues. Current campaigns focus on promoting fair trade, opposing sweatshops and labor exploitation, helping stop oil wars and curbing global warming. Global Exchange also offers a Reality Tour program, an intensive travel seminar that links travelers with activists and organizations from around the world who are working toward positive change. Established in 1988.

Volunteer Opportunities

Volunteers work in the San Francisco office in a variety of capacities. Programs/departments that utilize volunteers include media, IT, fundraising and development/membership, administration, reality tours, on line fair trade store, and the Cuba campaign. Global Exchange posts specialized opportunities on its website. Time commitments are flexible.

Contact Information

2017 Mission Street, 2nd Floor
San Francisco, CA 94110
(415) 255-7296

www.globalexchange.org
volunteers@globalexchange.org

------------------------------------★------------------------------------

HUMAN RIGHTS WATCH (HRW)

HRW exposes human rights violations and holds offenders accountable for their actions. In its mission to prevent discrimination and uphold political freedom, HRW offers objective investigations and advocacy, and puts international pressure on abusive governments and others who hold power to end abusive practices. Established in 1978.

Volunteer Opportunities

HRW offers academic internships at both the undergraduate and graduate level in its regional and thematic divisions, as well as its organizational support departments.

Undergraduate internships are primarily administrative and clerical in nature, but other projects can be assigned as they arise and match the student's interests and abilities, including research, drafting documents, translating, and helping researchers prepare for missions.

Graduate-level interns monitor human rights developments in various countries, draft reports on human rights conditions, and engage in advocacy efforts aimed at curtailing human rights violations. Internships are unpaid, except for certain funded graduate internships which are associated with specific universities.

While internships are generally unpaid, work-study funds are often available depending on the location of placement. Students are often able to arrange academic credit, as HRW internships frequently offer direct exposure to the workings of an international human rights organization, close supervision by the HRW staff, interaction with other U.S. and international organizations and foreign and domestic government officials, and opportunities to attend lectures, trainings, and special events relating to human rights. Students should check with their individual academic institutions for requirements.

Applicants should be well-organized, self-motivated and reliable, with a strong interest in international human rights. Relevant coursework is highly desirable, and knowledge of foreign languages is a plus. Computer skills (i.e., Microsoft Office, Internet applications) are required.

Internships are posted on the organization's website. Individuals can apply immediately by sending a letter of interest, resume, names or letters of reference, and a brief, unedited writing sample to the advertised email address included in the listing, with the name of the desired internship in the subject line. Only complete applications will be reviewed.

Contact Information
Headquarters: 350 Fifth Avenue, 34th Floor
New York, NY 10118-3299

(212) 290-4700
www.hrw.org

SOUTHERN CENTER FOR HUMAN RIGHTS (SCHR)

SCHR advocates for individuals affected by the criminal justice system in the South. The Center provides legal representation to prisoners facing the death penalty, works to end the use of the death penalty, challenges human rights violations in prisons and jails, seeks to improve legal representation for poor people accused of crimes, and fights for criminal justice system reforms. SCHR also publishes reports on such issues including developing more humane solutions to crime. Established in 1976.

Volunteer Opportunities

SCHR asks volunteers to commit to at least two hours of service a week for eight weeks. Positions are available in the following areas: impact (civil) litigation, capital litigation, fundraising, and administrative support. Activities range from assisting attorneys with the assembly of case notebooks to updating resource lists to data entry. To learn more, potential volunteers are asked to contact Renée Myers at rmyers@schr.org. Interested law students can apply to SCHR's internship program.

Contact Information
83 Poplar St. NW
Atlanta, GA 30303
(404) 688-1202

www.schr.org
info@schr.org

PEOPLE WITH DISABILITIES

THE ARC OF THE UNITED STATES

The Arc is an advocacy organization that protects and fights for the human rights of people with intellectual and developmental disabilities. Established in 1950.

Volunteer Opportunities

Contact the organization for details.

Contact Information

Main Office:
1660 L Street, NW, Suite 301
Washington, DC 20036

(202) 534-3700 or (800) 433-5255
www.thearc.org
info@thearc.org

BEST BUDDIES

Best Buddies is a volunteer-run international organization that provides one-on-one friendships, integrated employment and leadership development for people with intellectual and developmental disabilities (IDD). Established in 1989.

Volunteer Opportunities

Volunteers offer the gift of friendship to youth and adults with intellectual and developmental disabilities (IDD). The "Best Buddies" commit to seeing each other twice a month, for one year. Best Buddies asks individuals to contact a BB office located in their state for information on the volunteer opportunities offered in that area. To find the office near you, visit www.bestbuddies.org or email info@bestbuddies.org.

Contact Information:

Global Headquarters:
100 Southeast Second Street
Suite 2200
Miami, FL 33131

(305) 374-2233 or (800) 89 BUDDY
(28339)
www.bestbuddies.org

BREAD & ROSES

In an effort to boost spirits and support healing, Bread & Roses offers live music performances to isolated individuals, such as children undergoing chemotherapy and families in homeless shelters, in the San Francisco Bay Area. Established in 1974.

Volunteer Opportunities

Volunteers are needed throughout the year for daily shows, public benefit events, and to support Bread & Roses staff. Event volunteers assist with catering, photography, and a variety of other duties. Hosts emcee shows while musicians perform 45-minute sets of upbeat music. Office volunteers help Bread & Roses staff with archiving, data entry, research, and in other capacities in the organization's Corte Madera office. Applications and requirement details for each position are available on the website for Bread & Roses. All questions should be directed to Lisa Starbird at (415) 945-7120.

Contact Information

233 Tamalpais Drive
Suite 100
Corte Madera, CA 94925-1415

(415) 945-7120
www.breadandroses.org
info@breadandroses.org

NATIONAL ALLIANCE ON MENTAL ILLNESS (NAMI)

NAMI has a national organization as well as state organizations and local affiliates that work to improve the lives of individuals and families affected by mental illness. NAMI offers resources and information about mental disorders through its National Information HelpLine, NAMI Connection (a free recovery support program for adults living with mental illness), and its website. The alliance also advocates for treatment and research as well as state and federal policies that ensure an end to discrimination and the promotion of effective mental health services. Established in 1979.

Volunteer Opportunities

NAMI is mainly a volunteer organization so opportunities are plentiful at the national and local levels. The primary volunteer opportunity in NAMI's national headquarters office in Arlington, Virginia is serving as an information specialist for its National Information HelpLine. Volunteers answer calls, take down voice mail messages, return calls, respond to letters and emails, and perform some data entry. Law students or attorneys can volunteer their time by offering callers general legal information and providing referrals to local attorneys. Volunteers are asked to work at least one four-hour shift a week during HelpLine hours (weekdays 10 am-6 pm) for at least six months, but college student interns often work more shifts per week for a shorter time period of time, such as a semester. NAMI seeks applicants who have a good working knowledge of mental illness and recovery and solid oral and written communication skills. Training is provided.

Local and state volunteer opportunities are available with NAMI affiliates. Options vary according to an affiliate's size, activity level, staffing, support and education programs, and whether there's a designated volunteer coordinator. Tasks may range from stuffing envelopes or answering phones to writing for the newsletter, helping promote events or organizing an education meeting, to leading support groups or serving on the affiliate's board of directors.

Contact Information

Headquarters: 3803 N. Fairfax Dr.,
Ste. 100
Arlington, VA 22203

(703) 524-7600 or 800-950-6264
www.nami.org
info@nami.org

LIGHTHOUSE FOR THE BLIND AND VISUALLY IMPAIRED

The mission of the LightHouse is to help blind and visually impaired people in Northern California live independent and active lives. The LightHouse provides educational, recreational, rehabilitative and social services to youth, adults and seniors experiencing varying degrees of vision loss. Established in 1902.

Volunteer Opportunities

There are many opportunities for individuals to get involved, some from the comfort of one's own home. Volunteers can provide personal services (assisting a blind or visually impaired person in their home with reading, writing, and errands); record materials such as articles and manuals onto a cassette recorder; assist with the adult education and recreation program; provide tutoring or organize a class in an area of expertise; serve as a summer camp counselor or a youth program assistant; or help with clerical responsibilities. All volunteers must undergo vision loss awareness training and commit to working with the LightHouse for at least six months. Applications can be downloaded on the organization's website and questions can be directed to Don M. Franklin, dmfranklin@lighthouse-sf.org

Contact Information

Headquarters: 214 Van Ness Avenue
San Francisco, CA 94102
(415) 431-1481 or (888) 400-8933

www.lighthouse-sf.org
info@lighthouse-sf.org

NATIONAL CENTER FOR LEARNING DISABILITIES (NCLD)

NCLD works to ensure that the nation's 15 million children, adolescents and adults with learning disabilities have every opportunity to succeed in school, work and life. It provides essential information to parents, professionals and individuals with learning disabilities, promotes research and programs to foster effective learning, and advocates for policies to protect and strengthen educational rights and opportunities. Established in 1977.

Volunteer Opportunities

NCLD has various clerical and administrative opportunities year-round in its office. However, volunteers are most in-need at the beginning of each year to help with the organization's scholarship review and selection process for its Anne Ford and Allegra Ford Scholarship.

NCLD also invites individuals with learning disabilities, experience teaching children with LD, or with raising a child with LD to write for its blog, LD Insights.

Contact Information

381 Park Avenue South, Suite 1401
New York, NY 10016
(212) 545-7510 or (888) 575-7373

www.ncld.org
ncld@ncld.org

SPECIAL OLYMPICS

Special Olympics is a global nonprofit organization targeting individuals with intellectual disabilities. With a presence in over 200 countries, Special Olympics provides year-round sports training and competition for children and adults with intellectual disabilities. Established in 1963.

Volunteer Opportunities

Each one of Special Olympics' programs has different needs for volunteers, but across the board they are always looking for coaches, "Fans in the Stands", and help at games and tournaments. Those in the health-care industry can also contribute their efforts to the Healthy Athletes program which provides health screenings free of charge at Special Olympics competitions. Visit www.specialolympics.org to locate a Special Olympics near you and learn details of its specific opportunities.

Contact Information

Headquarters: 1133 19th Street, N.W.
Washington, DC 20036-3604 USA
(202) 628-3630 or (800) 700-8585

www.specialolympics.org
info@specialolympics.org

SENIORS

ALZHEIMER'S ASSOCIATION
The Alzheimer's Association is a voluntary health organization with goals to eliminate Alzheimer's disease with advanced research, reduce the risk of dementia, and to provide care and support for sufferers. The association serves individuals through its helpline, local chapters, message boards, emergency response service (MedicAlert +Alzheimer's Association Safe Return), online resources, published journal, and the Alzheimer's Association Green-Field Library, which is the nation's largest library dedicated to the disease. In addition, Alzheimer's Association hosts an annual international conference that unites scientists from around the world to discuss ideas and research. Established in 1980.

Volunteer Opportunities
The Alzheimer's Association encourages volunteers to contact their local chapters to learn about opportunities. Volunteers can usually help organize and work the day of special events (such as the Alzheimer's Association Memory Walk), participate in public education and awareness programs, provide office or helpline assistance, or assist with advocacy.

Contact Information
Headquarters: 225 N. Michigan Ave., Fl. 17
Chicago, IL 60601-7633

(312) 335-8700
www.alz.org
info@alz.org

----------------------------★----------------------------

EXPERIENCE CORPS
Experience Corps is a national program that connects older adults (typically age 55+) with elementary school students to serve as tutors and mentors. Members also assist teachers in the classroom and lead after-school enrichment activities. Established in 1995.

Volunteer Opportunities
Experience Corp operates in 22 states, with different time commitments and opportunities at each local chapter. Depending on the state, volunteers can provide individualized tutoring, conduct small reading groups, and develop parent and family outreach efforts.

Contact Information
Headquarters: 2120 L Street, NW, Suite 610
Washington, DC 20037

(202) 478-6190
www.experiencecorps.org
info@experiencecorps.org

LITTLE BROTHERS—FRIENDS OF THE ELDERLY (LBFE)

LBFE is a national network of non-profit, volunteer-based organizations committed to relieving isolation and loneliness among the elderly. Established in 1946.

Volunteer Opportunities

LBFE welcomes volunteers to help elders through a variety of activities, ranging from packing gift baskets and preparing food during the holidays to driving an elder to a special event or spending an hour visiting. Chapters are based in Boston, Philadelphia, Cincinnati, Chicago, Upper Peninsula of Michigan, Minneapolis/St. Paul, Omaha, and San Francisco.

Contact Information

There is no national office for LBFE. Visit www.littlebrothers.org to find your local chapter.

MEALS ON WHEELS ASSOCIATION OF AMERICA (MOWAA)

MOWAA is a national umbrella organization representing local, community-based senior nutrition programs with a goal to end senior hunger by 2020. These programs provide meals to seniors at their homes or at congregate locations like senior centers. Established in 1954.

Volunteer Opportunities

Volunteers can hold a variety of positions with their local Meals On Wheels program. Most help with actual deliveries, but many programs also need help with food preparation and office work.

Since all Meals On Wheels programs are independently run and operated, it's up to each one to require how much training is necessary before someone can fill a role.

Most programs don't have any time requirements, but regarding meal deliveries, ask that the volunteers complete at least one route during their volunteering session – which can sometimes take as little as an hour or less.

Contact Information

Headquarters: 203 S. Union Street
Alexandria, Virginia 22314
(703) 548-5558

www.mowaa.org
Mowaa@mowaa.org

NATIONAL GRAY PANTHERS

National Gray Panthers is an intergenerational organization that believes in civic participation and responsibility as fundamental means to achieving social and economic justice and peace. Some of the many issues the advocacy group focuses on is health care (reproductive choice, medical marijuana, stem cell research), family security (social security benefits and cap, welfare reform, Older Americans Act); peace (rebuilding Iraq, relations with Cuba, Middle East peace) education (access to education, the No Child Left Behind Act), jobs and worker's rights (living wage, right to organize, global trade) and the environment (sustainability, preservation, pollution). Established in 1970.

Volunteer Opportunities

Contact the organization for details.

Contact Information

Headquarters: 1612 K Street, NW, Suite 300
Washington, DC 20006

(202) 737-6637 or (800) 280-5362
www.graypanthers.org
info@graypanthers.org

★

SOCIAL WELFARE AND EMERGENCY RELIEF

AMERICAN RED CROSS

The American Red Cross is an emergency response organization providing care to the victims of war and natural disasters, and services to the needy and military members and their families. With nearly 700 locally supported chapters, the American Red Cross helps people prepare for and respond to emergencies with its health and safety educational programs. The organization also works to offer international relief and development programs. Due in part to its magnitude of blood donors, the Red Cross is the largest supplier of blood and blood products in the United States. Established in 1881.

Volunteer Opportunities

The American Red Cross relies on its many volunteers to teach classes in first aid, CPR and swimming, as well as assist with blood drives, deliver messages to members of the military, connect families displaced by disasters, and work in communities during emergency situations. Opportunities are arranged by local affiliates.

Contact Information

Headquarters: 2025 E Street, NW
Washington, DC 20006

(202) 303 5000
www.redcross.org

★

Name: Edward Hunkele

Location: Elmira, NY

Organization: Red Cross

Can you describe what you do as a volunteer for the blood drives at the Red Cross?

There are two jobs I perform at different times. One has to do with registering donors. I greet them, check their names against the appointment schedule, hand them reading materials and insure that they are assigned to technicians in order.

The other position is in the canteen. In addition to serving refreshments and handing out T-shirts, I also pre-register them for the next blood drive and insure that they are feeling well. If someone is feeling faint, I call a technician for assistance and assist with their recovery.

What inspired you to volunteer?

Blood supply is always at a critical stage. The drives we perform are important especially in times of disaster. Although my role is on the periphery of the actual drawing of blood, it is important that volunteers perform their roles to insure that the process flows smoothly. If these jobs were not handled by volunteers, the cost of the drives would increase due to the need for paid personnel. So, I take solice in the fact that it is a responsibility that I can do to help defray the overall cost of such an important endeavor.

From a personal standpoint, I personally benefited from a blood drive in 1986. I was hospitalized after losing a considerable amount of blood due to a bleeding ulcer. The plant, where I worked, dedicated the next blood drive to cover the blood I was given. Consequently, I tried to donate blood whenever I could and subsequently became a volunteer.

How has volunteering made an impact in your life?

I have always tried to set an example for my family with regards to stressing the importance of sharing the blessings we have with others that may be less fortunate. At Christmas, we deliver food baskets to low-income individuals through the church and distribute toys to underprivileged children. Volunteering also sets an example to them and their children on the basis that your time can be as important as monetary gifts.

I believe that my presence at the blood drives also serves as an example to others in the community since I am somewhat younger than most of the other volunteers. Hopefully this shows the people donating blood that they too can be a part of the process, regardless of their age. I also reinforce the importance of their donations by thanking them and encouraging them to sign up for future blood drives.

CATHOLIC CHARITIES USA

Catholic Charities USA is the national office for local Catholic Charities agencies and institutions nationwide that work to reduce poverty, support families and empower communities. Its members provide help to people of all faiths. Established in 1910.

Volunteer Opportunities

Contact the organization for details.

Contact Information

Sixty-Six Canal Center Plaza, Suite 600
Alexandria, Virginia 22314

(703) 549-1390
www.catholiccharitiesusa.org

SALVATION ARMY

The Salvation Army is a faith-based charity that helps people with all kinds of social needs. Amongst its services, the Christian organization provides relief efforts to communities impacted by both natural and man-made disasters. Established in 1878.

Volunteer Opportunities

Volunteers carry out numerous activities, including assisting with after-school programs, visiting nursing homes and hospitals, serving meals to the needy, providing instruction (such as piano lessons) to less fortunate children, and bell ringing at Christmas. Many units of the Salvation Army list their volunteer opportunities on VolunteerMatch.org. The organization also encourages individuals to contact their local Salvation Army.

Contact Information
National Headquarters: 615 Slaters Lane
P.O. Box 269

Alexandria, VA 22313
www.salvationarmyusa.org

--★--

U.S. COMMITTEE FOR REFUGEES AND IMMIGRANTS (USCRI)

USCRI addresses the needs and rights of persons in forced or voluntary migration worldwide by advancing fair and humane public policy, facilitating and providing direct professional services, and promoting the full participation of migrants in community life.

Volunteer Opportunities

Opportunities abound at the local level in USCRI's field offices in Albany, N.Y., Detroit, MI, Colchestser, VT, Erie, P.A., Raleigh, N.C., or through the organization's nationwide network of partner agencies. Volunteers can teach English as a Second Language (ESL) courses; provide translation and/or interpretation services; accompany refugees to appointments; conduct career, financial literacy, and similar workshops; welcome newly arrive refugees at the airport; and otherwise help refugees become acclimated to life in the United States.

Internships are also available and school credit can be arranged, with a minimum commitment of eight hours per week for at least three months.

Contact Information
2231 Crystal Drive, Suite 350
Arlington VA 22202-3711
(703) 310-1130

www.refugees.org
uscri@uscridc.org

--★--

Name: Deborah G. Taylor
Location: East Greenbush, NY
Organization: UUSCRI (Albany)

Can you describe what kind of work you do to as a volunteer for USCRI?

On a regular basis I see three different families and review their mail, help with job applications or social services forms, make doctor appointments, etc. I don't do this alone . . . my husband, Kevin Taylor, is also a USCRI volunteer who goes with me to assist. He loves the work as much as I do and helps the children with homework, drives them to the playground, and helps with the mail. In nice weather we try to bring the children (as many as we can fit in our cars) to the playground or get them out of the house as there are not many areas for them to play in their neighborhood.

What inspired you to do volunteer work?

For some time I had been meaning to volunteer. My children were grown and out of the house and it was always one of my New Years' resolutions. I didn't want to just write a check, but to make a difference and I was inspired to work with USCRI after reading an article in a local newspaper about the work they do to resettle refugees. I felt compelled to help welcome some of the neediest people to this country from some of the most deplorable conditions. So I contacted USCRI and attended a volunteer orientation. I work full time and was somewhat intimidated with volunteering to act as a mentor with a family but I also realized that this is where I could do the most good. As a resident in the outskirts of Albany I had no idea there were so many refugees in our area nor did I know where they came from.

Is there a particular experience you had as a volunteer that has left a lasting impression in your life?

The most profound experience I had was December 2009 when I was in the delivery room for the birth of the baby in the family I was assigned to help. I had taken the mother to doctor appointments and ultrasounds and the other children to the doctor. They have named the baby Debbie Meh, after me. They are all so appreciative, so gentle and kind and to be a friend to them is really very simple.

But there are many rewarding experiences. Last summer I spent many nights driving several carloads of children and adults over to my home to swim in our pool. At first they were afraid of the water because they did not have the opportunity to swim due to the lack of clean water in their countries. Now all of the children can swim to some degree and they tell me it is their favorite thing about America.

What advice would you give to someone interested in doing volunteer work in their community?

Make a commitment to make a difference. Both my husband and I spend several nights a week volunteering and get more from the experience than we give. Any type of commitment is worthwhile. I believe to learn from another culture is so rewarding for everyone. These people, all younger than me, have been through so much in their lives. They have lost everything yet they are optimistic and want the same things for their children that we want for ours. We all have so much and the opportunity to share is so rewarding.

YMCA (YOUNG MEN'S CHRISTIAN ASSOCIATION) OF THE USA

YMCA has more than twenty-six hundred local affiliates that serve communities across the country with health programs and activities. The organization strives to help children and youth deepen their positive values and motivation to learn, families build stronger bonds, and individuals improve their overall well-being. Established in 1851.

Volunteer Opportunities

Each YMCA in the U.S. is run by volunteers so a variety of opportunities exist, including programming (contributing as an exercise class instructor or a basketball coach), support (working at the front desk, office locker room or on the grounds), fundraising, policy (serving on the Y's board of directors), and managerial (act as a pro-bono accountant or PR specialist). Needs vary by location so volunteers should consult with their local YMCA to confirm opportunities and learn details.

Contact Information

Headquarters: 101 North Wacker Drive
Chicago, IL 60606

(800) 872-9622
www.ymca.net

YWCA (YOUNG WOMEN'S CHRISTIAN ASSOCIATION) OF THE USA

The YWCA is the oldest and largest multicultural women's organization in the world with more than 300 local associations in the nation. To accomplish its mission of empowering women and eradicating racism, each chapter provides a variety of services which may include childcare, domestic violence shelters, rape crisis intervention, career counseling, health and fitness, and social justice programs. Aside from its programs, the YWCA advocates for women's rights and civil rights in Congress. Established in 1859.

Volunteer Opportunities

Contact the organization for details.

Contact Information

Headquarters: 2025 M Street, NW
Suite 550
Washington, DC 20036

(202)-467-0801
www.ywca.org
info@ywca.org

VIOLENCE PREVENTION AND PEACE

AMERICAN FRIENDS SERVICE COMMITTEE (AFSC)

AFSC is a faith-inclusive Quaker organization that is committed to humanitarian service, social justice and peace programs throughout the world. AFSC applies a nonviolent approach in their programs and efforts, which currently include the elimination of nuclear weapons, immigrants' rights, withdrawing U.S. troops from Iraq and Afghanistan, and providing disaster relief to Haiti, amongst other global issues. Established in 1917.

Volunteer Opportunities

Contact the organization for details.

Contact Information

1501 Cherry St.
Philadelphia, PA 19102

(215) 241-7000
www.afsc.org

BRADY CAMPAIGN TO PREVENT GUN VIOLENCE AND BRADY CENTER TO PREVENT GUN VIOLENCE

The Brady Campaign strives to regulate the purchase and acquisition of guns in an effort to fight gun violence. The campaign applies grassroots activism to help pass and enforce federal and state gun laws, regulations and public policies. Its sister organization, The Brady Center, provides legal representation to victims of gun violence and educates the public through litigation, grassroots mobilization, and outreach. Established in 1974 and 1983, respectively.

Volunteer Opportunities

The organization relies heavily on volunteers to do research, make phone calls to legislative offices at the state and Federal level, represent the organization in speaking to local groups and school groups, attend rallies and press conferences, and many other activities. A one-hour per week time commitment is required.

Volunteers work in the organization's national office in Washington DC and in many offices of its affiliated chapters in 36 states. The largest numbers of volunteers work in New York City and Albany, New York; Los Angeles and Sacramento, California; Philadelphia, Pennsylvania; Chicago, Illinois; Denver, Colorado; Seattle, Washington.

Contact Information

1225 Eye Street, NW, Suite 1100
Washington, DC 20005
Brady Campaign: (202) 898-0792

www.bradycampaign.org
Brady Center: (202) 289-7319
www.bradycenter.org

★

COUNCIL FOR A LIVABLE WORLD (CLW)

Founded by nuclear physicist Lew Szilard and other scientists, CLW is an organization that advocates for the reduction of nuclear weapons and increase of national security. CLW provides members of Congress with scientific and technical information about topics of importance, including weapons of mass destruction and nuclear non-proliferation. It also employs legislation, lobbying, media and online outreach to find peaceful solutions to international conflict. Established in 1962.

Volunteer Opportunities

Supporters of nuclear disarmament and progressive national security policies are encouraged to become a member of Council for a Livable World and sign-up for its email alerts which include opportunities to sign petitions, participate in action alerts (such as calling your Senator about a policy issue) and make contributions to support candidates for Congress who also represent these values.

Full-time internships are available through CLW's sister organization, The Center for Arms Control and Non-Proliferation in Washington, D.C. Internship opportunities are for students of political science, international relations, the sciences, peace studies, or related fields.

Contact Information

322 4th Street NE
Washington, DC 20002

(202) 543-4100
www.livableworld.org

★

VIOLENCE PREVENTION AND PEACE

FAIR FUND

FAIR Fund, a D.C. based international nonprofit organization, works to prevent human trafficking and sexual violence in the lives of youth, especially girls, around the world. FAIR Fund builds the capacity of communities to better identify and assist youth aged 11 to 24 who are at high risk or have been exploited via human trafficking and sexual violence. FAIR Fund has active programs in Bosnia, Chicago, Illinois, Serbia, Russia, Washington, D.C, and Uganda.

Volunteer Opportunities
Contact the organization for details.

Contact Information
P.O. Box 21656
Washington, DC 20009
(202) 265-1505

www.fairfund.org
info@fairfund.org

MOVEON.ORG

MoveOn.org is comprised of two organizations: MoveOn.org Civic Action (formerly known just as MoveOn.org), a nonprofit that primarily focuses on education, advocacy and media, and MoveOn.org Political Action (formerly known as MoveOn PAC), a federal PAC that mobiles people across the country to engage with Congress to bring about change and to help elect desired candidates. In 2002 and 2003, MoveOn.org Civic Action conducted several important campaigns, including one to stop the Iraq war, and one that called to reduce America's dependence on oil. Established in 1998.

Volunteer Opportunities
Contact the organization for details.

Contact Information
www.moveon.org

NUCLEAR AGE PEACE FOUNDATION (NAPF)

NAPF's vision is a world free of violent conflict and weapons of mass destruction. It cites its core mission as one that helps "advance initiatives to eliminate the nuclear weapons threat to all life, to foster the global rule of law, and to build an enduring legacy of peace through education and advocacy." The foundation provides research and education and has created a national and international network of affiliates, associates and representatives in several continents and in the United Nations. Established in 1982.

Volunteer Opportunities

NAPF has many projects that volunteers can lend their skills and time to. Opportunities exist in NAPF's Santa Barbara, CA office, but the organization can also utilize volunteers who are willing to work remotely from anywhere. Interested individuals are instructed to email NAPF's Director of Programs, Rick Wayman, by completing a form at www.wagingpeace.org.

Contact Information
Physical address:
1622 Anacapa Street
Santa Barbara, CA 93101
(805) 965-3443

Mailing address:
Nuclear Age Peace Foundation
1187 Coast Village Road,
Suite 1, PMB 121
Santa Barbara, California 93108-2794
www.wagingpeace.org

★

PEACE ACTION

As the largest grassroots network working for peace and nuclear abolition, Peace Action has over 100 chapters in 34 states. It applies practices such as protest, direct action, Congressional lobbying and voter education to bring issues of peace and security and human rights to the forefront of U.S. foreign and domestic policy. The organization provides education on the effects of politics and current events on the global community through its quarterly newsletter, monthly e-Newsletter and weekly Action Alerts. Peace Action also organizes a student network, SPAN, which provides opportunities for high school and college youth to meet like-minded mentors and participate in regional conferences. Established in 1957.

Volunteer Opportunities

Volunteers can lend help to five different departments in the MD office:

- Development/Fundraising: data base work and mailings
- Office of the Executive Director: research and writing
- Finance: accounting and filing
- Program: writing, attending meetings, and helping with lobbying
- Communications: assisting with the website, writing blogs and press releases, and calling the media

Individuals living outside MD can contact any of the organization's many chapters and affiliates to learn of opportunities in their area.

Contact Information
8630 Fenton St Suite 524
Silver Spring, MD 20910

(301) 565-4050
www.peace-action.org

----------------------------★----------------------------

RAPE, ABUSE, AND INCEST NATIONAL NETWORK (RAINN)

RAINN is the nation's largest anti-sexual violence organization. Among its programs, RAINN created and operates the National Sexual Assault Hotline at 800.656.HOPE. This nationwide partnership of more than 1,100 local rape crisis centers provides victims of sexual assault with free, confidential services around the clock. The hotline has helped more than 1.4 million people since it began in 1994. In 2006, RAINN launched the National Sexual Assault Online Hotline, the nation's first secure web-based hotline. In addition, RAINN uses its community partnerships to put critical information into the hands of young women and men at concerts, on campus and in communities. Through these efforts, RAINN educates more than 120 million Americans each year about sexual assault. RAINN also publicizes the hotlines' free, confidential services and leads national efforts to improve services to victims and ensure that rapists are brought to justice.

Volunteer Opportunities

There are many ways to volunteer for RAINN — staff a hotline, volunteer at your local rape crisis center, raise money to support programs, and raise awareness through public education efforts like RAINN Day, the organization's college campaign on over 1000 campuses nationwide.

Contact Information
2000 L Street, NW, Suite 406
Washington, DC 20036
(202) 544-3064

www.rainn.org
info@rainn.org

----------------------------★----------------------------

WILDLIFE AND ANIMAL RIGHTS

AMERICAN SOCIETY FOR THE PREVENTION OF CRUELTY TO ANIMALS (ASPCA)

The American Society for the Prevention of Cruelty to Animals (ASPCA) was the first humane society to be established in North America and is, today, one of the largest in the world. The organization was founded on the belief that animals are entitled to kind and respectful treatment at the hands of humans, and must be protected under the law (ASPCA is granted legal authority to investigate and make arrests for crimes against animals). It provides local and national leadership in three key areas: caring for pet parents and pets, providing positive outcomes for at-risk animals and serving victims of animal cruelty. Headquartered in New York City, the ASPCA maintains a strong local presence, and with programs that extend its anti-cruelty mission across the country, it is recognized as a national animal welfare organization. Founded in 1866.

Volunteer Opportunities

Opportunities are available at the organization's administrative office and its shelter, both in New York City. Volunteers walk dogs or socialize (play) with them, assist in obedience and behavior modification training, or help socialize with cats and kittens. Volunteers can also help young, ill or frightened animals recuperate in foster homes and help find ASPCA's dogs and cats loving homes through its adoptions counselor training. Additionally, volunteers can perform clerical duties or assist with special projects or events. All volunteers receive training in each specific area of interest (dog, cat, adoptions, foster, etc) and volunteers are required to perform eight hours of volunteer service per month and sign up for at least a minimum of 6 months.

The ASPCA encourages anyone outside of the New York City area to volunteer at their local animal shelter or rescue group.

Contact Information

424 E. 92nd St
New York, NY 10128-6804

www.aspca.org

--★--

Name: Diane Wilkerson

Location: New York City

Organization: ASPCA

Director of the ASPCA's Adoption Center Volunteer Program

How did you get involved with the ASPCA?

When we moved to New York City four years ago for my husband's job, I wanted to do something with my time. Knowing that the ASPCA was nearby, I walked over one day. I adopted a kitten, and as a result of my positive experience, started volunteering as an Adoption counselor; this eventually led to getting my dream job!

What about working with volunteers and running a volunteer program appealed to you?

It was the perfect blend of the two things I love the most: people and animals.

What's a typical day at your job?

One of the things I like most about my job is that every day is different! But a typical day is making sure the adoptions center is appropriately staffed with volunteer adoptions counselors; being available for questions; scheduling classes, and helping to respond to the different requests that come in for volunteers, etc.

Can you recall a particularly memorable experience while working at the ASPCA?

To be honest, there are so many wonderfully memorable experiences, but if I had to pick one, it would be the example of one of our newest volunteers who started volunteering while she was on break from her teaching job. She so enjoyed her experience volunteering in the adoption center—working with our dogs, cats and adopters—that she decided to make a career change and was recently hired.

Do you find your work rewarding?

I consider myself truly blessed to have a job where I really feel I am making a difference in the lives of the wonderful animals here at the ASPCA. The volunteer program is essential in helping make our dogs and cats more adoptable, whether through socialization, training, or presenting the animals and their specific characteristics to potential adopters through the adoption counseling process.

What advice would you give to someone considering doing volunteer work? How about someone specifically interested in volunteering to help animals?

Volunteering provides that wonderful combination of doing something that makes you feel good while you are making a difference in the lives of people and animals!

HUMANE FARMING ASSOCIATION (HFA)

HFA's goals are to protect farm animals from cruelty, to protect the public from the dangerous misuse of antibiotics, hormones, and other chemicals used on factory farms, and to protect the environment from the impacts of industrialized animal factories. The association's programs include: anti-cruelty investigations and exposes, national media and ad campaigns, direct hands-on emergency care and refuge for abused farm animals. Founded in 1985.

Volunteer Opportunities

Contact the organization for details.

Contact Information

P.O. Box 3577
San Rafael, CA 94912
(415) 771-CALF

www.hfa.org
hfa@hfa.org

HUMANE SOCIETY OF THE UNITED STATES (HSUS)

Established in 1954, The HSUS seeks a humane and sustainable world for all animals. It works to reduce suffering and to create meaningful social change for animals by advocating for public policies, investigating cruelty and working to enforce existing laws, educating the public about animal issues, joining with corporations on behalf of animal-friendly policies, and conducting hands-on programs to make the world more humane. HSUS is also the lead disaster relief agency for animals, and it provides direct care for thousands of animals at its sanctuaries and rescue facilities, wildlife rehabilitation centers, and mobile veterinary clinics. The HSUS publishes All Animals, a membership magazine, and Animal Sheltering, a bi-monthly magazine for animal sheltering professionals.

Volunteer Opportunities

Volunteers work in emergency response, gather signatures for campaigns, and serve as online ambassadors who help spread the word about HSUS through the web. HSUS stresses that there are numerous ways for volunteers to get involved with the organization, but it also urges individuals to consider volunteering at local shelters for hands-on opportunities. People can sign up for action alerts through HSUS's website.

Contact Information

2100 L St., NW
Washington, D.C. 20037

(202) 452-1100
www.humanesociety.org

NATIONAL WILDLIFE FEDERATION

The National Wildlife Federation is America's largest conservation organization. It works with more than four million members, partners and supporters in communities across the country to protect and restore wildlife habitat, confront global warming and connect with nature.

MAKE A DIFFERENCE

Volunteer Opportunities

NWF provides a host of different opportunities, but warns that its volunteers do not directly handle wildlife. Interested parties should complete an online registration form at www.NWF.org. Positions include:

- **Habitat volunteers** work with their community member to learn about how to create, install and maintain wildlife-friendly backyards, schools, and other locations. There are three different types of opportunities:
  - *Hosts* serve as trainer for other volunteer opportunities in their community. Hosts need to be able to commitment at least six weeks to training and volunteer at least six hours a week.
  - *Stewards* are hand-on skill volunteers who are trained to assist community members with projects such as creating a wildlife garden. Stewards' opportunities are more physically demanding.
  - *Ambassadors* talk with community members and share information about how they can engage in programs or make a difference in their community. Ambassadors are on the ground spokespersons for NWF.
- **Wildlife advocates** volunteer in their communities to promote changes in laws or other policies. Virtual opportunities are available or volunteers can work in one of NWF's office to help staff with a variety of projects from research, marketing, writing, phone call or data entry (varies by location and need).
- **Special events volunteers** staff a table or help with a one-time event. Events are seasonal mainly in the Fall, Spring and Early Summer. Event volunteers give time to a specific event and are more generalist, helping in many different ways. Volunteers give their help over a short time frame, such as a few days or months. Volunteers need to be commitment to the duration of the event.
- **Behind-the-scenes volunteers** work with NWF staff members to help with office projects ranging from research to data entry. Volunteers can work either in an NWF office or virtual (from home). Volunteers need to be able to give at least four hours a week for a year.
- **Special situation volunteers** are on-call volunteers that can help with a variety of activities depending on their skills. Situation volunteers will be active as needed and may have an intense volunteer experience for a shorter term.
- **Corporate employee volunteers** are employees that can volunteer under their employer. Visit www.nwf.org for details.

- **"Be Out There" volunteers** work with parents and kids to get back outside and enjoy the outdoors.

Contact Information

11100 Wildlife Center Drive
Reston, VA 20190-5362

(800) 822-9919
www.NWF.org

---★---

PEOPLE FOR THE ETHICAL TREATMENT OF ANIMALS (PETA)

PETA focuses its attention on the four areas in which the largest numbers of animals suffer the most intensely for the longest periods of time: on factory farms, in laboratories, in the clothing trade, and in the entertainment industry. It also works on a variety of other issues, including the cruel killing of beavers, birds and other "pests," and the abuse of backyard dogs. PETA strives to achieve its mission through public education, cruelty investigations, research, animal rescue, legislation, special events, celebrity involvement, and protest campaigns. Founded in 1980.

Volunteer Opportunities

PETA provides opportunities at its Norfolk, Virginia, headquarters. Volunteers can get involved by attending outreach activities, including local tabling events at fairs and festivals and leafleting; critiquing medical and scientific research proposals; conducting online and library research; performing various types of office work, such as data entry, preparation of mailings, and faxing; and participating in PETA's weekly work party on Wednesday nights.

Individuals outside the VA area can join PETA's Action Team by completing an online form at www.peta.org. Participants receive information on upcoming events and demonstrations in their area, breaking news, urgent alerts and tips on how to improve the lives of animals every day.

Contact Information

501 Front Street
Norfolk, VA 23510

www.peta.org

---★---

PETCONNECT RESCUE AND WELLNESS

PetConnect Rescue was founded in 2005, in the wake of Hurricane Katrina, and has evolved into an all-breed animal rescue organization. Its mission is to save the lives of dogs and cats that have been abandoned and place them in loving and permanent homes. On a daily basis, PetConnect responds to email and phone pleas for help for dogs and cats imminently slated for euthanasia. The organization pulls these animals into rescue from over extended local shelters as well as rural shelters from West Virginia to Georgia. In the fall of 2009, PetConnect Rescue joined forces with The Kyra Macy Foundation, a nonprofit animal rescue organization.

Volunteer Opportunities

Opportunities are offered in Maryland and Virginia and include transporting animals, fostering, conducting home visits, assisting at adoption events as well as participating in the care of the rescues at PetConnect's two properties. In addition, those who wish to get involved can help with public relations, fundraising and administrative support. PetConnect asks potential volunteers to complete an online application on its website.

Contact Information

Virginia:
PetConnect Rescue and Wellness
The Kyra Macy Foundation
12054 North Shore Dr.
Reston, VA 20190

Maryland:
PetConnect Rescue and Wellness
P.O.Box 60714
Potomac, MD 20859
(877) 838-9171
www.petconnectrescue.org
info@petconnectrescue.org

THE STUDENT CONSERVATION ASSOCIATION

SCA provides college and high school-aged members with hands-on conservation service opportunities in virtually every field imaginable, from tracking grizzlies through the Tetons to restoring desert ecosystems and teaching environmental education at Washington, D.C.'s Urban Tree House. SCA's members protect and restore national parks, marine sanctuaries, cultural landmarks and community green spaces in all 50 states. Founded in 1957.

Volunteer Opportunities

SCA is looking for members who are motivated to serve the environment, eager to get their hands dirty while gaining real-world job experience, and make a difference for our planet. There are virtually no limits to the services and experiences offered by SCA. From wildlife management, habitat restoration, forestry, fisheries, hydrology, archaeology, trail construction, cultural interpretation, environmental education, visitor services... If it is practiced within the conservation field, there's a related position available at SCA.

Some specific examples of opportunities include: SCA members restoring areas of Angeles National Forest that were devastated by last year's Station Fire (they are preventing erosion by revegging burned out areas and reconstructing trails and camp sites); SCA interns at Yellowstone compiling an online database of all the park's geothermal features (information is being used by medical professionals seeking new cures to NASA officials pondering how life may exist under extreme conditions); interns working on climate change/sustainability outreach at the Field Museum.

SCA annually places thousands of members nationwide, covering all 50 states. It collaborates with partners including the National Park Service, US Forest Service, and Bureau of Land Management; numerous state and local resource management offices, and private organizations such as The Nature Conservancy and Audubon Society. Members do not ordinarily work at NH headquarters, but the organization's regional offices (Boise, Houston, Oakland, Pittsburgh, Seattle and Wash, DC) not only conduct local conservation programs for urban, often underrepresented populations, but often host interns in a variety of outreach and support positions.

As for specific terms, SCA's crew program for HS students operates each summer and the obligations runs from three to six weeks in length, depending upon the project. For individuals 18+, it offers internships that run from anywhere between 13 and 52 weeks (this also varies by project).

All SCA programs are tuition free and most are expenses-paid including transportation to and from site, housing, a cost of living stipend, insurance, and – upon completion of service – an AmeriCorps education award of up to $5,000.

Contact Information

689 River Road
P.O. Box 550
Charlestown, NH 03603

(603) 543-1700
www.thesca.org

--------------------------------------★--------------------------------------

THE WILDERNESS SOCIETY

Since its founding in 1935, The Wilderness Society has led the effort to permanently protect as wilderness nearly 110 million acres in 44 states. From the 1964 Wilderness Act to the landmark 2009 bill that permanently protected more than two million acres of wilderness across the country, The Wilderness

Society has been at the forefront of nearly every major public lands victory over the past 75 years.

Volunteer Opportunities

Duties typically include research to answer questions from staff members, legal and policy memos on technical issues, letters to federal agencies such as the Forest Service, and short updates for the organization's website. The Wilderness Society also has opportunities for office assistance.

Most volunteers work in the organization's national office in Washington, but sometimes there are opportunities in the largest regional offices, located in Seattle, San Francisco, Anchorage, Denver, Boise, and Bozeman (MT). Smaller offices are less likely to have volunteers.

Internships for school credit or stipends are also available.

Contact Information:

1615 M St, NW
Washington, DC 20036

(202) 833-2300
www.wilderness.org

★

WORLD WILDLIFE FUND (WWF)

WWF works in 100 countries and is supported by close to five million globally in its mission of protecting nature. The conservation organization combines global reach with a foundation in science, involves action at every level from local to global, and ensures the delivery of innovative solutions that meet the needs of both people and nature to preserve the diversity and abundance of life on Earth and the health of ecological systems. WWF focuses on three areas: protecting natural areas and wild populations of plants and animals (including endangered species), promoting sustainable approaches to the use of renewable natural resources and supporting more efficient use of resources and energy, and the maximum reduction of pollution. Its goal for the year 2020 is to conserve 19 of the world's most important natural places and significantly change global markets to protect the future of nature.

Volunteer Opportunities

WWF offers a volunteer program for people between the ages of 20-27. Participants work with WWF for several months in such countries as Madagascar, India, Paraguay, South Pacific and Bhutan.

For people outside the age requirements, WWF suggests contacting one's local county parks and recreation department for opportunities such as cleaning up local parks, monitoring stream quality or censuring migratory birds.

MAKE A DIFFERENCE

WWF also encourages interested individuals to join its online Conservation Action Network, to subscribe to its e-newsletter, and to regularly visit its website for information on how to support its mission.

Contact Information

1250 Twenty-Fourth Street, N.W.
P.O. Box 97180

Washington, DC 20090-7180
www.worldwildlife.org

WOMEN'S RIGHTS

CHOICE USA

Fifteen-years ago, renowned activist and author Gloria Steinem, along with other feminist leaders, founded Choice USA. As a national pro-choice organization, Choice USA gives emerging leaders the tools they need to organize, network, and exchange ideas to build a youth centered pro-choice agenda and mobilize communities for reproductive justice. Choice USA helps students and young activists build leadership and organizing skills through its institutes, trainings, and internships; mobile their communities for reproductive justice, by providing effective strategies for education and outreach; and win victories to increase the availability of reproductive and social justice information and services. Established in 1992.

Volunteer Opportunities
Contact the organization for details.

Contact Information
Headquarters: 1317 F Street, NW, Suite 501
Washington, DC 20004

(202) 965-7700 or (888) 784-4494
www.choiceusa.org

EQUALITY NOW

Equality Now was founded in 1992 to work for the protection and promotion of the human rights of women around the world. Working with national human rights organizations and individual activists, Equality Now documents violence and discrimination against women and mobilizes international action to support their efforts to stop these human rights abuses. Through its Women's Action Network of concerned groups and individuals around the world, Equality Now distributes information about human rights violations, takes action to protest these violations, and brings public attention to human rights violations against women. Issues of urgent concern to Equality Now include rape, domestic violence, reproductive rights, trafficking of women, female genital mutilation, and the denial of equal access to economic opportunity and political participation.

Volunteer Opportunities

Equality Now has research and campaign internships, media and outreach internships, and fundraising and accounting internships. Opportunities are available in London, New York, and Nairobi. Research and campaign interns generally conduct legal and fact-finding research and draft Women's Actions and campaign correspondence as the work requires. Media and outreach interns help out with media outreach, including assisting with drafting columns for newspapers and targeting other local media outlets. Outreach may also involve assisting in growing the Women's Action Network membership. Fundraising and accounting interns generally do research, report drafting, spreadsheets, special events work, filing and other office duties as assigned. Interns may also attend meetings at the United Nations and participate in other advocacy efforts to further Equality Now's work.

Summer interns spend 8-10 weeks full-time with Equality Now and semester interns spend approximately 10 hours a week with Equality Now. Please note that internships are unpaid and no arrangements can be made for housing or visas.

Application details can be found at www.equalitynow.org.

Contact Information

P.O. Box 20646
Columbus Circle Station
New York, NY 10023

www.equalitynow.org
info@equalitynow.org

GLOBAL FUND FOR WOMEN (GFW)

The Global Fund for Women is a nonprofit grantmaking foundation that advances women's human rights worldwide. GFW is a network of women and men who believe that ensuring women's full equality and participation in society is one of the most effective ways to build a just, peaceful and sustainable world. It raises funds from a variety of sources and makes grants to women-led organizations that promote the economic security, health, safety, education and leadership of women and girls.

Volunteer Opportunities

Opportunities are available in GFW's San Francisco office. Volunteers work regular business hours and occasionally help staff events. Volunteers handle basic administrative tasks including mailing, filing and data entry, assisting with global fund events, and translation.

Contact Information
222 Sutter Street, Suite 500
San Francisco, CA 94108
(415) 248-4800

www.globalfundforwomen.org
gfw@globalfundforwomen.org

NARAL PRO-CHOICE AMERICA

NARAL Pro-Choice America is committed to protecting a woman's right to choose and electing candidates who will promote policies to prevent unintended pregnancy. In its goal to protect women's reproductive freedom, NARAL Pro-Choice America educates and mobilizes voters, provides information about state bills, the enactment of new laws, and decisions handed down by state and federal courts related to reproductive rights, and works to stop anti-choice legislation. Established in 1966.

Volunteer Opportunities
Contact the organization for details.

Contact Information
1156 15th Street, NW Suite 700
Washington, DC 20005

(202) 973-3000
www.prochoiceamerica.org

NATIONAL NETWORK OF ABORTION FUNDS (NNAF)

NNAF is a network of over 100 grassroots groups in more than 40 states that help women pay for abortion services. Some of the network's initiatives include providing intensive training and support to its member Funds across the country, supporting the emergence of new abortion Funds in underserved areas, advocating on the state and national level for increased access to abortion, emergency contraception, and full reproductive health care for all women, coordinating funding for women needing financial assistance from more than one member Fund, and providing direct funding to women in need. Established in 1993.

Volunteer Opportunities
Although there are not many volunteer opportunities at the network's national office in Boston, NNAF is made up of 100 Funds, many of which are completely volunteer-run. Volunteers respond to calls from women in need, raise money, put on educational events, and in many cases do everything that makes a grassroots abortion Fund function. Opportunities range in terms of time commitment and skill-set required. NNAF encourages interested individuals to visit its website, www.nnaf.org, to learn more.

Contact Information

42 Seaverns Avenue
Boston, MA 02130-2865
(617) 524-6040

www.nnaf.org
info@nnaf.org

NATIONAL ORGANIZATION FOR WOMEN FOUNDATION (NOW FOUNDATION)

The NOW Foundation is devoted to furthering women's rights through education and litigation. The NOW Foundation is affiliated with the National Organization for Women, the largest women's rights organization in the United States, with a membership of over 500,000 contributing women and men dedicated to legal, political, social, and economic equality for women. NOW works on issues such as violence against women, racial and ethnic diversity, economic equality, welfare rights, health care and reproductive rights, lesbian and gay rights, and the Equal Rights Amendment. NOW urges activists to strive for equality and justice through mass action, lobbying, non-violent civil disobedience and direct action. Established in 1986.

Volunteer Opportunities

For those interested in taking an active role in the women's rights movement, NOW provides daytime and evening opportunities. Volunteer projects fall into several areas, including office support, public relations/communications and field organizing. Volunteers work under the direct supervision of national officers and staff members. Tasks vary depending on the needs and the skills of the volunteer but can include selecting and preparing materials to be archived at a library for women's history; office support such as bookkeeping or database entry; phoning members with information about an event, issue, or action; helping with mailings; responding to inquiries from the public; writing communications; or organizing events. Opportunities are available at the national office and local chapter. NOW asks daytime volunteers to work at least two to three hours per week. Interested parties can complete the online form at www.now.org/organization/volunt.html.

Contact Information

1100 H Street N.W., Third Floor
Washington, D.C. 20005

(202) 628-8669
www.nowfoundation.org

NATIONAL WOMEN'S POLITICAL CAUCUS (NWPC)

The National Women's Political Caucus is a multipartisan, multicultural grass-roots organization dedicated to increasing women's participation in the political field and creating a political power base designed to achieve equality for all women. Founded in 1971, the NWPC prides itself in increasing the number of pro-choice women elected and appointed into office every year. Through recruiting, training and financial donations, the NWPC provides support to women candidates running for all levels of office regardless of political affiliation. In addition, hundreds of state and local chapters reach out to women in communities across the country to better assist them in their dreams of being elected into office.

Volunteer Opportunities

NWPC is open to volunteers of all ages who share the goal of the organization. Opportunities abound at the local level but volunteers can also work at NWPC's national office in Washington, D.C.. At the state or local level, volunteers can help plan and staff events, assist on campaigns of endorsed candidates, and fundraise. At the national office, volunteers assist staff with research, writing and administrative tasks.

There are also opportunities to become directly involved on NWPC's board. All of its national board members are elected to serve, but serve in a volunteer capacity.

Contact Information

P.O. Box 50476
Washington, DC 20091
(202) 785-1100

www.nwpc.org
info@nwpc.org

Organizations by Type

If you're not sure where to start, or what exactly you have to offer, you can contact one of these organizations which can steer you in the right direction. In this section, you'll learn where to go if you're interested in advocacy or policy and issues. Faith-based organizations are a great place to check out if you belong to a church or synagogue (or simply have an affinity for a specific faith). The general resources are listed here, as well as organizations operating near or on campuses.

ADVOCACY ORGANIZATIONS

CORPORATE ACCOUNTABILITY INTERNATIONAL

Since 1977, Corporate Accountability International (formerly Infact) has waged—and won—campaigns that challenge irresponsible and dangerous actions by corporate giants. From bringing about significant reforms in the life-threatening marketing of infant formula in economically poor countries to pushing G.E. out of nuclear weaponsmaking to being a major contributing factor in the adoption of the world's first corporate accountability treaty, the Framework Convention on Tobacco Control, its work has influenced the way corporations are held accountable for the last 30 years.

Volunteer Opportunities

To receive action alerts, visit www.stopcorporateabuse.org to join the organization's online activist network.

Contact Information

Campaign Headquarters:
10 Milk Street, Suite 610
Boston, MA 02108

(800) 688-8797 or (617) 695-2525
www.stopcorporateabuse.org
info@stopcorporateabuse.org

DEMOCRACY FOR AMERICA (DFA)

Democracy for America, the people powered PAC, has over one million members nationwide. DFA is a grassroots powerhouse working to change our country and the Democratic Party from the bottom-up. It provides campaign training, organizing resources, and media exposure so its members have the power to support progressive issues and candidates up and down the ballot.

Volunteer Opportunities

Contact the organization for details.

Contact Information

P.O. Box 1717
Burlington, VT 05402
Physical Address: 38 Eastwood

Drive, Suite 300
South Burlington, VT 05403
(802) 651-3200
www.democracyforamerica.com

JOBS WITH JUSTICE (JWJ)

Jobs with Justice engages workers and allies in campaigns to win justice in workplaces and in communities where working families live. JwJ was founded in 1987 with the vision of lifting up workers' rights struggles as part of a larger campaign for economic and social justice.

Volunteer Opportunities
Contact the organization for details.

Contact Information
1325 Massachusetts Avenue NW, Suite 200
Washington, DC 20005

(202) 393-1044
www.jwj.org
jwjnational@jwj.org

NATIONAL LABOR COMMITTEE (NLC)

The mission of the National Labor Committee is to help defend the human rights of workers in the global economy. The NLC investigates and exposes human and labor rights abuses committed by U.S. companies producing goods in the developing world. It undertakes public education, research and popular campaigns that empower U.S. citizens to support the efforts of workers to learn and defend their rights.

Volunteer Opportunities
Student and recent graduate interns help with conducting corporate and trade research, updating NLC's donor database, and maintaining its website as well as social media network pages. NLC welcome volunteers and provides opportunities on a case-by-case basis depending on its project needs.

Contact Information
5 Gateway Center, 6th Floor
Pittsburgh, PA 15222
(412) 562-2406

www.nlcnet.org
nlc@nlcnet.org

PUBLIC CAMPAIGN

Public Campaign is a non-profit, non-partisan organization dedicated to sweeping campaign reform that aims to dramatically reduce the role of big special interest money in American politics. Public Campaign is laying the foundation for reform by working with a broad range of organizations, including local community groups, around the country that are fighting for change and national organizations whose members are not fairly represented under the current campaign finance system. Together they are building a network of national and state-based efforts to create a powerful national force for federal and state campaign reform.

Volunteer Opportunities

Public Campaign is always looking for people who want to support its efforts. Volunteers help with a variety of activities including phone banking, letter writing campaigns, and rallies, to name a few. Public Campaign deeply values the commitment of their supporters, and eagerly welcomes others who want to be involved in promoting Fair Elections policy.

Contact Information

1133 19th Street, NW Suite 900
Washington, DC 20036
(202) 293-0222

www.publiccampaign.org
info@pcactionfund.org

RESULTS AND RESULTS EDUCATIONAL FUND (REF)

RESULTS and RESULTS Educational Fund (REF) are sister organizations that, together, are a leading force in ending poverty in the United States and around the world. They create long-term solutions to poverty by supporting programs that address its root causes — lack of access to medical care, education, or opportunity to move up the economic ladder. They do this by empowering ordinary people to become extraordinary voices for the end of poverty in their communities, the media, and the halls of government. The collective voices of these passionate grassroots activists, coordinated with grass-tops efforts driven by the organizations' staff, leverage millions of dollars for programs and improved policies that give low-income people the tools they need to move out of poverty.

Volunteer Opportunities

The RESULTS website lists activist how-to's about engaging your elected official, working with your local media, and building a community coalition. The how-to's encompass the simple to the advanced and provide guidance on moving decision-makers toward becoming champions for the end of poverty. Available internships are also posted at www.results.org.

Volunteers can also join a local RESULTS advocacy group or start a new group in their area if one does not already exist. Volunteers meet monthly to become educated on the issues, trained on how to best advocate on them, and then take action. RESULTS has about 100 groups nationwide with around 800 active volunteers.

Contact Information

RESULTS / RESULTS Educational
  Fund
750 First Street NE Suite 1040
Washington, DC 20002
RESULTS: (202) 783-7100

RESULTS Educational Fund: (202)
  783-4800
www.results.org
results@results.org

---★---

TRUE MAJORITY

TrueMajority was founded by Ben Cohen, Co-founder of Ben and Jerry's. It is a grassroots education and advocacy joint project of UsAction and UsAction Education Fund.

Volunteer Opportunities

Once you register as a member with TrueMajority via its website, you will receive e-mail alerts about electoral campaign issues, activities, events, and critical topics. With one click of a button you can either send TrueMajority's suggested letters and petitions to local representatives or edit them yourself (and the organization will still send them for you.)

Contact Information

TrueMajority.org / USAction:
1825 K St. NW, Suite 210
Washington, DC 20006

(202) 263-4520
www.truemajority.org
info@truemajority.org

---★---

CAMPUS ORGANIZATIONS

AMNESTY INTERNATIONAL (AI)

Amnesty International is a worldwide movement of people who campaign for internationally recognized human rights for all. Amongst its areas of focus, AI takes action to stop violence against women, defend the rights and dignity of those trapped in poverty, regulate the global arms trade, and abolish the death penalty. AI has more than 2.8 million members and supporters in more than 150 countries and regions. Established in 1961.

Volunteer Opportunities

Becoming a member of AI gains you entry into local activist volunteer groups. Groups may work on freeing prisoners of conscience, economic justice, or the abolition of the death penalty, as well as other human rights campaigns. They also fundraise and organize meetings with members of congress. Volunteering in one of AI's local offices as an activist is also an option. Visit www.amnestyusa.org to search for groups or opportunities in your area or to view the AI activist toolkit.

Contact Information

5 Penn Plaza,16th floor
New York, NY 10001
(212) 807-8400

www.amnesty.org
admin-us@aiusa.org

★

Name: Becky Farrar

Location: Arlington, VA

Organization: Amnesty International

Can you describe what you do as a volunteer for Amnesty International?

I wear different hats with Amnesty International. I have a fantastic volunteer position as a Legislative Coordinator (LC). There are LCs around the country who work with Amnesty members and activists on lobbying members of Congress on human rights issues. I was the LC for Florida during law school, and have been LC for DC since I moved to DC last summer. I particularly enjoy leading lobbying trainings. I am also a member of a local Amnesty group and we are involved in several exciting projects. These have included taking part in rallies; hosting evening events and happy hours that raise awareness (and some funds); tabling at Eastern Market (to explain specific human rights abuses); and volunteering at arts festivals. And finally, I sit on one of the strategic member committees, which has allowed me to participate in some of the strategic planning for our Demand Dignity campaign.

So you don't work in an Amnesty office?

Much of my volunteer work is done from my home (sending emails, making phone calls) but I also attend meetings as a member of a local Amnesty group, and with other members on projects I am working on. I like the combination of things I can do from home and being in meetings and group gatherings.

How did you learn about this opportunity?

I decided to go to law school after several years in the work force, in part because I wanted to figure out how to make a bigger difference in the world on a global level. Years before, while living in Canada, I wrote letters on prisoners of conscience as an Amnesty member. But my law school didn't have an Amnesty chapter. Two of my fellow law students and I started one and I served as president. I became LC for Florida when my friend from the chapter graduated.

What appealed to you about volunteering with Amnesty?

I wanted to learn more about human rights from a credible source (and I knew Amnesty was that), and I wanted to give others the same information and awareness, and encourage them to get involved in human rights work.

What impact has volunteering made on your life?

It's important for me as a volunteer to feel passionate about what I'm working on, and it's also important to feel that what I give is valued and appreciated. Volunteering with Amnesty fulfills both of those needs. My personal goal is to do something for human rights every day, and with my Amnesty activities, that hasn't been a problem. The other key aspect in my volunteering is feeling appreciated. I have been very fortunate to work with staffers at Amnesty who have valued my contributions and that's been great.

Another huge joy for me is harder to put into words. I feel "akin" to the people involved in Amnesty. I've described that to people in the past by saying "This is my tribe." I feel that with my fellow LCs, and I feel it when I attend Amnesty meetings, conferences, and gatherings and meet other Amnesty members from around the country. It means I feel a part of a larger group—part of a community—that I identify with. That's very important to me as well.

What advice would you give to someone who wanted to volunteer in their community?

First, do it! Pick something you care about, something you really love or are passionate about, or something you think would be fun. Make sure there's an intrinsic joy in it—that's what keeps you going.

And then, research—figure out who does the kind of thing you want to do and do some research on the group itself. Make sure you're comfortable with what they do and how they operate, and see if they have a good opportunity for you. There's some chemistry involved so if you don't feel comfortable, look for another group. Every nonprofit organization can use help and needs talented and passionate volunteers!

CAMPUS PROGRESS

Campus Progress is a national organization that works with and for young people to promote progressive solutions to key political and social challenges. Through programs in activism, journalism, and events, Campus Progress engages a diverse group of young people nationwide, inspires them to embrace progressive values, provides them with essential trainings, and helps them to make their voices heard—and to push policy outcomes in a strongly progressive direction.

Volunteer Opportunities

The organization's campus and local activism work is done through the action alliance program. Action alliances consist of grants or help in executing an activism campaign, or both. Visit the website to apply for a grant (recipients receive up to $1,500 a year to help with websites, flyers, and other materials), or to apply for a progressive partnership (Campus Progress provides guidance, networking, strategic planning, and training for youth-led efforts). Campus Progress's national advocacy team works in Washington, D.C., and with young people around the country to promote and protect progressive solutions to key national policy challenges. The organization also offers funding, training and editorial guidance to a diverse network of print, online, and broadcast media on college campuses across the country. Interested individuals can also write for CP.org (stipends are provided) or sign petitions and contact public officials through the Campus Progress website. Contact the organization for more information on these opportunities.

Contact Information

Campus Progress
Center for American Progress
1333 H Street, NW 10th Floor
Washington, DC 20005

(202) 682-1611
www.campusprogress.com
campus@campusprogress.com

---★---

DEMOCRACY MATTERS

Democracy Matters, was founded in 2001 by NBA basketball player, poet, and activist Adonal Foyle and his parents, Joan and Jay Mandle, both of whom are Colgate University professors and life-long organizers. Its mission is to strengthen democracy by: training young people how to be effective grass-roots organizers and advocates, and supporting public financing of election campaigns ("fair elections") and other pro-democracy reforms. Democracy Matters is a non-partisan campus-based national student organization in partnership with Common Cause. Offering paid internships to undergraduates and affiliate internships to high school students, Democracy Matters mentors the next generation of leaders dedicated to strengthening democracy.

Volunteer Opportunities

Volunteers serve as liaisons between the organization and their own college campuses. Internships are also offered to undergraduates to do political organizing on their campuses.

In addition, interested individuals can download resources from the Democracy Matters website to start a campus action campaign. www.democracymatters.org also posts petitions and letters to local representatives that can be signed.

Contact Information

P.O. Box 157
Hamilton, NY 13346

(315) 824-4306
www.democracymatters.org

--------------------------------★--------------------------------

ENERGY ACTION COALITION

Energy Action Coalition is a coalition of 50 youth-led environmental and social justice groups working together to build the youth clean energy and climate movement.

Working with hundreds of campus and youth groups, dozens of youth networks, and hundreds of thousands of young people, Energy Action Coalition and its partners have united a burgeoning movement behind winning local victories and coordinating on state, regional, and national levels in the United States and Canada.

Volunteer Opportunities

There are a wide range of activity engagements through the coalition's partner organizations. Visit the Energy Action Coalition website to search the list of organizations.

Contact Information

1850 M St, Suite 1150
Washington, D.C. 20036
(202) 631-1992

www.energyactioncoalition.org
Theteam@energyaction.net

--------------------------------★--------------------------------

IDEALIST.ORG

Idealist is a project of Action Without Borders, a nonprofit organization founded in 1995 with offices in the United States and Argentina. Idealist is an interactive site where people and organizations can exchange resources and ideas and locate opportunities and supporters.

Volunteer Opportunities

Idealist.org offers an extensive search to help connect individuals with programs of interest.

Contact Information

New York City:
302 Fifth Avenue, 11th Floor
New York, NY 10001

Portland, OR:
1220 SW Morrison, 10th Floor
Portland, OR 97205
(503) 227-0803
www.idealist.org

NATIONAL STUDENT CAMPAIGN AGAINST HUNGER AND HOMELESSNESS

The Campaign is committed to ending hunger and homelessness in America by educating, engaging, and training students to directly meet individuals' immediate needs while advocating for long-term systemic solutions.

Volunteer Opportunities

Students who join the Campaign's network receive information on hunger and homeless issues and updates about upcoming events. The Campaign also provides advice and resources for students to help them organize on campus. Visit the organization's website to sign up or to view posted events.

Contact Information

National Organizing Office:
407 S. Dearborn, Suite 701
Chicago, IL 60605

(312) 291-0349 x302
www.Studentsagainsthunger.org
info@studentsagainsthunger.org

OXFAM AMERICA

An affiliate of Oxfam International, Oxfam America is a relief and development organization that strives to create lasting solutions to poverty, hunger, and injustice. Current campaigns focus on helping poor communities who are vulnerable to climate change and unfair practices by international oil, gas, and mining companies, and to ensuring US foreign aid is effective in fighting global poverty. Oxfam America also provides emergency relief around the world and helps communities rebuild and establish lasting change. Established in 1970.

Volunteer Opportunities

Founded by a group of volunteers in response to a humanitarian crisis, Oxfam America offers a long list of opportunities for interested volunteers. One way to get involved is by joining the Oxfam Action Corps. Volunteers work to improve national legislation and to fight poverty on a local level by collecting signatures, organizing petition drives, planning events, or joining a delegation to a lawmaker's local office. Other opportunities are regularly posted on the organization's website. To apply, Oxfam America requests a cover letter and resume emailed to internsandvolunteers@oxfamamerica.org with the name of the desired position in the subject line.

Contact Information

Headquarters: 26 Causeway St., 5th Floor
Boston, MA 02114-2206

(800) 77-OXFAM or (800)-776-9326
www.oxfamamerica.org

★

SIERRA STUDENT COALITION (SSC)

The Sierra Student Coalition (SSC) is a broad network of high school and college-aged youth from across the country working to protect the environment. The SSC is the youth-led chapter of the Sierra Club, the nation's oldest and largest grassroots environmental organization. The mission of the SSC is to "train, empower, and organize youth to run effective campaigns that result in tangible environmental victories and that develop leaders for the environmental movement."

Volunteer Opportunities

Check out the SSC website to sign up for the organization's monthly newsletter, SSC Update, which provides details on SSC campaigns and highlights. Interested individuals can also join the SSC Energy Forum to receive e-mails about energy campaigns and new opportunities and events.

In addition, the website provides information on becoming a campus organizer or community coordinator, registering a group as an SSC affiliate, and joining one the organization's national committees. Internships are also available.

Contact Information
www.ssc.sierraclub.org
info@ssc.org

---★---

STUDENT COALITION FOR ACTION ON LITERACY EDUCATION (SCALE)

SCALE supports campus-based literacy programs locally, statewide, and nationally through its Literacy Action Networks. In these programs, college students serve as literacy tutors or teachers in their community. It works with all types of program models, including America Reads, Family Literacy, Youth Literacy and Mentoring, and GED Preparation. The college students serving in these programs include volunteer/paid tutors or coordinators, AmeriCorps members, VISTA members, and service-learning students.

Volunteer Opportunities

Volunteers can get involved through the North Carolina Literacy Corps (a state AmeriCorps program). Through the Corps, Volunteers work for a one-year term beginning August 1 and concluding on July 31. They are placed in community and college-based literacy programs where they provide tutoring, train other volunteers to become tutors, and, depending on experience, work in program management. Part-time (900 hours) and full-time (1700 hours) participants receive a living allowance. Training is provided.

Volunteers can also get involved through Project Literacy, a program that connects students from the University of North Carolina with community based literacy organizations, or find opportunities through SCALE's partner organizations.

Contact Information

101 E. Weaver Street, Carr Mill Mall | (919) 962-1542
Suite 201 | www.readwriteact.org
Carrboro, NC 27510 | scale@unc.edu

---★---

STUDENT ENVIRONMENTAL ACTION COALITION (SEAC)

SEAC is a student and youth run national network of progressive organizations and individuals whose aim is to uproot environmental injustices through action and education. It defines the environment to include the physical, economic, political, and cultural conditions in which we live. By challenging the power structure which threatens these conditions, students in SEAC work to create progressive social change on both the local and global levels.

Volunteer Opportunities

Joining SEAC puts you in contact with SEAC resources and adds you to the organization's activist lists. Local groups can become affiliated with SEAC and individuals can become regional coordinators (regional coordinators are point people for their state or region. They are regularly communicating with the SEAC National Office as well as participating in and encouraging strategy and action among youth in their region) or chapter point people (each SEAC Chapter is encouraged to have a point person who keeps in touch regularly with SEAC National and learns strategy and skill for their group).

Internships are available in fundraising and graphic design. One can also become a SEAC blog contributor. Visit the organization's website to register.

Contact Information

2206 Washington Street E
Charleston WV 25311

(304) 414-0143
www.seac.org

STUDENT PUBLIC INTEREST RESEARCH GROUPS (PIRGS)

The PIRGs are independent statewide student organizations that work on issues like environmental protection, consumer protection, and hunger and homelessness.

Volunteer Opportunities

You can get involved with a variety of programs, including community service events, environmental campaigns, voter registration drives and local research projects. Visit the organization's website to complete a volunteer form. The website also discusses internships and features an activist toolkit for download.

Contact Information

407 S. Dearborn, Suite 701
Chicago, IL 60605
(312) 291-0349

www.studentpirgs.org
info@studentpirgs.org

UNITED STUDENTS AGAINST SWEATSHOPS (USAS)

United Students Against Sweatshops is a grassroots organization of youth and students who fight for the rights of working people, particularly campus workers and garment workers who make collegiate licensed apparel. USAS organizes campaigns protecting the right of workers to form unions, stopping tuition hikes, advocating for workers in higher education and in garment factories. Another focus of theirs, the Sweat-Free Campus Campaign, forces schools to require basic workers rights of corporations producing collegiate apparel.

Volunteer Opportunities

Opportunities are available at USAS's national office in D.C. Tasks vary from research to helping keep accounting records to calling supporters for donations. There are no time commitments or age restrictions.

Contact Information

Headquarters: 1150 17th Street NW, Washington, DC 20036 (202) NO-SWEAT

www.usas.org
staff@usas.org

UNITED STATES STUDENT ASSOCIATION (USSA)/ UNITED STATES STUDENT ASSOCIATION FOUNDATION (USSF)

The United States Student Association, the country's oldest, largest, and most inclusive national student-led organization, develops current and future leaders and amplifies the student voice at the local, state, and national levels by mobilizing grassroots power to win concrete victories on student issues.

The United States Student Association Foundation ensures the pipeline of effective student leadership by facilitating education, training and other development opportunities at national, state, and local levels in advocating for issues that affect students.

Volunteer Opportunities

USSA offers several internships each year that primarily focus on one of its two yearly conferences. USSA also helps coordinate student voter coalitions, which are groups of students who work on non-partisan get-out-the-vote efforts in a volunteer capacity on college campuses.

Contact Information

1211 Connecticut Ave., NW, Suite 406
Washington, DC 20036

(202) 640-6570
www.usstudents.org
ussa@usstudents.org

GENERAL RESOURCE ORGANIZATIONS

AMERICA'S PROMISE ALLIANCE

Founded in 1997 with General Colin Powell as Chairman and chaired today by Alma Powell, America's Promise Alliance is a cross-sector partnership of more than 300 corporations, nonprofits, faith-based organizations and advocacy groups that are passionate about improving lives and changing outcomes for children. The Alliance has made a top priority of ensuring that all young people graduate from high school ready for college, work and life. Its work involves raising awareness, encouraging action and engaging in advocacy to provide children the key supports the Alliance calls the Five Promises: Caring adults, Safe Places, A Healthy Start, An Effective Education and Opportunities to Help Others.

Volunteer Opportunities

America's Promise Alliance encourages interested individuals to visit its website to view the full list of Alliance Partners (corporations, nonprofit service organizations, foundations, policymakers, advocacy organizations, and faith groups) and contact those of interest to learn of their volunteer opportunities.

The Alliance also offers unpaid internships year-round.

Contact Information

1110 Vermont Avenue, N.W., Suite 900
Washington, DC 20005

(202) 657-0600
www.americaspromise.org

CORPORATION FOR NATIONAL & COMMUNITY SERVICE (CNS)

The Corporation is the nation's largest grantmaker supporting service and volunteering. Through its Senior Corps, AmeriCorps, and Learn and Serve America programs, it provides opportunities for Americans of all ages and backgrounds to express their patriotism while addressing critical community needs.

MAKE A DIFFERENCE

Volunteer Opportunities

Visit the CNS website to search for opportunities in your area.

See also "AmeriCorp" (p. TK) and "Volunteers In Service To America" (pg. TK) in Chapter TK.

Contact Information

1201 New York Avenue, NW
Washington, DC 20525
(202) 606-5000 or TTY: (202) 606-3472

www.nationalservice.org
info@cns.gov

★

EARTHSHARE

Founded by its member charities in 1988, EarthShare is an opportunity for employees and workplaces to support hundreds of environmental charities through workplace giving campaigns. A workplace giving campaign is an annual, employer-sponsored program that lets employees contribute a few dollars per paycheck as their charitable donation.

Volunteer Opportunities

EarthShare's website lists volunteer and event opportunities offered by EarthShare member charities and state affiliates across the country. It also provides a list of year-round volunteer opportunities offered by its members.

Contact Information

7735 Old Georgetown Road, Suite 900
Bethesda, MD 20814
(800) 875-3863 or (240) 333-0300

www.earthshare.org
info@earthshare.org

★

NETWORK FOR GOOD

Network for Good helps nonprofits (NPOs) raise money on their own websites and on social networks with free and low-cost fundraising tools. It also enables giving to any charity registered in the US at www.networkforgood.org, through fundraising widgets on social networks, and via partners' websites. Its "SixDegress.org" initiative links people with celebrity philanthropists.

Volunteer Opportunities

At www.networkforgood.org users can research any charity and search from among more than 40,000 volunteer opportunities. Individuals can also search for volunteer opportunities through Network for Good's state Volunteer Network sites: California, Louisiana and New York.

Contact Information

7920 Norfolk Avenue, Suite 520
Bethesda, MD 20814

(888) 284-7978
www.networkforgood.org

---★---

OPPORTUNITY KNOCKS

Opportunity Knocks is a national online job site, HR resource and career development destination focused exclusively on the nonprofit community. It is committed to lead and support efforts that help further nonprofit careers and promote a robust workforce that enables organizations to complete their missions.

Contact Information

50 Hurt Plaza, Suite 845
Atlanta, Georgia 30303
888-OKNOCKS

www.opportunityknocks.org
support@opportunityknocks.org

---★---

POINTS OF LIGHT INSTITUTE AND HANDSON NETWORK

Points of Light Institute inspires, equips and mobilizes people to take action that changes the world. The Institute has a global focus to redefine volunteerism and civic engagement for the 21st century, putting people at the center of community problem solving. It is organized to innovate, incubate and activate new ideas that help people act upon their power to make a difference. Points of Light Institute operates three business units that share its mission: HandsOn Network, MissionFish and the Civic Incubator.

HandsOn Network, the volunteer-focused arm of Points of Light Institute, is the largest volunteer network in the nation and includes more than 250 HandsOn Action Centers in 16 countries. HandsOn includes a powerful network of more than 70,000 corporate, faith and nonprofit organizations that are answering the call to serve and creating meaningful change in their communities. Annually, the network delivers approximately 30 million hours of volunteer service valued at about $600 million.

Volunteer Opportunities

The HandsOn Network action centers connect volunteers with projects in their geographical areas. Visit www.handsonnetwork.org to search opportunities in your area or to find a local HandsOn Action Center.

MAKE A DIFFERENCE

Contact Information

Atlanta Office, Headquarters:	**Washington, D.C. Office:**
600 Means Street, Suite 210	1875 K St NW 5th Floor
Atlanta, GA 30318	Washington, DC 20006
(404) 979-2900	Volunteer Info: 1-800-Volunteer

PROGRESSNOW

Since 2003, ProgressNow has been developing its network of state partner organizations to fill a unique and critical role in the progressive infrastructure of key states. ProgressNow state partners serve as non-stop, multi-issue advocacy organizations. Year-round, ProgressNow promotes progressive ideas and causes with creative earned media strategies, targeted email campaigns, and cutting-edge new media. Working with its allies, the organization has significantly improved the communications effort of the entire progressive community in its states.

Volunteer Opportunities

ProgressNow is located in about 13 states. To get involved, visit www.progressnow.org and find the link to your state to view action items.

Contact Information

1536 Wynkoop St., Suite 203
Denver, CO 80202
(303) 991-1900

www.progressnow.org
info@progressnow.org

PROGRESSIVE FUTURE

Progressive Future promotes progressive values through grassroots action. It is a nonprofit organization advocating for core progressive principles such as community, fairness, and security; and working for progress on critical issues such as providing health care for all Americans, promoting a clean energy economy, and ending the war in Iraq.

Volunteer Opportunities

Progressive Future lists actions, such as contacting local representatives, on its website.

Contact Information

218 D Street SE, Suite 250
Washington, DC 20003
(202) 543-3332

www.progressivefuture.org
info@progressivefuture.org

VOLUNTEERMATCH

VolunteerMatch strengthens communities by making it easier for good people and good causes to connect. The organization offers a variety of online services to support a community of nonprofit, volunteer and business leaders committed to civic engagement. Its popular service, www.volunteermatch.org, welcomes millions of visitors a year and has become the preferred internet recruiting tool for more than 73,000 nonprofit organizations.

Volunteer Opportunities

The organization is best-known for its public web site, www.volunteermatch.org, which makes it possible for volunteers to search from a variety of volunteer roles and projects based on skills, cause, time commitment, and other requirements. VolunteerMatch also has opportunities available in its San Francisco office, which are posted in the organization's own account on its website.

Contact Information

717 California St., Second Floor
San Francisco, CA 94108

(415) 241-6868
www.volunteermatch.org

★

FAITH-BASED ORGANIZATIONS

AMERICAN JEWISH CONGRESS (AJC)

The American Jewish Congress is an association of Jewish Americans organized to defend Jewish interests at home and abroad through public policy advocacy—using diplomacy, legislation, and the courts. Established in 1918.

Volunteer Opportunities

Contact the organization for details.

Contact Information

National Headquarters: 115 East 57 Street, Suite 11
New York, NY 10022

(212) 879-4500
www.ajcongress.org
contact@ajcongress.org

---★---

ASSOCIATION OF JEWISH FAMILY AND CHILDREN'S AGENCIES (AJFCA)

AJFCA is a membership organization of over 130 Jewish Family and Children's Agencies, and specialized Jewish human service agencies, in the United States and Canada. Member JF&CS agencies provide social services to children, adults and the elderly in the Jewish and general community. Tracing their roots back to the 19th century, JF&CS agencies began by assisting Jewish refugees and immigrants, orphans, and the poor and needy. Today, JF&CS agencies continue to provide preventative as well as social services to people of all ages and to those with special needs.

Volunteer Opportunities

Contact the organization for more information.

Contact Information

5750 Park Heights Avenue
Baltimore, MD 21215

(800) 634-7346
www.ajfca.org

---★---

CATHOLIC CAMPAIGN FOR HUMAN DEVELOPMENT

The Catholic Campaign for Human Development is the domestic anti-poverty, social justice program of the U.S. Catholic bishops. Its mission is to address the root causes of poverty in America through promotion and support of community-controlled, self-help organizations and through transformative education. Founded in 1969.

Volunteer Opportunities

Visit the website to learn about supporting the campaign's mission.

Contact Information

3211 Fourth St. NE
Washington DC 20017
(202) 541-3210

www.usccb.org/cchd/
cchdpromo@usccb.org

CATHOLIC NETWORK OF VOLUNTEER SERVICE (CNVS)

Catholic Network of Volunteer Service (CNVS), established in 1963, is a non-profit membership organization of 200 domestic and international volunteer and lay mission programs. Currently, more than 10,000 volunteers and lay missioners serve in these programs throughout the U.S. and in 108 other countries.

CNVS publishes and distributes RESPONSE, a comprehensive handbook of lay mission volunteer opportunities. The network also provides its member programs with recruitment services, training and technical assistance resources including its National Conference, Formation Workshops, Renewal Workshops, and its web based Resource Library.

Volunteer Opportunities

Catholic and Christian volunteer programs can be found by using the CNVS RESPONSE directory. It allows individuals to search all volunteer opportunities offered by CNVS's 200 member programs by type of placement; region, state, or country; length of service; financial arrangements; living arrangements; size of program; and participation in the AmeriCorps Education Awards Program (AEAP).

CNVS also seeks Volunteer Associates to provide administrative and project support in its national office in Takoma Park, Maryland. Long-term and short-term opportunities are available annually to help with team projects, assist in various administrative tasks, maintain databases and resource materials, support projects, and assist with mailings, writing reports and record-keeping. Applicants must be at least 21 years old, have some understanding of mission and role of the laity, and a commitment to Christian values. Desirable qualities include excellent interpersonal, organizational, computer and writing skills, ability to work independently and previous volunteer experience. Housing and stipend is available for year-long volunteers and handled on a case-by-case basis for short-term volunteers. Applicants should contact Jim Lindsay at jlindsay@cnvs.org for more information.

Contact Information

6930 Carroll Avenue, Suite 820
Takoma Park, MD 20912-4423
(301) 270-0900 or (800) 543-5046

www.cnvs.org
cnvsinfo@cnvs.org

★

CATHOLIC WORKER MOVEMENT

The Catholic Worker Movement began on May 1, 1933, when a journalist named Dorothy Day and a philosopher named Peter Maurin teamed up to publish and distribute a newspaper called "The Catholic Worker." This radical paper promoted the biblical promise of justice and mercy.

Grounded in a firm belief in the God-given dignity of every human person, their movement was committed to nonviolence, voluntary poverty, and the Works of Mercy as a way of life. It wasn't long before Dorothy and Peter were putting their beliefs into action, opening a "house of hospitality" where the homeless, the hungry, and the forsaken would always be welcome.

Over many decades the movement has protested injustice, war, and violence of all forms. Today there are some 185 Catholic Worker communities in the United States.

Volunteer Opportunities

All Catholic Worker communities welcome volunteers to work in many capacities, including helping with gardening, letter-writing, and bookkeeping. Contact a local community for details or visit www.catholicworker.org to learn of specific opportunities.

Contact Information

www.catholicworker.org lists communities by state.

★

CENTER FOR COMMUNITY ACTION FOR B'NAI B'RITH INTERNATIONAL

The B'nai B'rith International (BBI) Center for Community Action (CCA) helps BBI serve individual Jewish communities and the world, providing disaster relief and services to those in need, promoting respect for others and celebrating diversity, and offering a helping hand. Established in 1843.

Volunteer Opportunities

The center provides activities (such as food distributions for Chanukah and Passover) for individuals who wish to get involved in programs that assist those-in-need. Activities are locally based in communities across the U.S. and the world. Many of the programs are part of an annual calendar and are coordinated by local chair people who also run the programs. Other examples of possible opportunities include working with a daily food rescue program in Los Angeles, CA or participating in Christmas Eve or Christmas Day hospital visits. The center also provides opportunities through some of its partnerships with other organizations. For more information about getting involved with B'nai B'rith programs, email cca@bnaibrith.org or call (212) 490-3290.

Contact Information

Headquarters: B'nai B'rith
International
2020 K Street, NW, 7th Floor
Washington, DC 20006
(202) 857-6600 or (888) 388-4224
www.bnaibrith.org

Center for Community Action:
(212) 490-3290
www.bnaibrith.org/centers/cca.cfm
cca@bnaibrith.org

---★---

CHRISTIAN RELIEF SERVICES (CRS)

Incorporated in 1985, Christian Relief Services was founded on the belief that community partnerships are the best way to solve problems related to poverty, both here in the United States and around the world. The Mission of Christian Relief Services is to work through partnerships and in collaboration with grassroots charitable organizations to connect the vast resources of the United States with communities in need to enable the people of these communities to help themselves.

Volunteer Opportunities

Opportunities are available on Indian reservations in South Dakota and Montana, working with Native American youth. CRS asks volunteers for a three to four week commitment and housing is provided.

Volunteers can also perform general clerical work in the CRS office in Alexandria, VA.

Contact Information

2550 Huntington Avenue, Suite 200
Alexandria, VA 22303
(703) 317-9086 or (800) 33-RELIEF

www.christianrelief.org
info@christianrelief.org

★

CITYTEAM MINISTRIES

CityTeam Ministries is a non-profit organization serving the poor and homeless in San Jose, San Francisco, Oakland, Portland, Philadelphia, and actively training church planters and planting churches in 82 other countries around the world. Since 1957, CityTeam has provided life-saving food, shelter, clothing, recovery programs, youth outreach, camp for at-risk inner city kids, discipleship and other essential care 365 days a year.

Volunteer Opportunities

Volunteers are vital to the heartbeat of CityTeam Ministries. Visit the organization's website to learn of volunteer events and to find contact information for volunteer coordinators in CityTeam Ministries' offices.

Contact Information

Headquarters: 2304 Zanker Road
San Jose, CA 95131
(408) 232-5600

www.cityteam.org
sanjose@cityteam.org or info@
cityteam.org

★

CRISTA MINISTRIES

CRISTA describes its mission as "to love God by serving people—meeting practical and spiritual needs —so that those we minister to will be built up in love, united in faith and maturing in Christ."

Volunteer Opportunities

There are many opportunities for volunteers. Ministries include senior living, world concern, Seattle Urban Academy, broadcasting, veterinary missions, CRISTA camps, and King's Schools. Visit the organization's website or contact CRISTA for details.

Contact Information

19303 Fremont Avenue N
Seattle, WA 98133
(206) 546-7200

www.crista.org
info@crista.net

★

FELLOWSHIP OF RECONCILIATION (FOR)

The FOR seeks the company of people of faith who will respond to conflict nonviolently, searching for reconciliation through compassionate action. Its campaigns include abolishing nuclear weapons, ending U.S. Military aid in Colombia, opposing any future military drafts, and promoting nonviolence in Iran.

Volunteer Opportunities

FOR has several dozen local chapters and affiliates across North America, so one way to become active in FOR's work is by participating in those local expressions of activism. FOR also coordinates campaigns on various issues toward peace, justice, human rights, and interfaith engagement, and regularly invite all of its members and supporters to participate.

Contact Information

521 N. Broadway
Nyack, New York 10960

(845) 358-4601
www.forusa.org

GENERAL BOARD OF CHURCH AND SOCIETY, THE UNITED METHODIST CHURCH (GBCS)

The General Board of Church and Society (GBCS) is one of four international general program boards of The United Methodist Church. The General Board is defined by its five areas of ministry: public witness and advocacy, administration, ministry of resourcing congregational life, United Nations ministry, and communications.

Volunteer Opportunities

Contact the organization for details.

Contact Information

100 Maryland Ave, NE
Washington, D.C. 20002

(202) 488-5600
www.umc-gbcs.org

LUTHERAN SERVICES IN AMERICA (LSA)

Lutheran Services in America creates opportunities with people in thousands of communities throughout the United States and the Caribbean as an alliance of the Evangelical Lutheran Church in America, The Lutheran Church--Missouri Synod, and their over 300 health and human service organizations.

Working neighbor to neighbor through services in health care, aging and disability supports, community development, housing, and child and family strengthening, these organizations together touch the lives of one in 50 Americans each year and have aggregated annual incomes over $16.6 billion.

Volunteer Opportunities

LSA seeks people who want to be partners in supporting social ministry and social change, people who can help create relationships, work groups, think tanks, and innovation sessions with philanthropists, universities, corporations, and social entrepreneurs. It looks for volunteers to help it leverage the Lutheran social ministry network to create better communities and more opportunities for all people. If you are interested in how your experience and interests can intersect with those of Lutheran social ministry at the national level, contact Cynthia Osborne at cosborne@lutheranservices.org or (410) 230-3546.

Individuals can also volunteer with one of LSA's member organizations. Volunteers have many opportunities to work with member organizations, from working with clients to offering management expertise or support behind the scenes. Similarly, LSA's denominational members, the Evangelical Lutheran Church in America and The Lutheran Church-Missouri Synod, have multiple volunteer options. Visit LSA's website for more information.

Contact Information

National headquarters: 700 Light Street
Baltimore, MD 21230-3850

(800) 664-3848
www.lutheranservices.org
lsa@lutheranservices.org

MISSIONS DOOR

Missions Door exists to assist local churches and Christ followers in their efforts to evangelize, disciple and plant churches around the world.

Volunteer Opportunities

For short-term or long-term mission work around the world, visit Missions Door website to complete an online form.

Contact Information

2530 Washington Street
Denver, CO 80205-3142
(303) 308-1818

www.missionsdoor.org
info@missionsdoor.org
NATIONAL BENEVOLENT

ASSOCIATION OF THE CHRISTIAN CHURCH (NBA)/ DISCIPLES BENEVOLENT SERVICES (DBS)

NBA—which is now doing business as Disciples Benevolent Services (DBS), but holds onto NBA as its legal name—is a nonprofit organization headquartered in the St. Louis suburb of Maryland Heights, Missouri. The organization has programs and facilities in nine states. Included in its services are chaplaincy care ministry for residents of older adult facilities as well as alcohol and drug treatment facilities; residential facilities and programs for at-risk children and youth; family unification programs; and community based supportive-living programs for developmentally disabled adults.

Volunteer Opportunities

Opportunities vary by location. The organization asks that interested individuals email the headquarters office to be put in contact with a representative at the appropriate location.

Contact Information

149 Weldon Parkway, Suite 115
Maryland Heights, MO 63043-3103
(314) 993-9000

www.nbacares.org
grp-nba@nbacares.org

PRESBYTERIAN HUNGER PROGRAM (PHP)

The Presbyterian Hunger Program is a ministry of the Presbyterian Church working with congregations and partners around the globe to alleviate hunger and eliminate its causes. To achieve this mission of the church, PHP provides grants to programs addressing hunger and its causes in the United States and around the world. It also provides special educational, mission and action programs and campaigns for Presbyterians.

Volunteer Opportunities

One way of offering volunteer service to the hunger program is through creative events that raise funds for PHP that in turn allow the organization to give more grants to organizations doing direct food relief. A list of our grantees from 2008 and 2009 (for 2010 work) are listed here. http://gamc.pcusa.org/ministries/hunger/grants/. Contacting the local congregation or a grantee in their area would be a good way of making contact.

In addition, PCP encourages individuals to get involved with local bodies doing work surrounding hunger issues, such as local presbytery hunger committees. Also through its work with the Campaign for Fair Food there are opportunities to support the work of some of PCP's partners like the CIW. Its international work is done through a program called Joining Hands and those networks have opportunities to get connected locally and internationally. Visit http://gamc.pcusa.org/ministries/fairfood/ to learn more about the work PHP does with the Campaign for Fair Food and CIW. Contact the organization for further details.

Contact Information

100 Witherspoon Street
Louisville, KY 40202

http://archive.pcusa.org/hunger/

★

SOJOURNERS

Sojourners—publisher of a monthly magazine of the same name—is a voice and vision for social change. Founded in 1971 as a faith-based organization, Sojourners provides an alternative perspective on faith, politics, and culture through its magazine, Web site, e-mail services, media commentaries, and public events. It nurtures community by bringing together people from the various traditions and streams of the church and also hosts an annual program of voluntary service.

Volunteer Opportunities

Sojourners strives to provide an internship program of Christian discipleship, with a focus on life and faith, prayer and formation, and work and mission.

Life and Faith: Participants live together as a community in Washington, D.C. Together, the interns design the structures for maintaining their shared household. Through weekly house meetings, the interns worship, conduct business, pray, and experience city life as a community.

Prayer and Formation: Interns receive a structured curriculum and monthly educational seminars on a wide range of topics designed to provoke and challenge their perspectives on personal and social issues of faith. Interns are matched with mentors to provide spiritual and vocational guidance during their year-long experience. Time for personal reflection, contemplation, and community building is offered at retreats given throughout the year.

Work and Mission: Participants develop skills by working full-time in the ministry of Sojourners. Skilled staff members challenge interns as supervisors in a variety of departments including editorial, marketing and circulation and development. Also, volunteer opportunities are encouraged to enhance interns' experience of Washington D.C.'s diverse activities and culture.

The program is open to anyone 21 years or older who is single or married without dependents. Room, board, health insurance, city transportation, and a $100 monthly stipend for clothing, travel, and recreation are provided. Sojourners interns commit themselves to one year of service, starting in early September and ending in mid-August the following year.

In addition, actions (such as signing petitions) are posted on the website.

Contact Information
3333 14th St. N.W., Suite 200
Washington, D.C. 20010
(202) 328-8842 or (800) 714-7474

www.sojo.net
sojourners@sojo.net

UNITARIAN UNIVERSALIST ASSOCIATION (UUA)

The Unitarian Universalist Association (UUA) is a religious organization that combines two traditions: the Universalists, who organized in 1793, and the Unitarians, who organized in 1825. They consolidated into the UUA in 1961. Unitarian Universalism is a liberal religion with Jewish-Christian roots. It has no creed. Amongst other things, Unitarian Universalists have been at the forefront of the same-sex marriage debates, advocating for the right for each person to marry the partner of his or her choice.

Volunteer Opportunities
Congregations are self-governing and volunteer opportunities are based on the interests and needs of local chapters. Visit the UUA website to find local congregations to contact for more information.

Contact Information
25 Beacon Street
Boston, MA 02108
(617) 742-2100

www.uua.org
info@uua.org

UNITARIAN UNIVERSALIST SERVICE COMMITTEE (UUSC)

UUSC, the activist arm of the Unitarian Universalist church, is a nonsectarian organization that advances human rights and social justice in the United States and around the world. Through a combination of advocacy, education, and partnerships with grassroots organizations, UUSC promotes economic rights, advances environmental justice, defends civil liberties, and preserves the rights of people in times of humanitarian crisis. It also engage local communities through two experiential-learning programs, JustWorks and JustJourneys, which introduce participants to the work of its domestic and overseas partners — who are often on the front lines of addressing social-justice issues.

Volunteer Opportunities

The most popular way for individuals to engage with UUSC's work is through its experiential learning, or JustWorks, program. Through JustWorks camps, participants work directly with people in local communities on direct-service projects, learning about human-rights issues firsthand.

These camps included projects such as helping to rebuild the homes and lives of survivors of the 2005 Gulf Coast hurricanes, rebuilding African-American churches in the South that were destroyed by racially motivated arson, renovating schools and community facilities on Native -American reservations, and working on local service projects in migrant farmworker communities.

JustWorks camps generally are short-term (usually weeklong) projects that help participants examine and understand the root causes and damaging effects of injustice, with an eye to promoting intercultural understanding. Participants are taught advocacy skills for addressing issues of poverty, discrimination, and racism in their own communities.

In addition to JustWorks camps, UUSC has a limited number of opportunities for volunteers interested in its human-rights mission, including those who have expertise in the organization's specific program focus areas. These individuals contribute their time and efforts to helping UUSC in many valuable ways, from basic data entry to research and analysis of human-rights issues.

Individuals interested in volunteering their time and skills to further UUSC's mission are invited to e-mail employment@uusc.org with a resume and a short description of one's interests and availability.

Contact Information

National **Headquarters:** 689
   Massachusetts Avenue
Cambridge, MA 02139-3302

(617) 868-6600 or (800) 388-3920
www.uusc.org

★

POLICY AND ISSUES ANALYSIS ORGANIZATIONS

ALLIANCE FOR RETIRED AMERICANS

The mission of the Alliance for Retired Americans is to ensure social and economic justice and full civil rights for all citizens so that they may enjoy lives of dignity, personal and family fulfillment and security. The Alliance believes that all older and retired persons have a responsibility to strive to create a society that incorporates these goals and rights and that retirement provides them with opportunities to pursue new and expanded activities with their unions, civic organizations and their communities. Established in 2001.

Contact Information

815 16th Street, NW 4th floor
Washington, DC 20006

(202) 637-5399
www.retiredamericans.org

------------------------------------★------------------------------------

AMERICAN ASSOCIATION OF PEOPLE WITH DISABILITIES (AAPD)

The American Association of People with Disabilities (AAPD), the country's largest cross-disability membership organization, organizes the disability community to be a powerful voice for change – politically, economically, and socially. AAPD was founded in 1995 to help unite the diverse community of people with disabilities, including their family, friends and supporters, and to be a national voice for change in implementing the goals of the Americans with Disabilities Act (ADA).

Contact Information

1629 K Street NW, Suite 950
Washington, DC 20006

(202) 457-0046 (V/TTY) or
(800) 840-8844 (Toll Free V/TTY)

------------------------------------★------------------------------------

AMERICAN FEDERATION OF TEACHERS (AFT)

The American Federation of Teachers, an affiliate of the AFL-CIO, was founded in 1916 and represents nearly 3,000 local affiliates nationwide, 43 state affiliates and 1.5 million members.

Five divisions within the AFT represent the broad spectrum of the AFT's membership: pre-K through 12th-grade teachers; paraprofessionals and other school-related personnel; higher education faculty and professional staff; federal, state and local government employees; and nurses and other healthcare professionals. In addition, the AFT represents approximately 80,000 early childhood educators and nearly 250,000 retiree members.

The mission of the American Federation of Teachers includes improving the lives of its members and their families; giving voice to its members' legitimate professional, economic and social aspirations; bringing together all members to assist and support one another; and promoting democracy, human rights and freedom throughout the world.

Contact Information

555 New Jersey Ave., N.W.   (202) 879-4400
Washington, DC 20001   www.aft.org

---★---

AMERICAN PSYCHOLOGICAL ASSOCIATION (APA)

Based in Washington, DC, the American Psychological Association (APA) is a scientific and professional organization that represents psychology in the United States. With 150,000 members, APA is the largest association of psychologists worldwide. The mission of the APA is to advance the creation, communication and application of psychological knowledge to benefit society and improve people's lives. Established in 1892.

Contact Information

750 First Street, NE   (800) 374-2721 or (202) 336-5500
Washington, DC 20002-4242   www.apa.org

---★---

AMERICANS FOR FINANCIAL REFORM

Americans for Financial Reform is a coalition of more than 250 national, state and local consumer, labor, investor, civil rights, community, small business, and senior citizen organizations that have come together to spearhead a campaign for reform. Together, they are fighting for a banking and financial system based on accountability, fairness and security. The organizations that make up Americans for Financial Reform bring together expertise in policy, advocacy, mobilization, public outreach, media relations and legislative strategy.

Contact Information
1825 K Street NW, Suite 210   www.ourfinancialsecurity.org
Washington, DC 20006   info@ourfinancialsecurity.org
(202) 263-4533

CAMPAIGN FOR AMERICA'S FUTURE

The Campaign for America's Future is the strategy center for the progressive movement. Its goal is to "forge the enduring progressive majority needed to realize the America of shared prosperity and equal opportunity that our country was meant to be."

To attain its ultimate goal, the campaign spearheads a progressive agenda that addresses the kitchen-table issues working families face. It regularly convenes and educates progressive thinkers, organizers and community activists so their voices will be coordinated, cogent and potent. And it incubates national campaigns on the critical issues that will define America for generations to come. Established in 1996.

Contact Information
1825 K Street, NW, Suite 400   (202) 955-5665
Washington, DC 20006   www.ourfuture.org

CENTER FOR AMERICAN PROGRESS

The Center for American Progress is dedicated to improving the lives of Americans through progressive ideas and action. Building on the achievements of progressive pioneers such as Teddy Roosevelt and Martin Luther King, its work addresses 21st-century challenges such as energy, national security, economic growth and opportunity, immigration, education, and health care. The center develops new policy ideas, critiques the policy that stems from conservative values, and challenges the media to cover issues that truly matter and shape the national debate. Founded in 2003.

Contact Information
1333 H Street NW, 10th Floor
Washington DC, 20005

(202) 682-1611
www.americanprogress.org

----------------------------------★----------------------------------

CENTER FOR AUTO SAFETY

Consumers Union and Ralph Nader founded the Center for Auto Safety (CAS) in 1970 to provide consumers a voice for auto safety and quality in Washington and to help lemon owners fight back across the country. Among its accomplishments, the organization has achieved numerous legal victories over government agencies that have saved vital consumer, safety and environmental laws under assault by industry.

Contact Information
1825 Connecticut Ave, NW, Suite 330
Washington, DC 20009-5708

(202) 328-7700
www.autosafety.org

----------------------------------★----------------------------------

CENTER FOR COMMUNITY CHANGE (CCC)

The mission of the Center for Community Change (CCC) is to build the power and capacity of low-income people, especially low-income people of color, to change their communities and public policies for the better. CCC strengthens, connects and mobilizes grassroots groups to enhance their leadership, voice and power. It works to amplify community voices and ensure that grassroots voices are heard in Washington and shape the national conversation about building a better America. Founded in 1968 to honor the life and values of Robert F. Kennedy, the Center is one of the longest-standing champions for low-income people and communities of color.

Contact Information
Main Office:
1536 U Street NW
Washington, DC 20009

(202) 339-9300
www.communitychange.org
info@communitychange.org

----------------------------------★----------------------------------

CENTER FOR SCIENCE IN THE PUBLIC INTEREST (CSPI)

The Center for Science in the Public Interest (CSPI) is a consumer advocacy organization whose twin missions are to conduct innovative research and advocacy programs in health and nutrition, and to provide consumers with current, useful information about their health and well-being. Its award-winning newsletter, Nutrition Action Healthletter, with some 900,000 subscribers in the United States and Canada, is the largest-circulation health newsletter in North America.

Contact Information

1875 Connecticut Ave. N.W., Suite 300 | (202) 332-9110
Washington, D.C. 20009 | www.cspinet.org

CENTER ON BUDGET AND POLICY PRIORITIES (CBPP)

The Center on Budget and Policy Priorities (CBPP) is a policy organizations working at the federal and state levels on fiscal policy and public programs that affect low- and moderate-income families and individuals. It conducts research and analysis to help shape public debates over proposed budget and tax policies and to help ensure that policymakers consider the needs of low-income families and individuals in these debates. CBPP also develops policy options to alleviate poverty.

In addition, the Center examines the short- and long-term impacts of proposed policies on the health of the economy and the soundness of federal and state budgets. Among the issues it explores are whether federal and state governments are fiscally sound and have sufficient revenue to address critical priorities, both for low-income populations and for the nation as a whole. Established in 1981.

Contact Information

820 First Street, NE, Suite 510 | www.cbpp.org
Washington, DC 20002 | center@cbpp.org
(202) 408-1080

CITIZENS FOR TAX JUSTICE

Citizens for Tax Justice, founded in 1979, is a public interest research and advocacy organization focusing on federal, state and local tax policies and their impact upon our nation. CTJ's mission is to give ordinary people a greater voice in the development of tax laws. Against special interest lobbyists for corporations and the wealthy, CTJ fights for:

- Fair taxes for middle and low-income families
- Requiring the wealthy to pay their fair share
- Closing corporate tax loopholes
- Adequately funding important government services
- Reducing the federal debt
- Taxation that minimizes distortion of economic markets

Contact Information

1616 P Street NW	(202)299-1066
Suite 200	www.ctj.org
Washington, DC 20036	ctj@ctj.org

COALITION ON HUMAN NEEDS (CHN)

The Coalition on Human Needs (CHN) is an alliance of national organizations working together to promote public policies which address the needs of low-income and other vulnerable populations. The Coalition's members include civil rights, religious, labor and professional organizations and those concerned with the well being of children, women, the elderly and people with disabilities. Established in 1981.

Contact Information

1120 Connecticut Avenue, NW	(202) 223-2532
Suite 312	www.chn.org
Washington, DC 20036	djohnson@chn.org or info@chn.org

CONSUMER FEDERATION OF AMERICA (CFA)

The Consumer Federation of America (CFA) is an association of non-profit consumer organizations that was established in 1968 to advance the consumer interest through research, advocacy, and education. Today, nearly 300 of these groups participate in the federation and govern it through their representatives on the organization's Board of Directors.

Contact Information

1620 I Street, NW—Suite 200	www.consumerfed.org
Washington, DC 20006	cfa@consumerfed.org
(202) 387-6121	

CORPORATION FOR SUPPORTIVE HOUSING (CSH)

The Corporation for Supportive Housing (CSH) is a national nonprofit organization and community development financial institution that helps communities create permanent housing with services to prevent and end homelessness. CSH advances its mission by providing advocacy, expertise, leadership, and financial resources to make it easier to create and operate supportive housing. The organization is committed to a ten-year plan of creating 150,000 new units of supportive housing by 2012. CSH has offices in eleven states and provides limited assistance to many other communities. Established in 1991.

Contact Information
Headquarters: 50 Broadway, 17th
  Floor
New York, NY 10004

(212) 986-2966
www.csh.org
info@csh.org

---★---

CORPWATCH

CorpWatch provides non-profit investigative research and journalism to expose corporate malfeasance and to advocate for multinational corporate accountability and transparency. It works to foster global justice, independent media activism and democratic control over corporations. The organization seeks to expose multinational corporations that profit from war, fraud, environmental, human rights and other abuses, and to provide critical information to foster a more informed public and an effective democracy. Established in 1997.

Contact Information
2958 24th Street
San Francisco, CA 94110

(415) 641-1633
www.corpwatch.org

---★---

DEMOS

Demos is a non-partisan public policy research and advocacy organization founded in 2000. Headquartered in New York City, Demos works with advocates and policymakers around the country in pursuit of four overarching goals:

- A more equitable economy with widely shared prosperity and opportunity

- A vibrant and inclusive democracy with high levels of voting and civic engagement
- An empowered public sector that works for the common good
- Responsible U.S. engagement in an interdependent world

Contact Information

National Office:
220 Fifth Avenue, 5th Floor
New York, New York 10001

(212) 633-1405
www.demos.org
info@demos.org

DISABILITY RIGHTS ADVOCATES (DRA)

DRA is a non-profit legal center whose mission is to ensure dignity, equality, and opportunity for people with all types of disabilities throughout the United States and worldwide.

DRA's national advocacy work includes high-impact class action litigation on behalf of people with all types of disabilities, including mobility, hearing, vision, learning and psychological disabilities. Through negotiation and litigation, DRA has made thousands of facilities throughout the country accessible and has enforced access rights for millions of people with disabilities in many key areas of life, including access to technology, education, employment, transportation and health care. DRA also engages in non-litigation advocacy throughout the country, including research and education projects focused on opening up access to schools, the professions and health care. DRA publishes a variety of reports that provide information and guidance on disability rights and obligations of entities as well as statistics that address the status of people with disabilities. Established in 1993.

Contact Information

2001 Center Street, Fourth Floor
Berkeley, CA 94704-1204
(510) 665-8644 or (510) 665-8716
  (TTY)

www.dralegal.org
general@dralegal.org

DO SOMETHING (DOSOMETHING.ORG)

DoSomething.org is one of the largest organizations in the US that helps young people rock causes they care about. A driving force in creating a culture of volunteerism, DoSomething.org is on track to activate two million young people in 2011. By leveraging the web, television, mobile, and pop culture, DoSomething.org inspires, empowers and celebrates a generation of doers: teenagers who recognize the need to do something, believe in their ability to get it done, and then take action. Established in 1993.

Contact Information

24-32 Union Square East
4th Floor
New York, NY 10003
Contact: Mike Fantini

(212) 254.2390 x232
www.dosomething.org
mfantini@dosomething.org
6399 Wilshire Blvd #600
Los Angeles, CA 90048

ECONOMIC POLICY INSTITUTE (EPI)

EPI is an independent, non-profit and non-partisan research institute founded in 1986 on the belief that every working family deserves a better future: a good job, fair pay, affordable health care and access to a quality education. To that end, its staff of Ph.D economists and policy analysts conducts rigorous research on the economic issues that impact working families, and works to promote policies that are good for working Americans.

EPI was the first organization to focus on these issues, and remains the premier institute publishing research on the economic condition of low- and middle-income American families.

Contact Information

1333 H Street, NW
Suite 300, East Tower
Washington, DC 20005-4707

(202) 775-8810
www.epi.org
epi@epi.org

FAMILIES USA

Families USA is a national nonprofit, non-partisan organization dedicated to the achievement of high-quality, affordable health care for all Americans. Working at the national, state, and community levels, it has earned a national reputation as an effective voice for health care consumers for 25 years. Along with other tasks, the organization manages a grassroots advocates' network for organizations and individuals working for the consumer perspective in national and state health policy debates, produces healthy policy reports, acts as a watchdog over government actions affecting health care, and conducts public information campaigns. Established in 1982.

Contact Information

1201 New York Avenue NW, Suite 1100
Washington, DC 20005

(202) 628-3030
www.familiesusa.org
info@familiesusa.org

---★---

FAMILY VIOLENCE PREVENTION FUND (FVPF)

For more than three decades, the Family Violence Prevention Fund (FVPF) has worked to end violence against women and children around the world. Instrumental in developing the landmark Violence Against Women Act passed by Congress in 1994, the FVPF has continued to break new ground by reaching new audiences including men and youth, promoting leadership within communities to ensure that violence prevention efforts become self-sustaining, and transforming the way health care providers, police, judges, employers and others address violence. Established in 1980.

Contact Information
Main Office:
383 Rhode Island St., Suite #304
San Francisco, CA 94103-5133
(415) 252-8900 or (800) 595-4889 (TTY)

www.endabuse.org
info@endabuse.org

---★---

FOOD RESEARCH AND ACTION CENTER (FRAC)

The Food Research and Action Center (FRAC) is a national nonprofit organization working to improve public policies and public-private partnerships to eradicate hunger and undernutrition in the United States. FRAC works with hundreds of national, state and local nonprofit organizations, public agencies, corporations and labor organizations to address hunger, food insecurity, and their root cause, poverty. Established in 1970.

Contact Information

1875 Connecticut Avenue NW
Suite 540
Washington, DC 20009

(202) 986-2200
www.frac.org

---★---

HOUSING ASSISTANCE COUNCIL (HAC)

A nonprofit corporation headquartered in Washington, D.C., the Housing Assistance Council (HAC) has been helping local organizations build affordable homes in rural America since 1971. HAC emphasizes local solutions, empowerment of the poor, reduced dependence, and self-help strategies. HAC assists in the development of both single- and multi-family homes and promotes homeownership for working low-income rural families through a self-help, "sweat equity" construction method. The Housing Assistance Council offers services to public, nonprofit, and private organizations throughout the rural United States. HAC also maintains a special focus on high-need groups and regions: Indian country, the Mississippi Delta, farmworkers, the Southwest border colonias, and Appalachia. Established in 1971.

Contact Information
National Office:
1025 Vermont Ave., N.W.
Suite 606
Washington, D.C. 20005

(202) 842-8600
www.ruralhome.org
hac@ruralhome.org

★

INDEPENDENT SECTOR

Independent Sector serves as the premier meeting ground for the leaders of America's charitable and philanthropic sector. Since its founding in 1980, it has sponsored ground-breaking research, fought for public policies that support a dynamic, independent sector, and created unparalleled resources so staff, boards, and volunteers can improve their organizations and better serve their communities.

Contact Information
1602 L Street, NW, Suite 900
Washington, DC 20036
(202) 467-6100

www.independentsector.org
info@independentsector.org

★

INSIGHT CENTER FOR COMMUNITY ECONOMIC DEVELOPMENT

Formerly National Economic Development and Law Center, The Insight Center for Community Economic Development is a national research, consulting, and legal organization dedicated to building economic health in vulnerable communities. It develops and promotes innovative solutions that help people and communities become and remain economically secure. Program work includes legal services, savings and asset building, early care and education, and workforce development. Established in 1969.

Contact Information

Oakland, CA:
2201 Broadway, Suite 815
Oakland, CA 94612-3024

Los Angeles, CA:
3701 Wilshire Boulevard, Suite 208
Los Angeles, CA 90010-2826
(510) 251-2600
www.insightcced.org
info@insightcced.org

INSTITUTE ON RACE AND POVERTY (IRP)

The Institute on Race & Poverty (IRP) investigates the ways that policies and practices disproportionately affect people of color and the disadvantaged. A core purpose for IRP's work is to ensure that people have access to opportunity. Another is to help the places where people live develop in ways that both promote access to opportunity and help maintain regional stability. The Institute is directed by Myron Orfield, associate professor of law at the University of Minnesota Law School. Established in 1993.

Contact Information

Institute on Race & Poverty
University of Minnesota
N150 Walter Mondale Hall
229 South 19th Avenue

Minneapolis, MN 55455
(612) 625-8071
www.irpumn.org

LEADERSHIP CONFERENCE ON CIVIL AND HUMAN RIGHTS (LCCR) AND LEADERSHIP CONFERENCE ON CIVIL RIGHTS EDUCATION FUND (LCCREF)

The Leadership Conference on Civil and Human Rights (formerly called the Leadership Conference on Civil Rights) is a coalition charged by its diverse membership of more than 200 national organizations to promote and protect the civil and human rights of all persons in the United States. Through advocacy and outreach to targeted constituencies, The Leadership Conference works toward the goal of a more open and just society. It was founded in 1950 and has coordinated national lobbying efforts on behalf of every major civil rights law since 1957.

The Leadership Conference Education Fund builds public will for federal policies that promote and protect the civil and human rights of all persons in the United States. The Education Fund's campaigns empower and mobilize advocates around the country to push for progressive change in the United States. Founded in 1969 as the education and research arm of The Leadership Conference.

Contact Information

LCCR/LCCREF
1629 K Street NW
10th Floor
Washington, DC 20006

LCCR: (202) 466-3311
LCCREF: (202) 466-3434
www.civilrights.org

LEAGUE OF WOMEN VOTERS OF THE UNITED STATES (LWV)

The League of Women Voters, a nonpartisan political organization, encourages informed and active participation in government, works to increase understanding of major public policy issues, and influences public policy through education and advocacy. Established in 1920.

Contact Information

1730 M Street NW, Suite 1000
Washington, DC 20036-4508

(202) 429-1965
www.lwv.org

MEDIA MATTERS FOR AMERICA

Media Matters for America is a web-based, not-for-profit, progressive research and information center dedicated to comprehensively monitoring, analyzing, and correcting conservative misinformation in the U.S. media.

Launched in May 2004, Media Matters for America put in place, for the first time, the means to systematically monitor a cross section of print, broadcast, cable, radio, and Internet media outlets for conservative misinformation—news or commentary that is not accurate, reliable, or credible and that forwards the conservative agenda — every day, in real time.

Using the website mediamatters.org as the principal vehicle for disseminating research and information, Media Matters posts rapid-response items as well as longer research and analytic reports documenting conservative misinformation throughout the media. Additionally, Media Matters works daily to notify activists, journalists, pundits, and the general public about instances of misinformation, providing them with the resources to rebut false claims and to take direct action against offending media institutions.

Contact Information

455 Massachusetts Ave. NW, Suite 600
Washington, DC 20001

(202) 756-4100
www.mediamatters.org

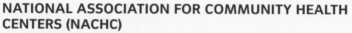

NAACP LEGAL DEFENSE AND EDUCATIONAL FUND, INC. (LDF)

The NAACP Legal Defense and Educational Fund, Inc. is America's premier legal organization fighting for racial justice. Through litigation, advocacy, and public education, LDF seeks structural changes to expand democracy, eliminate disparities, and achieve racial justice in a society that fulfills the promise of equality for all Americans. LDF also defends the gains and protections won over the past 70 years of civil rights struggle and works to improve the quality and diversity of judicial and executive appointments. Established in 1940.

Contact Information

National **Headquarters:** 99 Hudson Street, Suite 1600
New York, NY 10013

(212) 965-2200
www.naacpldf.org

NATIONAL ASSOCIATION FOR COMMUNITY HEALTH CENTERS (NACHC)

Established in 1970, NACHC works with a network of state health center and primary care organizations to serve health centers in a variety of ways:

- Provide research-based advocacy for health centers and their clients.
- Educate the public about the mission and value of health centers.
- Train and provide technical assistance to health center staff and boards.
- Develop alliances with private partners and key stakeholders to foster the delivery of primary health care services to communities in need.

Contact Information

7200 Wisconsin Ave, Suite 210
Bethesda, MD 20814

(301) 347-0400
www.nachc.org

NATIONAL CENTER FOR BICYCLING AND WALKING (NCBW)

The NCBW is the major program of the Bicycle Federation of America, Inc. (BFA), a national, nonprofit corporation. The NCBW works with local, state, and national bicycle, pedestrian, and transportation advocates to bring about changes in government policies, programs, and procedures to help create more bicycle-friendly and walkable communities.

Several of NCBW's many activities include providing specialized community-based workshops, consulting services in the areas of long-range planning, policy development, public involvement, and route selection. Established in 1977.

Contact Information
www.bikewalk.org
info@bikewalk.org

NATIONAL CONGRESS FOR COMMUNITY ECONOMIC DEVELOPMENT (NCCED)

Founded in 1970, The National Congress for Community Economic Development is the trade association for community development corporations (CDCs) and the community economic development (CED) industry. Its mission is to promote, support and advocate for CDCs and the CED Industry, whose work creates wealth, builds healthy and sustainable communities and achieves lasting economic viability.

Contact Information

1030, 15th ST. NW, Suite 325
Washington, DC 20005

(202) 289-9020 or (877) 44-NCCED (62233)
www.ncced.org

NATIONAL CONSUMER LAW CENTER

The National Consumer Law Center is a nonprofit advocacy organization that seeks to build economic security and family wealth for low-income and other economically disadvantaged Americans. It promotes access to quality financial services and protects family assets from unfair and exploitive transactions that wipe out resources and undermine self-sufficiency. For over 40 years NCLC has used its expertise to write the rules of a fair marketplace.

Contact Information
Headquarters: 7 Winthrop Square
Boston, MA 02110-1245
(617) 542-8010

www.nclc.org
consumerlaw@nclc.org

POLICY AND ISSUES ANALYSIS ORGANIZATIONS

NATIONAL COUNCIL OF CHURCHES (NCC)

Since its founding in 1950, the National Council of the Churches of Christ in the USA has been the leading force for ecumenical cooperation among Christians in the United States. The NCC's member faith groups — from a wide spectrum of Protestant, Anglican, Orthodox, Evangelical, historic African American and Living Peace churches — include 45 million persons in more than 100,000 local congregations in communities across the nation. Amongst its working groups/task forces, the NCC has an eco-justice program, health task force, special commission for the gulf coast, and living wage campaign.

Contact Information

475 Riverside Drive, 8th floor
New York, NY 10115

www.nccusa.org
info@ncccusa.org

NATIONAL EDUCATION ASSOCIATION (NEA)

The mission of the NEA is to advocate for education professionals and to unite the organization's members and the nation to fulfill the promise of public education to prepare every student to succeed in a diverse and interdependent world. Established in 1857.

Contact Information

1201 16th Street, N.W.
Washington, DC 20036-3290

(202) 833-4000
www.nea.org

NATIONAL ENERGY ASSISTANCE DIRECTORS' ASSOCIATION (NEADA)

NEADA is the primary educational and policy organization for the state and tribal directors of the Low-Income Home Energy Assistance Program (LIHEAP). LIHEAP is a federal program providing formula grants to states to help low-income families pay their heating and cooling bills. Established in 1990.

Contact Information

1232 31st Street N.W.
Washington, DC 20007

(202) 333-5915
www.neada.org
info@neada.org

NATIONAL HEAD START ASSOCIATION (NHSA)

The National Head Start Association is a private not-for-profit membership organization dedicated exclusively to meeting the needs of Head Start children and their families (Head Start is the longest-running national school readiness program in the United States. It provides comprehensive education, health, nutrition, and parent involvement services to low-income children and their families). NHSA represents more than 1 million children, 200,000 staff and 2,600 Head Start programs in the United States. The Association provides support for the entire Head Start community by advocating for policies that strengthen services to Head Start children and their families; by providing extensive training and professional development to Head Start staff; and by developing and disseminating research, information, and resources that enrich Head Start program delivery. Established in 1965.

Contact Information

1651 Prince Street
Alexandria, VA 22314

(703) 739-0875
www.nhsa.org

--------------------------------★--------------------------------

NATIONAL RESOURCES DEFENSE COUNCIL (NRDC)

NRDC uses law, science and the support of 1.3 million members and online activists to protect the planet's wildlife and wild places and to ensure a safe and healthy environment for all living things. It works to foster the fundamental right of all people to have a voice in decisions that affect their environment and also aims to solve pressing environmental issues: curbing global warming, getting toxic chemicals out of the environment, moving American beyond oil, reviving our oceans, and helping China go green. Established in 1970.

Contact Information

Headquarters: 40 West 20th Street
New York, NY 10011

(212) 727-2700
www.nrdc.org
nrdcinfo@nrdc.org

--------------------------------★--------------------------------

PHYSICIANS FOR SOCIAL RESPONSIBILITY (PSR)

Physicians for Social Responsibility is a non-profit advocacy organization that is the medical and public health voice for policies to prevent nuclear war and proliferation and to slow, stop and reverse global warming and toxic degradation of the environment. PSR's 50,000 health professionals and concerned citizen members and e-activists, 31 PSR chapters, and 41 student PSR chapters at medical and public health schools, along with national and chapter staff, form a unique nationwide network committed to a safer and healthy world. Established in 1961.

Contact Information

1875 Connecticut Avenue, NW, Suite 1012
Washington, DC, 20009

(202) 667-4260
www.psr.org
psrnatl@psr.org

PLOUGHSHARES FUND

Ploughshares Fund works to create a safe, secure, and nuclear weapon-free world. Combining high-level advocacy, an enhanced grantmaking capacity and the organization's own expertise, Ploughshares Fund is helping to fundamentally change nuclear weapons policy. Established in 1981.

Contact Information

Headquarters: Fort Mason Center B-330
San Francisco, CA 94123

(415) 775-2244
www.ploughshares.org

POLICYLINK

PolicyLink is a national research and action institute advancing economic and social equity. It connects the work of people on the ground to the creation of sustainable communities of opportunity that allow everyone to participate and prosper. The organization shares its findings and analysis through its publications, website and online tools, convenings, national summits, and in briefings with national and local policymakers. Established in 1999.

Contact Information

Headquarters: 1438 Webster Street, Suite 303
Oakland, CA 94612

(510) 663-2333
www.policylink.org
info@policylink.org

POPULATION ACTION INTERNATIONAL (PAI)

Population Action International uses advocacy and research to improve access to family planning and reproductive health care across the world. PAI believes that by ensuring couples are able to determine the size of their families, poverty and the depletion of natural resources are reduced, improving the lives of millions across the world. Established in 1965.

Contact Information

1300 19th Street, NW Suite 200
Washington, DC 20036-1624

(202) 557-3400
www.populationaction.org
pai@popact.org

PUBLIC EDUCATION NETWORK (PEN)

PEN is a national association of local education funds (LEFs) and individuals working to advance public school reform in low-income communities across the country. PEN and its members are building public demand and mobilizing resources for quality public education on behalf of 12 million children in 32 states, the District of Columbia and Puerto Rico. It has expanded its work internationally to include members in Mexico, Peru, the Philippines, South Africa and Tanzania. Established in 1983.

Contact Information

601 Thirteenth Street NW
Suite 710 South
Washington, DC 20005-3808
(202) 628-7460

www.publiceducation.org
PEN@PublicEducation.org

TRUTHDIG

Truthdig is a news web site that provides expert coverage of current affairs as well as a variety of thoughtful, provocative content assembled from a progressive point of view. The site is built around reports by authorities in their fields who conduct in-depth exploration of contemporary topics. To offer frequent change and surprise, the site also presents a diversity of original reporting and aggregated content culled by the site's editors and staff.

Contact Information

1158 26th St., No. 443
Santa Monica, CA 90403-4698

www.truthdig.com
info@truthdig.com

USACTION

USAction builds power by uniting people locally and nationally, on-the-ground and online, to win a more just and progressive America. It promotes a guarantee of quality, affordable health coverage for everyone in the U.S., an end to the war in Iraq, and new commitments to strengthen public education and promote safe, clean energy to end America's dependence on oil. Established in 1999.

Contact Information

1825 K Street NW
Suite 210
Washington, DC 20006

(202) 263-4520
www.usaction.org
usaction@usaction.org

★

SERVICE ORGANIZATIONS

KIWANIS INTERNATIONAL

Kiwanis is a global organization of volunteers dedicated to changing the world one child and one community at a time. Its members develop youth as leaders, build playgrounds and raise funds for pediatric research. In addition, Kiwanis helps shelter the homeless, feed the hungry, mentor the disadvantaged and care for the sick. Established in 1915.

Volunteer Opportunities

Visit the Kiwanis web site to find a club in your area.

Contact Information

3636 Woodview Trace
Indianapolis, IN 46268-3196

(317) 875-8755 [dial 411] or (800) 549-2647 [dial 411]
www.kiwanis.org

LIONS CLUB INTERNATIONAL

Lions Clubs International is the world's largest service club organization, with 1.35 million members in more than 45,000 clubs worldwide. The organization is best known for fighting blindness, but it also volunteers for many different kinds of community projects – including caring for the environment, feeding the hungry and aiding seniors and the disabled. Its community projects often support local children and schools through scholarships, recreation and mentoring. Along with the Lions Club International Foundation (which helps to fund Lions humanitarian projects) Lions Club International helps communities following natural disasters by providing for immediate needs such as food, water, clothing and medical supplies—and aiding in long-term reconstruction. Established in 1917.

Volunteer Opportunities

Lions Club International has community clubs that meet in person, cyber clubs that meet online, and special interest clubs that can be based on a member's profession or hobby. Each club matches the needs of its members to help them support their community. Membership is by invitation, but it is also possible to start a new club. Visit the Lions Club website to find a club near you or learn more about beginning a club. To learn more about becoming a Lion, contact the club's membership team at memberops@lionsclubs.org.

Contact Information

International Headquarters: 300 W. 22nd Street
Oak Brook, IL 60523-8842

(630) 571-5466
www.lionsclub.org

----------------------------------★----------------------------------

NATIONAL ASSOCIATION OF JUNIOR AUXILIARIES (NAJA)

Junior Auxiliary is a national non-profit organization that encourages members to render charitable services which are beneficial to the general public with particular emphasis on children. NAJA has more than 14,000 active, associate and life members in 101 chapters in Alabama, Arkansas, Florida, Louisiana, Mississippi, Missouri, Tennessee and Texas. Junior Auxiliaries are all-women organizations.

Volunteer Opportunities

Opportunities vary chapter so contact your local chapter.

Contact Information

Headquarters: P.O. Box 1873
Greenville, MS 38702-1873
845 South Main Street
Greenville, MS 38701

(662) 332-3000
www.najanet.org
najanet@bellsouth.net

----------------------------------★----------------------------------

ROTARY INTERNATIONAL

Rotary International is the world's first service club organization, with more than 1.2 million members in 33,000 clubs worldwide. Rotary club members are volunteers who work locally, regionally, and internationally to combat hunger, improve health and sanitation, provide education and job training, promote peace, and eradicate polio under the motto Service Above Self. Established in 1905.

Volunteer Opportunities

Rotary club membership is by invitation and club members must hold or be retired from a professional, proprietary, executive, or managerial position and live or work within the locality of the club or surrounding areas. Visit the website to complete a Prospective Member form and find a club near you.

Contact Information
Headquarters: One Rotary Center
1560 Sherman Ave.
Evanston, IL 60201

(847) 866-3000
www.rotary.org

---★---

YOUTH SERVICE AMERICA (YSA)

Youth Service America (YSA) seeks to improve communities by increasing the number and the diversity of young people, ages 5-25, serving in important roles. Founded in 1986, YSA is an international nonprofit resource center that partners with thousands of organizations in more than 100 countries to expand the impact of the youth service movement with families, communities, schools, corporations, faith-based organizations, nonprofits, the media, and governments. Through this network, it works to increase the quality and quantity of service opportunities and to make service and service-learning the common expectation and common experience of all young people. YSA also operates Servenet.org, a website that includes a searchable database of local volunteer opportunities.

Volunteer Opportunities

YSA provides grants to help individuals coordinate their own volunteer projects.

Volunteers can also check out www.Servenet.org to find opportunities matching their needs.

Contact Information
1101 15th St NW, Suite 200
Washington, DC, 20005

www.YSA.org
info@ysa.org

---★---

CENTER FOR GLOBAL EDUCATION (CGE)

The Center for Global Education collaborates with colleges, universities and other organizations around the world to promote international education and raise cross-cultural awareness. CGE works to create and enhance existing study abroad programs, integrate international perspectives in the US education system, increase the ethnic diversity of study abroad participants, and encourage research in the area of international education. Established in 1982.

Volunteer Opportunities
Contact the organization for details.

Contact Information
Loyola Marymount University
1 LMU Drive
University Hall, Suite 1840
Los Angeles, California 90045-2659

(310) 980-6971
www.globaled.us
globaled@lmu.edu

★

Acknowledgments

Any book is, to some extent, a collaboration between author, editor, and publisher. In this respect I have been fortunate as Ann Treistman and Tony Lyons could not have been more supportive and generous at each stage of the development of this project. Helen Matatov has done a superb job of researching a substantial part of the book and it would be incomplete without her efforts.

Judy MacLean's editing, editorial suggestions, and common sense insights are invaluable. Marla Wilson and Lee Patterson have provided exceptional technological and word processing support. Stan and Sidney Shuman, as well as Mary-Ann and Philip Hobel have provided their friendship and gracious hospitality that has given me the space to reflect upon and design this project.

I am also deeply appreciative of the time and effort that the following individuals have put forth to write reflective and insightful essays about their personal volunteer experiences. They are, in alphabetical order: Sam Beard, Sabrina Bornstein, Juan Cruz, John Garamendi, Sophia Harris, Sara Hobel, Paul Marienthal, Martine Makower, Anna McCorvey, Julie Morial, Elliot Naishat, Susan Patricof, Matthew Piepenbury, Laura Polacheck, Tom Powers, Bruce

Reaves, William Rhodes, Casey Rogers, Michael Roth, Rosemary Shahan, Mehan Voorhees, Ashley Wiltshire, Susan Ford Wiltshire

I also wanted to thank Robert Bellah and William M. Sullivan for their contribution to the Final Report of the National Advisory Council on Economic Opportunity, which is the basis for chapter three of this book.